DEBATING
THE KENNEDY
PRESIDENCY

Debating Twentieth-Century America
Series Editor: James T. Patterson, Brown University

Debating American Immigration, 1882–Present
by Roger Daniels and Otis L. Graham
Debating Southern History: Ideas and Action in the Twentieth Century
by Bruce Clayton and John Salmond
Debating the Civil Rights Movement, 1945–1968
by Steven F. Lawson and Charles Payne
Debating the Origins of the Cold War
by Ralph B. Levering, Vladimir O. Pechatnov,
Verena Botzenhart-Viehe, and C. Earl Edmundson,
Debating the Kennedy Presidency
by James N. Giglio and Stephen G. Rabe

Forthcoming in the series:

Debating the American Welfare State, 1945–Present
by Nelson Lichtenstein, Sonya Michel, and Jennifer Klein
Debating FDR's Foreign Policy, 1932–1945
by Justus Doenecke and Mark Stoler,
Debating the New Deal
by Robert McElvaine and Anthony Badger
Debating the "Negro Problem"
by Barbara J. Ballard and Marcus C. Bruce

DEBATING
THE KENNEDY
PRESIDENCY

JAMES N. GIGLIO
and
STEPHEN G. RABE

ROWMAN & LITTLEFIELD PUBLISHERS, INC.
Lanham • Boulder • New York • Oxford

ROWMAN & LITTLEFIELD PUBLISHERS, INC.

Published in the United States of America
by Rowman & Littlefield Publishers, Inc.
A Member of the Rowman & Littlefield Publishing Group
4720 Boston Way, Lanham, Maryland 20706
www.rowmanlittlefield.com

PO Box 317
Oxford
OX2 9RU, UK

British Library Cataloguing in Publication Information Available

Library of Congress Cataloging-in-Publication Data

Giglio, James N., 1939–
    Debating the Kennedy presidency / James N. Giglio and Stephen G. Rabe.
        p. cm. — (Debating twentieth-century America)
    Including bibliographical references and index.
        ISBN 0-7425-0833-1 (alk. paper) — ISBN 0-7425-0834-X (pbk. : alk.
    paper)
        1. United States—Politics and government—1961–1963. 2. United
    States—Politics and government—1962–1963—Sources. 3. Kennedy, John
    F. (John Fitzgerald), 1917–1963. I. Rabe, Stephen G. II. Title. III.
    Series
        E841 .G538 2003
        973.922'092—dc21
                                                                2002010084

Printed in the United States of America

♾™ The paper used in this publication meets the minimum requirements of
American National Standard for Information Sciences—Permanence of Paper
for Printed Library Materials, ANSI/NISO Z39.48-1992.

CONTENTS

INTRODUCTION

Despite the brevity of the John F. Kennedy presidency, its significance endures. The Cold War reached its pinnacle in the Kennedy years when the United States successfully confronted the Soviet Union over its installation of nuclear-tipped missiles in Cuba. The world was on the verge of a nuclear holocaust. The crisis over Berlin also escalated dangerously, with the Soviets constructing a wall that physically divided the former German capital. That communist symbol remained until German citizens demolished it in 1989. Moreover, in the name of anticommunism, President Kennedy rapidly expanded U.S. covert capabilities, destabilizing governments throughout Latin America; sanctioning sabotage and terrorism in Cuba; and perhaps even planning an assassination of Fidel Castro. Kennedy also extended U.S. commitments in South Vietnam, creating the context for the disastrous military decisions made during the Lyndon B. Johnson and Richard M. Nixon presidencies. Domestically, the Kennedy era witnessed the Second Reconstruction, with a flurry of civil rights activities the likes of which had not been seen since the Reconstruction Era of the 1860s and 1870s. Spurred by young black and white activists who engaged in voter registration drives, sit-ins, and freedom rides, President Kennedy proclaimed the commitment a moral one and pushed for racial justice. His efforts culminated in the momentous Civil Rights Act of 1964, which President Johnson signed following Kennedy's assassination.

1

James N. Giglio and Stephen G. Rabe have spent much of their professional careers studying the Kennedy years. Rabe, a historian of U.S. foreign relations, depicts Kennedy as a relentless cold warrior who perpetuated the Cold War more than he resolved it. Rabe gives particular attention to the nuclear arms race; the Soviet-American confrontations over Berlin and Cuba; and Kennedy's war against Fidel Castro, Latin America, and Vietnam. Giglio, a U.S. political historian, sympathetically surveys domestic policies, including Kennedy's successful efforts to promote economic growth and his quest to provide health care for the aged, federal aid for education, economic equality for women, and civil rights for blacks. Giglio recognizes the broadening scope of Kennedy's New Frontier agenda to include the successful Peace Corps program and the Apollo lunar-landing project. Although foreign and domestic policies are analyzed in separate essays, both scholars recognize their interrelationship.

What is provocative about the two essays is that scholars conventionally treat Kennedy's domestic performance more harshly or dismissively than they assess his foreign policies. That is not the case in the Giglio and Rabe essays. Giglio defends the Kennedy record by emphasizing the constraints under which the president had to operate. Such constraints are especially applicable to domestic matters. They include Kennedy's narrow election victory, a recalcitrant Congress, the conservative nature of the American public until 1963, the dominant foreign-policy problems, and the prevailing view that Democrats were soft on communism. Rabe acknowledges those constraints but argues that Kennedy adopted an orthodox approach to the Cold War and failed to exercise presidential leadership.

Despite obvious differences in interpretation, Giglio and Rabe nevertheless agree on several significant points. They believe that Kennedy made winning the Cold War his administration's highest priority. Giglio and Rabe also note that Kennedy's presidency set into motion powerful forces for change. His youthful charisma and lofty rhetoric inspired countless young Americans to join the Peace Corps and engage in other forms of public service. No other president in the post–World War II era has had that sort of impact. Kennedy was an effective manager of crises, but performed less satisfactorily in resolving or avoiding them. In a rapidly changing world, the Kennedy administration played a transitional role, paving the way for the Vietnam War, the nuclear arms race, and the civil rights and education legislation of the mid-1960s. Students of this important presidency will have to decide whether Kennedy's legacy is a positive, negative, or ambiguous one.

JOHN F. KENNEDY AND THE WORLD

Stephen G. Rabe

He faced down communist aggression in Berlin and Cuba. He made the world a safer place, negotiating a nuclear-test-ban treaty with the Soviet Union. He championed nationalism, identifying the United States with the emerging nations of Asia, Africa, and Latin America. And he reached out to the world's poor and needy with programs like the Alliance for Progress, the Peace Corps, and Food for Peace. In less than a thousand days in office, "he had accomplished so much." Historian and presidential aide Arthur M. Schlesinger Jr. wrote those words, in his worshipful memoir of President John F. Kennedy. In Schlesinger's judgment, history had rarely witnessed a leader so capable of combining toughness and restraint, of will, nerve, and wisdom. Moreover, the president had galvanized international diplomacy and dazzled citizens both at home and abroad with his idealism and breathtaking eloquence. His inaugural address in 1961 and his declaration of solidarity with the people of Berlin in 1963 inspired many to "bear any burden" in the defense of liberty. Other members of the president's staff sustained Schlesinger's testimony. Roger Hilsman wrote of working for a "leader" and a "hero." Theodore Sorensen, who composed many of the president's speeches, predicted that history would remember Kennedy not only for his grace, wit, and style but also his "substance—the strength of his ideas and ideals, his courage and judgment."[1]

3

Schlesinger and his colleagues can perhaps be forgiven for their effusive praise of their boss. They loved and admired the man they served. Writing in the mid-1960s, they may also have been traumatized by Kennedy's assassination. But their memoirs have transcended time and place. Over the past four decades, their fellow citizens have affirmed that President Kennedy represented the best America had to offer. Although he barely captured the presidency, defeating Richard Nixon in November 1960 by less than 1percent, Kennedy enjoyed solid job approval ratings from the public. By mid-1963, 59 percent of Americans claimed to have voted for him. After his assassination, that voting figure rose to 65 percent. At the beginning of the twenty-first century, it would probably be difficult to find any American, now over sixty years of age, admitting to having voted for Nixon over Kennedy. Beyond distorting electoral results, Americans have honored President Kennedy with countless monuments, naming airports, schools, and buildings after him. Indeed, monuments to him abound throughout the world. Major urban areas in Western Europe and Latin America have important boulevards and avenues named after the U.S. president.

Americans also continue to believe that what their country and the world needs is another John Kennedy. In 1996 a *New York Times*/CBS News public-opinion poll found that if U.S. voters could pick any former president to govern the country, they would choose Kennedy. The Massachusetts Democrat easily outpolled Franklin Delano Roosevelt, surely the most influential political leader of the twentieth century. The poll's respondents even preferred Kennedy over those who had their faces sculpted on Mount Rushmore—George Washington, Thomas Jefferson, Abraham Lincoln, and Theodore Roosevelt. When asked to explain their choice, the respondents cited Kennedy's quality of leadership.

The Kennedy magic also seems to have bewitched U.S. historians. In professional surveys conducted in the 1980s and 1990s, historians rated him as an "above average" or "average (high)" president, remarkable ratings in view of his brief tenure in office. My colleague, Professor James Giglio, agrees that Kennedy merits his above average presidential rating.[2] To be sure, historians are not yet prepared to recommend resuming the blasting and cutting of rock at Mt. Rushmore. But that time may come. In a survey of fifty-eight presidential scholars conducted by public-affairs cable channel C-SPAN and released on President's Day, 21 February 2000, Kennedy earned an eighth-place rating out of the first forty-one U.S. presidents. In terms of presidential leadership, he finished just behind

Woodrow Wilson and Thomas Jefferson and in front of Andrew Jackson and James Madison.

Scholars have speculated on the enduring and growing popularity of John Kennedy. Professor Alan Brinkley of Columbia University notes that Kennedy was a man of the television age—gifted, witty, and articulate. When contemporary Americans see him on film they are "struck by how smooth, polished, and spontaneously eloquent he was, how impressive a presence, how elegant a speaker." Kennedy also stands out by comparison with other presidents. After the assassination, Americans endured the Vietnam debacle under Lyndon Baines Johnson and the lying, corruption, and abuse of power dubbed "Watergate" under Richard M. Nixon. Although good men, neither Gerald Ford nor Jimmy Carter could cope with the national economic malaise engendered by the Vietnam War. The pleasant Ronald Reagan had the good fortune to preside over the end of the Cold War, but even his closest advisors conceded that Reagan lacked intellectual depth. President Bill Clinton proved an adept manager of the nation's economy and a tireless worker for reconciliation in Northern Ireland, the Middle East, and southeast Europe. But Clinton's lack of personal restraint tarnished the peace and prosperity he had achieved. Brinkley concludes that Americans believe Kennedy's death "marked the end of an age of confidence and optimism and the beginning of an era of conflict and disenchantment." Kennedy's mission and idealism stands, in Brinkley's opinion, "as an appealing contrast to what seems the emptiness and aimlessness of today's public world."[3]

John Kennedy serves, as Brinkley astutely observes, as "an important figure in our national imagination." Whether intended or not, his presidency set in motion powerful forces for change. Countless Americans devoted their lives to public service, remembering Kennedy's inaugural day challenge and asking themselves what they could do for their country and the world. These idealists included college students, black and white alike, who risked their lives, marching in demonstrations, sitting in at lunch counters, and registering people to vote, as they sought simple justice for African Americans living in the segregated, "Jim Crow" South. Kennedy's children also included Lt. Philip Caputo, a young Marine Corps officer who landed in Danang, South Vietnam, in March 1965 as part of the first U.S. combat unit sent to Indochina. Caputo recalls that as he marched through the rice paddies he was imbued by "the missionary idealism he [Kennedy] had awakened in us." Along with his rifle and pack, Caputo carried with him the conviction that the Vietcong would be quickly beaten and that "we were doing something altogether noble and good."[4] Ironically, those youth who left their college campuses and took to the streets to oppose the war in Vietnam similarly believed that they were upholding the idealism and commitment that John Kennedy demanded. Long after the tumultuous 1960s, the Kennedy spirit continued to infuse Americans. In 1992, at the Democratic Party's national convention, the delegates collectively gasped when they saw, in a campaign biography film, President Kennedy reach out into a crowd of young men and shake the hand of the teenaged Bill Clinton. Clinton, almost seventeen, met the president while attending a leadership conference in Washington, D.C., sponsored by the American Legion. To Democratic loyalists, however, it might have seemed as if the young Clinton had ascended to Camelot to be knighted by King Arthur!

Without doubt, innumerable Americans took up public service, becoming kindergarten teachers, university professors, elected officials, diplomats, U.S. Marines, community activists, and Peace Corps volunteers, because they took seriously Kennedy's inaugural day challenge to spurn self-indulgent careerism and to ask what they could do for their country and fellow human beings. The United States is a more humane and progressive society because of this public service. Scholars are right to consider the impact of Kennedy's idealism on his and subsequent generations when they assess his presidency. But ultimately scholars must judge public leaders by what they were and what they did, not by what they might have been. My focus in this essay is on the Kennedy administration's foreign policies. In my judgment, President Kennedy does not merit the acclaim he has received from some scholars and most citizens for his conduct of U.S. foreign policy.

A fair examination of the Kennedy administration's foreign-policy record reveals a mixed and ambiguous history. In the context of the Soviet-American confrontation, or the Cold War (1945–1989), Kennedy cannot be considered a historically significant figure. Presidents Harry S. Truman, Dwight D. Eisenhower, Nixon, and perhaps Reagan developed policies and made decisions that shaped the course, conduct, and eventual end of the Cold War. Kennedy did not conduct a fundamental reassessment of U.S. foreign policy and remained attached to the core of Cold War thinking. Kennedy affirmed that the Soviet Union directed an international communist movement that threatened the security of the United States. Like Secretaries of State Dean Acheson (1949–1953) and John Foster Dulles (1953–1959), Kennedy believed that only a tough, determined response grounded in military superiority, could ensure the nation's survival. To be sure, President Kennedy successfully managed the Cuban missile crisis, the most dangerous conflict of the Cold War. But his heedless, often reckless, actions helped precipitate the showdown over Soviet missiles in Cuba. Indeed, an aggressive, militaristic, confrontational attitude often characterized his approach to waging Cold War. He and his brother, Attorney General Robert F. Kennedy, demonized Fidel Castro, authorizing sabotage, terrorism, and perhaps assassination of the Cuban leader. Under the banner of anti-communism, the administration also repeatedly intervened in the internal affairs of other nations, destabilizing popularly elected governments. The president bears some responsibility for the Vietnam War, the signal policy failure of the Cold War and a debacle virtually unprecedented in U.S. history. However well intentioned, his Alliance for Progress program proved poorly conceived and overly ambitious and did not create the democratic, economically vibrant, socially just Latin America that Kennedy promised. Kennedy merits credit for negotiating the nuclear test ban treaty and calling, during the last year of his life, for improved relations with the Soviet Union. But his military policies had already dangerously accelerated the nuclear arms race. In sum, President Kennedy had not made the world a safer place during his brief time in office. He had waged Cold War.

In analyzing and assessing the foreign policy of the Kennedy presidency, this essay will first look at the president's foreign-policy background, his core beliefs, and the way he organized his foreign-policy team. The essay will then address some of the key policies, issues, events, and crises of the period: U.S. relations with the Soviet Union, Cuba, Vietnam, and Latin America; the Berlin crisis and the Cuban missile crisis; military spending and nuclear arms policy; and the Alliance for Progress. Although not a complete examination of Kennedy's foreign policies, the essay offers one perspective on the Kennedy presidency, one reasoned judgment of its historical significance in international affairs. Certainly, the president also pressed his Cold War agenda in such far-flung areas as the former Belgian Congo (Zaire), British Guiana (Guyana), and Laos. And he continued the U.S. policy of nonrecognition and intense hostility toward Communist China. But a thorough examination of those policies would confirm, not refute, the critical analyses offered in this essay.

BELIEFS AND EXPERIENCE

When John Kennedy took command of the presidency on 20 January 1961, he brought to the Oval Office a core of beliefs about the duties of the United States in the world, the challenges the United States faced in the international arena, and the role the president should play in directing the foreign policies of the United States. Kennedy espoused "internationalism." Like Presidents Theodore Roosevelt and Woodrow Wilson, he understood that the peace and prosperity of the United States depended upon peace and prosperity in the world. Given its size, wealth, and power, the United States had a natural obligation to take a leadership role in promoting international peace and prosperity. Kennedy was also a cold warrior. Like virtually all his political contemporaries, he accepted the premise that the Soviet Union and the international communist movement threatened the survival of the United States. The United States had to confront the communist menace. Kennedy confidently professed, however, that he could wage Cold War far more effectively than the Truman and Eisenhower administrations. Winning the Cold War depended, in Kennedy's view, on the president personally taking charge of U.S. foreign policies.

As a young man, Kennedy grew to be comfortable in the international arena. Having the good fortune of growing up in a wealthy and powerful family, he had the opportunity to travel abroad. Kennedy toured Europe during the time his father, Joseph P. Kennedy, served as Franklin Roosevelt's ambassador in London. During the war years, he served with distinction in the South Pacific as the commander of a patrol-torpedo (PT) boat. He also visited Argentina and Cuba and, in the mid-1950s, took his bride, Jacqueline Bouvier Kennedy, to the resort city of Acapulco, Mexico.

Kennedy displayed his first intellectual interest in international affairs in 1940 with his senior thesis at Harvard University. The study, *Why England Slept,* asked why the United Kingdom had not immediately and forcefully confronted the Nazi Germany of Adolf Hitler. The British, led by Prime Minister Neville Chamberlain, had tried to appease Hitler at Munich in 1938 by permitting him to seize part of Czechoslovakia. This appeasement only fed Hitler's appetite for aggression, leading to World War II. Although Kennedy did not especially criticize British leaders in his senior thesis, his study fit well into the intellectual consensus that developed in the postwar period. U.S. foreign-policy elites believed that seminal lessons were to be learned from what happened at Munich. The United

States needed to be actively engaged in international affairs, militarily prepared, and ready to resist criminal nations. The Soviet Union's domination of Poland and Romania in 1945, like Hitler's aggression in Austria and Czechoslovakia, might have been the first hint of a master plan to conquer the world. Kennedy's reputation was enhanced not only by his timely decision to analyze a critical historical event but also by his father's backing of the project. Joseph Kennedy asked prominent journalists to rewrite the thesis, and then he arranged for its publication.

During his time in the U.S. House and Senate (1947–1960), Kennedy supported key Cold War initiatives designed to contain the Soviet Union—the Truman Doctrine, the Marshall Plan, the North Atlantic Treaty Organization (NATO). He would have affirmed the central ideas in National Security Council Memorandum No. 68 (NSC 68), which the Truman administration secretly adopted in mid-1950.[5] According to NSC 68, the Soviet Union directed the international communist movement and was bent on world domination. Indeed, the Soviet Union allegedly planned to enslave the United States. NSC 68 depicted the ongoing Cold War in apocalyptic terms, or, as Kennedy put it in 1960, "a struggle for supremacy between two conflicting ideologies: Freedom under God versus ruthless, godless tyranny." The United States needed to remember the lessons of Munich. The Soviet Union was another Nazi Germany and Josef Stalin was as evil as Hitler had been. Only by building a military power "second to none," with hydrogen bombs, intercontinental bombers, and nuclear-powered submarines, could the United States hope first to contain and then to overwhelm the Soviet Union. NSC 68 also anticipated a globalist foreign policy; the United States must respond wherever communism reared its ugly head. U.S. vital interests included not just Western Europe but such distant areas as British Guiana, the Congo, and South Vietnam.

Senator Kennedy accepted the lessons of Munich and the Cold War verities of NSC 68, but he further believed he had insights and proposals that would hasten the defeat of the Soviet Union. By the mid-1950s, he had gained a seat on the prestigious Senate Foreign Relations Committee, which was a superb platform for promoting his ideas. Kennedy advised that the United States needed to appeal to Asians, Africans, and Latin Americans—the people of the developing world. The old order of European colonialism was crumbling; in 1960 alone eighteen new nations would appear. Speaking on the Senate floor in July 1957, Kennedy gained national and international attention by denouncing France for its suppression of Algerian independence.

He identified nationalism as "the most powerful force" in the world and Soviet and Western imperialists as the enemies of freedom. He reasoned that "the single most important test of American foreign policy today is how we meet the challenge of imperialism." One legacy of Western imperialism was U.S. control over the Panama Canal. Kennedy privately sympathized with Panamanian demands for the return of their canal, although he understood he would have difficulty persuading U.S. citizens to accommodate Panamanian nationalism. The senator also argued that the United States needed to finance economic development in poor regions and introduced legislation in 1958–1959 to give special assistance to India.

By proposing that the United States befriend impoverished, nonwhite people, Kennedy also revealed something about his character. Unlike many who had preceded him to the White House, Kennedy was a racial egalitarian who had a genuine concern for the poor. Although his $20 billion Alliance for Progress program for Latin America had strong anticommunist overtones, it also underscored Kennedy's belief that wealthy nations had a duty and responsibility to help their neighbors. For example, in 1963 while touring Costa Rica, Kennedy noticed an unoccupied hospital and ordered aides to find funds to staff it. Kennedy delighted in the company of Latin Americans and became fast friends with several Latin American leaders. Although not passionate about the issue of civil rights, Kennedy considered racism, like colonialism, to be anachronistic and irrational. As president, he consoled African diplomats who encountered discriminatory treatment in states like Maryland and Virginia. When Kennedy decided in 1963 to back civil rights legislation wholeheartedly, he knew that the abolition of segregation in the American South would aid the United States in its ideological struggle with the Soviet Union for the hearts and minds of people of color throughout the world.

However, Kennedy qualified his fervor for nationalism and economic justice and his opposition to colonialism and racism. Like most Democrats, he knew that his party had paid a terrible political price for "losing" China in 1949. Republicans blamed the Truman administration for the triumph of Mao Zedong and his Communist forces, and they rode the issue to electoral triumphs throughout the 1950s. The "fall" of China also fueled the hysteria associated with Senator Joseph McCarthy and his movement, dubbed "McCarthyism." McCarthy and his retinue alleged that disloyal Americans, usually Democrats, had undermined support for the anticommunist Chinese Nationalist forces. Kennedy was absolutely determined not to lose another country to communism.

During the 1960 campaign he repaid the Republicans for the China issue by blaming the Eisenhower/Nixon team for Fidel Castro's rise to power in Cuba. The political and intellectual problem for Kennedy was how to respond to figures like Nelson Mandela of South Africa, Cheddi Jagan of British Guiana, João Goulart of Brazil, or Salvador Allende of Chile. These nationalist leaders fought against imperialism, racism, and economic injustice, but they held left-wing political and economic views and gave credence to Marxist critiques of capitalist societies. They also accepted support from local Communist parties. For example, Mandela's African National Congress worked with South African Communists. Wedded to the NSC 68 analysis of the Soviet-American global struggle and forever fretting about his domestic political fortunes, Kennedy concluded that he could not work with progressive leaders who tolerated radical ideas. Fighting and winning the Cold War proved to be Kennedy's paramount concern. He inevitably chose an anticommunist dictator over a popularly elected leader who was not a zealous anticommunist. Under Kennedy, the United States ignored Mandela, destabilized Goulart's government, secretly spent millions of dollars to influence Chilean elections, and bluntly told the British to preserve colonialism in British Guiana in order to prevent Jagan from legitimately gaining power.

A speech by Soviet Premier Nikita Khrushchev reinforced Kennedy's ambivalent attitude toward Asia, Africa, and Latin America. On 6 January 1961, just prior to Kennedy's inauguration, Khrushchev promised to support "wars of national liberation." Presumably the Soviets would mask their conspiracies by infiltrating legitimate nationalist movements for freedom and justice. But scholars have pointed out that the Soviet leader only briefly raised the issue in the lengthy speech and that he may have been addressing doctrinal disputes within the Communist world. Nonetheless, Kennedy took Khrushchev's boast as a personal affront and direct challenge to the United States, and he ordered his new foreign-policy team to study the speech. He called it "one of the most important speeches of the decade," and in 1962 he reminded his advisors that Khrushchev "had made clear the pattern of military and paramilitary subversion which could be expected under the guise of 'wars of liberation.'" These fears prompted Kennedy to temper his sophisticated analysis of the dynamics of societies emerging from colonialism and poverty and to promote counterinsurgency doctrines and new military units, such as the U.S. Special Forces or "Green Berets." But military-aid programs for the developing world had the distinct possibility of bolstering the extremist, conservative groups that Kennedy professed to deplore.

Kennedy had the opportunity to present his views on the U.S. role in the world more fully during the 1960 presidential campaign. Foreign-policy issues dominated the debates between Kennedy and Vice President Richard Nixon. This focus on foreign policy probably aided Kennedy's election, because, in the late 1950s, many U.S. citizens worried that the U.S. standing in the world had declined. In 1957, the Soviet Union stunned the world by launching *Sputnik,* placing an artificial satellite into orbit around the earth. Thereafter, the Soviets displayed their scientific prowess and rocket and missile technology through several other impres-sive space missions. In 1958, Nixon had an unhappy tour of South Amer-ica, where he was greeted by protests in several counties and was nearly killed by a howling mob in Caracas, Venezuela. Latin Americans de-nounced the United States for its past support of anticommunist dictators. In 1959, Fidel Castro triumphantly rode on a tank into Havana and trans-formed his Cuban Revolution into a bitterly anti-American movement. The next year, the Soviets shot down a U-2 spy plane and captured the U.S. pilot. The U-2 incident turned into an immense propaganda victory for Khrushchev because the Eisenhower administration initially denied that the United States had intentionally violated Soviet airspace. The U-2 inci-dent further wrecked the May 1960 summit meeting in Paris between Eisenhower and Khrushchev. The president had hoped to use the summit to tame the nuclear arms race. That same year Eisenhower also had to can-cel a goodwill trip to Japan because of predicted protests and riots.

Kennedy relentlessly criticized the Eisenhower/Nixon stewardship of U.S. foreign policy. While speaking in Nashville, Tennessee, he pointed out the new danger of "a Communist satellite ninety miles off the coast of Florida, eight minutes by jet." In a press release, he suggested he would take steps to assist the overthrow of Castro. He repeatedly charged that the ad-ministration, by being parsimonious with military spending, had permit-ted a "missile gap" to develop. With numerical superiority in interconti-nental ballistic missiles, the Soviets might have the capability of starting and winning a nuclear war. Kennedy's charge was specious. Ironically, the photographs taken during the U-2 missions proved that the United States retained a sizable strategic nuclear advantage over the Soviets. Beyond spe-cific issues, Kennedy wanted the public to know that he grasped the mo-mentous nature of the Soviet-American confrontation and that he calcu-lated that the United States was losing the Cold War. The enemy, "the Communist system itself," was, in Kennedy's words, "lean and hungry" and "implacable, insatiable, unceasing in its drive for world domination." And the Communists might fulfill their master plan. As Kennedy told an audience in Alexandria, Virginia, history might judge "that these were the days when the tide began to run out for the United States. These were the times when the Communist tide began to pour in." Such dramatic rhetoric reverberated, of course, with the lessons of Munich and the ominous tone of NSC 68.

Presidential leadership, Kennedy promised, could rescue the United States and the world from the red tide of communism. The organization of the foreign-policy team would determine whether the president could carry out the bold, decisive actions necessary for winning the Cold War. The president-elect and his followers were convinced that Eisenhower had produced an organizational scheme guaranteeing ponderous thinking and torpid foreign policies. Drawing on his military experience, he had created an elaborate staff system to recommend policies and monitor their execution. Eisenhower made critical policy decisions at often lengthy National Security Council meetings. During his two terms, the NSC met 366 times, with Eisenhower presiding over 339. From the Kennedy administration's perspective, this process guaranteed endless talk and little action. But Eisenhower supplemented the NSC with regular gatherings in the Oval Office with his closest advisors, such as Secretary of State John Foster Dulles. Eisenhower used these meetings to coordinate national security policy with diplomacy, the day-to-day conduct of international relations. Presidential scholars have disagreed with Kennedy's assessment of the Eisenhower system and have given Eisenhower high marks for the way he organized his foreign policy. They have concluded that his organizational design prevented rash action, allowed the free exchange of ideas, and permitted the president to make the important decisions.

President-elect Kennedy's appointments reflected his disdain for elaborate committee structures and organizational charts and his desire to make the president, in his words, "the vital center of action in our whole scheme of government." He wanted to be a foreign-policy president and his own secretary of state. Moreover, he insisted on discussing his policy options and making his decisions in small, intense meetings. His appointment of McGeorge Bundy, as the president's assistant for national security affairs, signaled Kennedy's intentions. Bundy, who became Kennedy's chief foreign-policy counselor, centralized decision making in the White House and controlled the flow of information to the president. Bundy's appointment also demonstrated Kennedy's wish to consult with brilliant, relatively young men who enjoyed making decisions. Bundy, at forty-one, was a former dean at Harvard University who had also worked in government. Journalists tagged Kennedy's men the "action intellectuals" or the "best and the brightest." In this group was Robert S. McNamara, the president of Ford Motor Company, who was renowned for his computerized intelligence, "an IBM machine with legs." McNamara became secretary of defense. Kennedy named Dean Rusk, who had extensive diplomatic experience with Asian affairs, to be his secretary of state. But Kennedy considered the State Department to be conservative and unimaginative and did not work closely with Rusk. Beyond Bundy, the president relied on his brother, Attorney General Robert F. Kennedy, for advice. He especially appreciated his brother's fierce loyalty and readiness to discipline any U.S. official who challenged the administration's policies. With these appointments and arrangements, John Kennedy had placed himself in "the vital center of action" in the making of U.S. foreign policy.

THE NUCLEAR ARMS RACE, BERLIN, AND THE SOVIET UNION

Like other U.S. leaders in the Cold War era, President Kennedy defined his primary foreign-policy goal as containing and ultimately defeating the Soviet Union. Because he reckoned that the Soviet Union had taken the lead in the ideological struggle for the hearts and minds of the world's people, Kennedy argued that the United States needed to act boldly and decisively in the international arena. It had to speak unflinchingly about the dangers the United States faced, and it had to proclaim the political and moral superiority of the United States. It also had to defend its interests in contested areas of the world, such as West Berlin. Furthermore, the United States needed to curb Soviet expansionism by embarking on a robust buildup of its nuclear and conventional forces. Kennedy's assertive foreign policy had unforeseen consequences, intensifying the Soviet-American rivalry and making the world a more perilous place than it had been.

During his first months in office, President Kennedy demonstrated that he was a politician who would keep his campaign promises. Throughout the presidential race, Senator Kennedy had warned that the Soviet Union was winning the Cold War and that the Eisenhower/Nixon team had imperiled the security of the United States with its lax diplomatic and military policies. Most U.S. citizens remember the president's eloquent and stirring inaugural address, with its call to duty, greatness, and national self-sacrifice. But the president's address to a joint session of Congress ten days later, on 30 January 1961, set the tone for the administration's approach to international affairs. The new president revisited the apocalyptic language of his political campaign. It was the "hour of national peril." Whatever domestic problems existed, they paled compared to "those which confront us around the world." The Soviet Union and Communist China still harbored ambitions for world domination. Each day, the United States drew nearer "the hour of maximum danger." The administration would "reappraise our entire defense strategy," for "weapons spread and hostile forces grow stronger." Kennedy somberly reported that "I feel I must inform the Congress that our analyses over the last ten days make it clear that, in the principal areas of crisis, the tide of events has been running out—and time has not been our friend."

In order to convince the Communists that "aggression and subversion will not be profitable routes to pursue," the United States would have to rearm. During his first year in office, Kennedy, in three separate budgetary requests, asked for a total increase in military spending of 15 percent. By 1963, defense spending would be up to $54 billion, a substantial increase over President Eisenhower's final defense budget of $46 billion. The new spending transformed the U.S. military. Between 1961 and 1964, the number of nuclear weapons increased by 150 percent. The delivery vehicles for those nuclear weapons, intercontinental ballistic missiles (ICBMs), increased from 63 to 424, with the administration setting a goal of 1,000 ICBMs. The administration further accelerated the building of Polaris submarines and missiles. Conventional forces also benefited from the new spending. The army divisions increased from eleven to sixteen, the number of ships in the fleet doubled, and tactical air squadron numbers increased by 30 percent. The president took a special interest in counterinsurgency warfare. He instructed the Special Warfare Center at Fort Bragg, North Carolina, to accelerate training. The number of Special Forces personnel increased from fewer than one thousand to over twelve thousand by the end of 1963. The president actually chose the "green beret" as the symbol of the Special Forces.

This new military muscle allowed the United States to project power around the world. The nuclear firepower of the North Atlantic Treaty Organization increased by 60 percent between 1961 and 1963. By 1963, the United States had 275 major military bases in thirty-one countries. Sixty-five countries hosted U.S. armed forces, and U.S. military personnel trained armed forces from seventy-two countries. A total of 1.25 million members of the armed forces were stationed abroad. The Kennedy administration coupled the U.S. military buildup with a substantial increase in military aid to anticommunist nations. Between 1961 and 1964, U.S. military aid to Latin America, for example, averaged more than $77 million a year, a 50 percent increase over the average of the Eisenhower years.

In his alarmist address of 30 January 1961, Kennedy explicitly repudiated the national security policies of the Eisenhower administration. Eisenhower had outlined his approach to Cold War in NSC 162/2 (1953). In the document, Eisenhower implied that President Truman had not thought through the momentous implications of NSC 68. NSC 68 called for a massive, rapid military buildup, predicted that 1954 would be the year of "maximum danger," and called on the United States to amass a preponderance of power. Indeed, Paul Nitze, a principal author of NSC 68, suggested that the United States needed to take "increased risks of general war" in order to reach a satisfactory relationship with the Soviet Union. (Nitze now advised Kennedy on nuclear weapons, and Kennedy had used the "maximum danger" reference in his January 30 speech.) Eisenhower shared the Democrats' virulent anticommunism, but he rejected their doomsday scenarios. Eisenhower constantly preached that nuclear war would be catastrophic and that peace could be waged through nuclear deterrence. He predicted that the Cold War would last for decades but that victory was inevitable. Eisenhower judged Soviet leaders, like Nikita Khrushchev, as expansionists but also as rational men who loved their country and understood the consequences of general war. The Soviets would respect firmness and resolve. The key for Eisenhower was to have a strategy that was sustainable and would not bankrupt the nation. Excessive military spending would undermine "the American way of life." Federal funds allocated for aircraft carriers meant fewer dollars for schools, hospitals, and national parks. National security included having a healthy economy and resources to assist allies and woo nations emerging from colonialism. The United States would avoid rash confrontations that could provoke general war. It would deter Soviet aggression with nuclear weapons and challenge Soviet probes in Asia, Africa, and Latin America with military and economic aid and covert interventions.

Eisenhower underscored his thinking with his diplomatic and military policies, especially during his second presidential term. He feared that new military technologies, such as intercontinental ballistic missiles and submarine-launched ballistic missiles, raised the risk of thermonuclear war and the end of civilization. The successful launching of *Sputnik I* in 1957 by the Soviets had demonstrated the accuracy and power of these new missiles. In October 1958, Eisenhower suspended the testing of U.S. nuclear weapons, and, in 1959, he met with Khrushchev at Camp David, the presidential retreat, and had satisfactory discussions. Eisenhower envisioned reaching an agreement with the Soviet leader that would permanently ban the testing of nuclear weapons. The U-2 incident ruined Eisenhower's Paris summit meeting with Khrushchev in May 1960. Nonetheless, Eisenhower revisited his concerns about excessive military spending and the nuclear arms race in his farewell address on 17 January 1961, when he warned U.S. citizens about the dangers of the "military-industrial complex." President Kennedy's call to arms two weeks later stood in stark contrast to Eisenhower's plea for caution.

Politicians and military leaders criticized Eisenhower for restraining military spending, and some military officers resigned their commissions in public protest. In *Uncertain Trumpet* (1959), General Maxwell Taylor charged that Eisenhower had shortchanged U.S. conventional forces and left the nation too dependent on its nuclear deterrent. (President Kennedy would appoint Taylor as chairman of the Joint Chiefs of Staff.) As a candidate, Kennedy had alleged, of course, that Eisenhower had permitted a "missile gap" to develop. With the photographic evidence obtained by the U-2 spy planes, Eisenhower knew the facts. The first generation of ICBMs developed by the Soviets proved cumbersome and unwieldy. The United States—with two thousand bombers, one hundred ballistic missiles of varying ranges, and over eighteen thousand warheads in its nuclear stockpile—exercised an enormous strategic advantage over the Soviets. The United States had attained massive "overkill" capabilities, able to reduce the Soviet Union to a hulking, radiating ruin. Indeed, Eisenhower had never been able to curb the appetites of bureaucracies such as the Joint Chiefs of Staff, Defense Department, and Atomic Commission for new nuclear technologies and weapons. His "military-industrial complex" speech can, in part, be interpreted as an admission of failure. Eisenhower chose, however, not to flaunt U.S. nuclear prowess. Boasts and threats would only heighten global tensions and invite the Soviets to accelerate their nuclear weapons programs. And he never called Khrushchev's bluff, ignoring his blustering about Soviet military power.[6]

The new Kennedy administration gained access to the intelligence data that had informed Eisenhower's thinking on nuclear weapons. On 6 February, Secretary of Defense McNamara blurted out to correspondents: "There is no missile gap." The administration quickly retreated from that statement, recognizing that it would be denounced for having made false and misleading charges during the presidential campaign. The president qualified McNamara's admission by noting that it would be "premature to reach a judgment." But throughout 1961, Kennedy received intelligence estimates that persistently downgraded Soviet nuclear strength. U.S. intelligence analysts were aided by reports that they were receiving from Colonel Oleg Penkovsky, a Soviet military intelligence officer working for the West. By September, Kennedy was informed that the Soviet missile force was negligible. That same month he visited the Strategic Air Command (SAC) headquarters in Omaha, Nebraska, and listened as military commanders spoke of SAC's ability to deploy its bombers and missiles to hit nearly four thousand targets with nuclear warheads. Despite this information, the president went forward with his ambitious military expansion program. He justified his goal of one thousand ICBMs by explaining that he did not want to signal weakness to the Soviets.

President Kennedy took care to ensure that Khrushchev and other Soviet leaders knew about U.S. missile superiority. In the fall of 1961, in news conferences and interviews, the president, Secretary of State Rusk, and McNamara boasted in general terms that the United States had "nuclear power several times that of the Soviet Union." More important, the president authorized Roswell Gilpatric, the deputy secretary of defense, to enumerate U.S. nuclear power. Gilpatric's speech, which was given on 21 October 1961, provoked and humiliated Khrushchev, who was meeting with Communist officials in Moscow at the Twenty-Second Party Congress. Gilpatric provided specifics on U.S. bombers, ICBMs, and Polaris submarines. He assured his audience of U.S. businessmen that the United States could survive a surprise nuclear attack and retaliate with a devastating blow. From Gilpatric's presentation, however, the Soviets could draw the conclusion that the United States had achieved the capacity to begin, fight, and "win" a nuclear war. In the arcane world of strategic planning and doctrine, the United States possessed a "first-strike" capability. However unintentionally, Secretary McNamara may have reinforced that impression when he briefed NATO members in Athens, Greece, in May 1962 and indirectly suggested that the United States had a blueprint for a nuclear first strike.

In retrospect, the Kennedy administration had undermined U.S. national security with its rhetoric and the reality of its massive military buildup. Secretary of Defense McNamara has conceded that he and his boss had unnecessarily threatened the Soviet Union. The administration had publicly exposed the military weakness of the Soviet Union. It had further indicated that it now perceived nuclear weapons not just as a tool to deter war but also as an instrument of war. Soviet military planners might have surmised that the United States now believed it could survive a nuclear war. The Soviets were also angered by the administration's decision in mid-1961 to deploy fifteen medium-range ballistic missiles, Jupiters, to Turkey, a neighbor of the Soviet Union. President Eisenhower had authorized the Jupiters in 1959 but had delayed their deployment. The Kennedy administration had created the impression that it was backing the Soviet Union into a corner. Inevitably, the Soviets responded. Khrushchev's decision in mid-1962 to send nuclear missiles to Cuba can, in part, be explained by his desire to achieve the appearance of nuclear parity with the United States. In the 1960s, the Soviets would also embark on their own rapid, massive expansion of nuclear weaponry to match, even surpass, the Kennedy-era buildup. By the 1970s and 1980s, both superpowers had the ability to hit over ten thousand targets with strategic nuclear weapons. By the mid-1980s, there were fifty thousand nuclear warheads in the world on average, thirty times more powerful than the atomic bomb that annihilated Hiroshima in August 1945. President Kennedy and his advisors sought security through nuclear weapons. More nuclear weapons produced, however, more insecurity for U.S. citizens.

During his first months in office, President Kennedy managed to unnerve not only Soviet leaders but also his constituents. On 25 July 1961, the president gave another somber speech to the nation. This came a month after his unpleasant meeting with Khrushchev in Vienna, Austria. Beyond announcing he would ask Congress to add $3 billion to the defense budget, Kennedy requested that Congress appropriate $207 million to begin a civil-defense, fallout shelter program. In Kennedy's words, he "hoped to let every citizen know what steps he can take without delay to protect his family in case of attack." He added: "The lives of those families which are not hit in a nuclear blast and fire can still be saved—if they can be warned to take shelter, and if that shelter is available." The administration discussed building five to six million shelter spaces by early 1962 and over fifty million spaces over the next several years. The president's proposal sparked words and actions that can only be characterized as macabre. Children practiced "duck and cover" drills, hiding beneath their school desks. Citizens debated whether those who could afford to build their own shelters should arm themselves to keep out their unfortunate neighbors. Good judgment eventually took hold of the U.S. public. To enter a shelter would be to enter a tomb. The firestorms generated by thermonuclear war would burn so intensely they would consume available oxygen and asphyxiate living things. Indeed, that had been the fate of the residents of Dresden, Germany, when their city was firebombed during World War II. Even if a shelter program could save 30 million U.S. citizens, it might be in the context of losing 140 million people. In such a world, the living would envy the dead. Kennedy's civil defense program received little congressional support. The administration reconsidered and dropped its foolhardy plan.

President Kennedy's doomsday proposals reflected both his fears about the aggressive designs of the Soviet Union and his assessment of the bellicose nature of its leader, Nikita Khrushchev. Khrushchev, whose official title was Chairman of the Council of Ministers of the Union of Soviet Socialist Republics, was a veteran Communist who was twenty-three years older than Kennedy. Khrushchev came from a classic "peasant and worker" background and had only a rudimentary education. His father labored on a small farm, and Khrushchev worked for a time as a miner and a locksmith. In 1918, at the age of twenty-four, Khrushchev joined the Communist party and fought in the civil war. Over the next decades, he rose through the party ranks and became the party boss in the Ukraine. Those who gained status and power in the Communist party were loyal to Josef Stalin (1928–1953), the paranoid, murderous dictator of the Soviet Union. Khrushchev enforced Stalin's repressive polices. At the time of Stalin's death in 1953, Khrushchev was the leader of the party in Moscow. He used his party ties to become a national leader, and by 1957–1958 he had pushed aside rivals and took complete control of the Soviet Union.

Khrushchev's rise to power led to meaningful change in the Soviet Union. In a speech delivered to the Twentieth Party Congress in 1956, he denounced Stalin for his monstrous crimes. He subsequently ordered the release of millions of Soviet citizens from Stalin's prisons. He also relaxed censorship and promoted science. Khrushchev could take personal credit for the Soviet Union's crowning achievement—the launch of Sputnik—because he freed from a labor camp the scientist, Sergei Korolov, who designed the satellite. Khrushchev also began to curtail his country's military-industrial complex, devoting more resources to consumer goods. Reflecting his peasant background, he tried to boost agricultural production and alleviate the abysmal living conditions in the countryside. When he visited the United States in 1959, Khrushchev inspected a farm in Iowa and was dumbfounded by America's agricultural abundance. He vowed to reform Soviet agricultural practices and boasted that, under communism, the Soviet Union would soon surpass the United States in the production of milk, butter, and meat. He also planned to introduce corn production to his country. Khrushchev's good intentions did not, however, improve the diet of Soviet citizens. He lacked the scientific and technical expertise to plan properly, and, with his authoritarian personality, he refused to consult with experts. His corn production scheme proved a spectacular failure.

Khrushchev's foreign policies presented both challenges and opportunities to the United States. The Soviet leader initially suggested that he took a flexible attitude toward various paths to socialism, and he reconciled with the independent Communist nation of Yugoslavia, led by Joseph Tito. But he sent tanks in Budapest in October 1956 to crush Hungarian patriots who fought to free their country from Soviet domination. He also quarreled with Chinese leaders about doctrinal issues in the communist world. Notably, Khrushchev criticized Mao Zedong for not accepting the reality that a thermonuclear war would be catastrophic for global civilization. He preached a peaceful but competitive coexistence with the West. Khrushchev blathered on endlessly about the eventual triumph of communism and backed up his rhetoric by expanding Soviet economic and military contacts with developing nations such as Egypt and Indonesia. But his formula of coexistence meant that he had implicitly rejected the communist doctrine that armed conflict with capitalist nations was inevitable. In fact, he tried to restrain Soviet military spending. Although a fervent Communist, Khrushchev did not have a "blueprint" for the destruction of the United States and the domination of the world—the premise of both NSC 68 and the ominous speeches delivered by President Kennedy on 30 January and 25 July 1961.

U.S. officials and citizens found it difficult to comprehend Khrushchev, because he cloaked his actions in coarse behavior and crude language. They tired of hearing about the accuracy and power of Soviet rockets and Soviet achievements in space, which included putting a cosmonaut, Yuri Gagarin, into orbit around the earth in early 1961. They were astounded when Khrushchev punctuated an aggressive speech at the

United Nations in October 1960 by taking off his shoe and pounding the podium with it. U.S. citizens were also frightened by Khrushchev's decision to resume atmospheric testing of nuclear weapons on 30 August 1961. In part, Khrushchev's move was a reaction to Kennedy's massive expansion of nuclear weaponry. Over the next sixty days, the Soviets conducted fifty tests, including one fifty-eight-megaton (the equivalent of fifty-eight million tons of TNT) explosion. Khrushchev further bellowed that the Soviet Union might conduct a one-hundred-megaton explosion, enough to consume the state of Maryland in a firestorm. It was typical Khrushchev. His warlike propaganda could not be made tangible, because no country had delivery vehicles that could carry such massive bombs. Nonetheless, in September 1961, Kennedy ordered the resumption of underground tests of nuclear warheads, and U.S. atmospheric tests resumed in March 1962.

Mutual fear, suspicion, and distrust characterized the Soviet-American confrontation during the Cold War and especially during the Kennedy presidency. Neither superpower practiced the virtue of empathy. Khrushchev apparently assumed that Kennedy possessed telepathic powers and would understand that the "wars of national liberation" affirmation of early January 1961 was directed at the Chinese Communists. Kennedy inferred, however, that Khrushchev had declared war against the United States at the dawn of his presidency. Similarly, Kennedy must have thought Soviet intelligence analysts were so capable that they knew the president, in confidential discussions with U.S. civilian and military advisors, expressed extreme skepticism about the concept of "limited nuclear war" or "winning" a nuclear war. Khrushchev and his advisors predictably examined the public statements by prominent Defense Department officials such as Gilpatric and McNamara. They concluded that the United States contemplated a preemptive nuclear strike against Mother Russia. This fear and loathing served as the context for the Kennedy-Khrushchev confrontations at Vienna and over Berlin and Cuba.

The two leaders held extended discussions at Vienna on 3–4 June 1961. After opening pleasantries, the talks immediately degenerated into the diplomatic equivalent of a shouting match. Kennedy began by noting that the two powers could be peaceful rivals if they respected each other's basic strategic interests. But the Soviet Union, Kennedy averred, "was seeking to eliminate free systems in areas that are associated with us." Khrushchev denied that his nation promoted communism throughout the world, although he boasted that "what the Soviet Union says is that communism will triumph." Just as the French Revolution swept away feudal-ism, so communism, in a "victory of ideas," would overwhelm capitalism. The United States, Khrushchev implied, was like the Spanish Inquisition, which "burned people who disagreed with it. . . ." However, he continued, "ideas did not burn and eventually came out as victors." After this stale de-bate about ideology, the two leaders talked about their allies. President Kennedy gave a tortured defense of U.S. support for tyrants such as Fran-cisco Franco of Spain and the Shah of Iran. Chairman Khrushchev made the ludicrous points that Poland had freely chosen communism and that "its election system is more democratic than that in the United States." Hyperbole and distortion similarly characterized their exchanges about Cuba, Vietnam, and nuclear testing. Kennedy later confessed to aides and journalists that he felt Khrushchev had overwhelmed him and had tried to take advantage of his relative youth and inexperience. He reportedly re-ferred to Khrushchev as a "barbarian." The memorandums of the conver-sations reveal, however, that Kennedy gave as good as he got, countering each of Khrushchev's accusations with his own allegation. He also managed to remain calm, whereas Khrushchev, befitting his style, blustered. The ten-sion was broken only at the luncheons and dinners. The Soviet chairman enjoyed conversing with the elegant and intelligent Jacqueline Kennedy, the president's wife.

Berlin became the burning issue at the Vienna talks and erupted into a Soviet-American crisis in the summer of 1961. On the second day of talks, Khrushchev stunned Kennedy when he demanded that the United States abandon its position in West Berlin by the end of the year. He threat-ened to terminate the agreements of World War II and sign a separate peace treaty with East Germany. East Germany would then be in a position to cut off Western access to the city, because Berlin was situated entirely within East Germany, 110 miles from the border of West Germany. The word "war" actually arose in the talks. Kennedy noted that "he had gained the impression that the USSR was presenting him with the alternative of accepting the Soviet act on Berlin or having a face to face confrontation." Khrushchev responded "that if the U.S. wanted war, that was its problem." He reiterated, however, his "firm and irrevocable" decision to sign a peace treaty in December. President Kennedy concluded the exchange "by ob-serving that it would be a cold winter."

Competing visions of the past, present, and future encompassed the Soviet-American confrontation over Berlin.[7] Berlin's unique international position resulted from the defeat of Nazi Germany and wartime agreements. Germany and its capital city were divided among the four Allied powers, pending a comprehensive settlement. The United States, Great Britain, and France merged their respective sectors, creating West Germany (Federal Republic of Germany) in 1949 and West Berlin. Bonn became the capital of West Germany. The Soviet sector became East Germany (German Democratic Republic) and East Berlin. The four powers, based on occupation rights, retained privileges in all Berlin. Legally, Berlin was part of neither West nor East Germany. For example, West Germany did not govern West Berlin, although West Berliners were citizens of West Germany, and the divided city and the nation maintained close ties.

West Germany had made remarkable progress since 1945. The United States, through its Marshall Plan (1947–1952) economic aid program, had reconstructed the defeated nation, made it prosperous, and turned it into a bulwark against communism. Konrad Adenauer (1949–1963) gave West Germany determined leadership. Adenauer, who had opposed Adolf Hitler and the Nazis, tied his nation to the West and its anticommunist policies. In 1955, West Germany became part of NATO, the military alliance against the Soviet Union. Adenauer also foresaw the day when Germany would be reunified and have a democratic, capitalist system. He refused to acknowledge East Germany, deeming it an illegitimate state. The Western powers officially favored the reunification of Germany, although some U.S. and Western European officials privately expressed misgivings about the restoration a powerful, unified Germany.

Chairman Khrushchev did not hesitate to assert his nation's adamant opposition to a unified Germany. In the twentieth century, Germany had twice invaded Russia. Nazi Germany's invasion and destruction of the Soviet Union during World War II arguably represented the most barbarous act in the history of international relations. Hitler's forces killed as many as twenty-five million Soviet citizens and destroyed everything in their path. At Vienna, Khrushchev spoke emotionally of losing his son in the war. With little exaggeration, he added: "There is not a single family in the USSR or the leadership of the USSR that did not lose one of its members in the war." From Khrushchev's perspective, that sacrifice was being dishonored by U.S. policy. West Germany had become part of the anti-Soviet military alliance, and former Nazi officers served in the NATO command. A unified, anticommunist Germany with access to nuclear weapons would undermine national security and signify that the Soviet Union had gained nothing from its victory in World War II. Although public opinion polls were not a feature of the Communist system, Khrushchev probably spoke the views of most Russians when it came to their former enemy.

The prospect of a unified Germany was not beyond imagination, because East Germany, a client state or satellite of the Soviet Union, was collapsing in 1961. In the past decade, more than two million East Germans had fled the country via West Berlin, with many then moving on to West Germany. In July 1961 alone, the month after the Vienna summit, thirty thousand East Germans entered West Berlin. They left East Germany because they resented Soviet domination of their country, opposed communism, believed in parliamentary government, or wanted to work in the dynamic West German economy. They represented the best and brightest of their society—doctors, engineers, students, skilled workers. Soviet officials joked that soon only German Communist leader Walter Ulbricht and his mistress would be left in East Germany. Khrushchev vowed that he would eliminate the "sore spot," "ulcer," and "thorn." West Berlin had become a "bone in the Soviet throat."

President Kennedy could scarcely meet Khrushchev's demands. He had to honor the moral obligation the United States had to the two million West Berliners and their inspired leader, Mayor Willy Brandt. Moreover, Kennedy's predecessors had made the defense of West Berlin a keystone of U.S. foreign policy. In 1948–1949, President Truman, by sending a massive airlift of food and supplies, overcame Stalin's effort to blockade the city. In 1958–1959, President Eisenhower rejected Khrushchev's first ultimatum on Berlin. Eisenhower conceded that Berlin's status was "abnormal," but he was unwilling to negotiate a substantive change in the U.S. position. He stayed calm and deliberate during the crisis, counting on the idea that neither side wanted a nuclear war. As Kennedy explained to Khrushchev, defending Berlin had taken on a larger meaning. If the Soviets unilaterally drove the United States out of West Berlin, the status of the United States as a world power would be diminished. Western Europeans would question the U.S. pledge to defend them. In Kennedy's words, "US commitments would be regarded as a mere scrap of paper." An astute politician, Kennedy also knew that his citizens overwhelmingly supported a tough stance on Berlin. One public opinion survey in July 1961 reported that 82 percent of the U.S. public favored using force to defend West Berlin.

U.S. citizens might have tempered their enthusiasm for military action if they fully understood the potential consequences. Because Berlin was so exposed, U.S. military planners were not persuaded that the United States could defend it with conventional weapons. War plans included the United States being the first to use nuclear weapons. In a review of military contingency plans in case of a Berlin conflict, Assistant Secretary of Defense Paul Nitze actually advised Kennedy to consider launching a preemptive nuclear attack on the Soviet Union, arguing that "we could in some real sense be victorious in the series of nuclear exchanges." Secretary of Defense McNamara doubted a meaningful victory could be achieved. Secretary of State Rusk reminded the president that "the first side to use nuclear weapons will carry a very grave responsibility and endure consequences before the rest of the world."

Although he exacerbated Soviet-American tensions in his first months in office and initiated a new and ominous nuclear arms race, President Kennedy managed the Berlin crisis. His speech of 25 July, with its calls for a military buildup, fallout shelters, and mobilization of military reservists did not ease international anxieties. The Soviet Union officially labeled the speech as "warlike." Khrushchev protested that Kennedy had just declared "preliminary war" against his nation. But Kennedy avoided excessive options. Some advisors, such as the influential former Secretary of State Dean Acheson, urged the president to declare a national emergency and take provocative actions such as dispatching a division of U.S. troops from West Germany along the highway, or autobahn, through East Germany to West Berlin. Acheson opposed compromises, wanting the Berlin crisis to be a "test of will." Astute analysts might have also noticed that the president refrained from calling for the unification of Germany or the right of East Berliners to travel to West Berlin. He simply vowed to preserve surface access from West Germany to West Berlin, to maintain a military presence in the city, and to defend West Berlin. Shortly thereafter, Senator J. William Fulbright (D-Ark.), the chair of the Senate Foreign Relations Committee, publicly suggested that the Soviets and the East Germans treat the refugee issue as a domestic issue. Fulbright said, "I don't understand why the East Germans don't close their border, because I think they have a right to close it."

During the night of 12–13 August 1961, the East Germans, with Soviet approval, closed the border between East and West Berlin, tearing up roads and installing roadblocks and barbed wire. On that last day, four thousand East Germans had fled to West Berlin. A few days later, the East Germans began to construct what came to be known as the "Berlin Wall," a permanent installation of concrete, barbed wire, and watchtowers, bordered by minefields. The Berlin Wall, which reached one hundred miles in length, surrounded West Berlin, sealing it off from East Berlin and neighboring parts of East Germany. About fifteen thousand East German troops guarded the wall. East Germans continued trying to enter West Berlin, but only a few thousand ever managed to get over the wall or through the minefields. The border guards shot about six hundred East Germans trying to escape. In one appalling incident in August 1962, Peter Fechter, an East German, was shot by border guards and then bled to death at the foot of the wall.

President Kennedy did not launch a frontal assault on the Berlin Wall. His policy was encapsulated in his remark to aides that "a wall is a hell of a lot better than a war." He kept silent about the wall in the week following its construction and, until June 1963, mentioned it only three times. To signal his concern, he dispatched Vice President Johnson and General Lucius Clay, the hero of the Berlin airlift of 1948–1949, to West Berlin. He also ordered a small battle group of fifteen hundred military men to travel on trucks down the autobahn through East Germany to West Berlin to insure that the West preserved its access to the city. The battle group received a tumultuous welcome from Berliners when it rolled down the *Kurfürstendamm,* the glittering shopping street of West Berlin, and the soldiers were personally saluted by the vice president. Kennedy concluded that Khrushchev would not challenge the U.S. position in West Berlin.

After August 1961 the Berlin crisis gradually wound down, without a definitive settlement. Kennedy essentially adopted Eisenhower's approach of 1958–1959. He toned down his rhetoric, most notably in a speech he gave at the United Nations in September, when he spoke eloquently about the dangers of nuclear war. He and Khrushchev began a personal correspondence about Berlin, and he authorized high-level discussions about the status of the city. The subsequent talks produced nothing of substance. Kennedy had to face a potential crisis in late October 1961, when a dispute over the right of a U.S. diplomat to cross into East Berlin flared into a confrontation. U.S. and Soviet tanks faced one another at "Checkpoint Charlie," a border crossover point. Through an intermediary, the president suggested a face-saving formula to Khrushchev; both sides withdrew their tanks.

Chairman Khrushchev gained some short-term advantages from the ugly Berlin Wall. By halting the flight of refugees, he preserved East Germany, a buffer state for the Soviet Union. He may have also contained the

East German leadership. Khrushchev distrusted all Germans, including German Communists. He perhaps worried that a desperate Ulbricht might drag the Soviet Union into a conflict by ordering East German troops to attack a U.S. military convoy. Khrushchev surely noticed that President Kennedy did not protest about East Berlin and downplayed Chancellor Adenauer's demand for free elections and the unification of Germany. On 17 October 1961, Khrushchev withdrew the ultimatum he had issued at the Vienna summit. Fundamentally, both he and Kennedy feared thermonuclear war. Khrushchev may have also had the same problem as Kennedy, controlling irresponsible military and civilian advisors who talked about emerging victorious from nuclear exchanges. Nonetheless, a year later both he and Kennedy would come much closer to nuclear war in the Cuban missile crisis.

However it may have resolved some immediate political difficulties, the Berlin Wall proved politically disastrous for the Soviet system. International observers admired both the Soviet Union's valiant battle against Nazi Germany and their scientific achievements in outer space. They also approved of Khrushchev's denunciation of Joseph Stalin's crimes. But fairminded people judged the Berlin Wall, in the words of Mayor Willy Brandt, as "an offense not only against history, but an offense against humanity." The hideous scar that stretched across the city separated families, divided husbands and wives, brothers and sisters, and kept a national people apart. The Berlin Wall came to symbolize the political and socioeconomic failures of communism. Many reasoned thereafter that Stalin's gross violations of basic human rights were not particular to a paranoid megalomaniac but endemic to the communist system. When jubilant Berliners pushed the wall over in November 1989, it heralded the end of the Soviet domination of Eastern Europe and the collapse of the Soviet Union two years later.

Only once did President Kennedy seize the propaganda bonanza that Khrushchev had handed the West, but he did so in a memorable way. On 26 June 1963, he addressed a gigantic, delirious crowd of West Berliners from a platform mounted on the steps of the *Rathaus,* or city hall. That morning Kennedy had seen the wall for the first time. He sent the crowd into a frenzy, proclaiming that "today, in the world of freedom, the proudest boast is *Ich bin ein Berliner* [I am a Berliner]!" His answer to anyone who questioned the moral superiority of the West was: "Let them come to Berlin!" The "Free World" had problems, "but we have never had to put a wall up to keep our people in, to prevent them from leaving us!" Kennedy told the crowd that he foresaw the day when Berlin and Germany would be joined again. When that day comes, "the people of West Berlin can take sober satisfaction in the fact that they were in the front lines."

Kennedy's triumphant performance in Berlin garnered him adulation both at home and abroad. But the president, who had an appreciation of irony, might have reflected on what he had done. He had consigned the Soviet Union and communism to the dustbin of history. Kennedy had done exactly what he had objected to when Nikita Khrushchev gave his "wars of national liberation" speech and when he proclaimed the inevitable victory of communism at the Vienna summit.

FIDEL CASTRO AND CUBA

If one issue defined John F. Kennedy's presidency, it would be his conduct of relations with Cuba under Fidel Castro. From the public's perception, U.S. policy toward Cuba represented both the high and low points of the Kennedy years. The president achieved a striking triumph in October 1962, when he forced the Soviet Union to dismantle and remove nuclear-tipped missiles from the Caribbean island. This diplomatic victory came a little more than a year after Kennedy suffered a humiliating defeat. In April 1961, Castro's forces routed the U.S.-backed invasion force of Cuban exiles at the Bay of Pigs. But Kennedy's Cuban policy can be measured in more than just success and failure. During the Cuban crises, he displayed his leadership talents, his decision-making abilities, and crisis-management skills. Kennedy's stability and judgment can also be examined, in light of his administration waging a campaign of sabotage and terrorism against Cuba and trying to assassinate the Cuban leader. The war against Castro left an enduring legacy. Nearly four decades after President Kennedy's death, the United States remains obsessed with Castro's Cuba.

On 19 January 1961, the day before the transfer of presidential power, President Eisenhower bluntly informed the president-elect that "in the long run the United States cannot allow the Castro Government to continue to exist in Cuba." Kennedy listened well. He spent his limited time in office trying to overthrow Castro. He shared his predecessor's insight that the United States could not accept a radical regime in the Western Hemisphere, the traditional U.S. sphere of influence.

Fidel Castro and his band of bearded guerrillas rode on tanks into Havana in the first days of 1959. Their triumphant entry into the capital city marked the culmination of Castro's six-year struggle against dictator Fulgencio Batista. The Cuban strongman had dominated national life since 1934 and had directly ruled since 1952, when he seized power. Castro and his youthful followers opposed Batista's tyrannical rule. They also envisioned a socially just, progressive Cuba that addressed the nation's problems of poverty and deep social and racial inequities. Like other educated Cubans, Castro held ambivalent views about the United States. He appreciated the wealth and technological prowess of the United States and admired its heroes, such as Abraham Lincoln. He also enjoyed U.S. popular culture, playing baseball and following major league teams like the New York Yankees. But Cubans deeply resented the role that the United States had played in Cuba's history and political and economic life. After assisting Cuba's struggle for independence in the War of 1898, the United States attached the Platt Amendment (1903–1934) to the Cuban constitution, giving the United States the right to oversee Cuba's internal affairs. U.S. military forces repeatedly invaded the island. With their money guaranteed by the bayonets of U.S. Marines, U.S. investors came to dominate Cuba's economic life. With approximately $900 million invested in Cuba by 1959, U.S. investors accounted for 40 percent of the country's critical sugar production. U.S. companies also controlled public utilities, oil refineries, mines, railroads, and the tourist industry. Trade treaties granted Cuban sugar producers a guaranteed, subsidized market in the United States but simultaneously gave the United States enormous leverage over the Cuban economy and ensured that U.S. firms would supply most of Cuba's imports. Cubans took further offense that U.S. tourists considered Havana their playground for gambling, narcotics, and prostitution. Cubans also could not forget that the Eisenhower administration fawned over Batista and armed him with U.S. weapons because the dictator protected foreign investments, voted with Washington at the United Nations, and professed to be an anticommunist. In fact, the unscrupulous Batista quietly worked with the Cuban Communist party.

Reforming Cuban society inevitably meant altering the U.S. presence in Cuba. Like many Cubans, Fidel Castro blamed the United States for Cuba's backwardness and international insignificance. As an astute politician, he understood that anti-Americanism would strike a responsive chord among the Cuban public. His agrarian reform law, which was promulgated in April 1959, set the tone for U.S.-Cuban relations. The law expropriated farmlands larger than one thousand acres, with compensation to be paid in Cuban bonds and based on the land's declared value for taxes in 1958. Sugar barons, both foreign and domestic, had predictably undervalued their land in Batista's Cuba. The new law—which was to be administered by a Cuban Communist, Antonio Núñez Jiménez—also prohibited foreigners from owning agricultural land. Sympathetic observers judged agrarian reform as a legitimate effort to address the crushing poverty and injustice that characterized the Cuban countryside. But from Washington's perspective, the Agrarian Reform Law of 1959 smacked both of anti-Americanism and communism.

Fidel Castro moved only progressively toward communism. On 1 December 1961, he publicly declared: "I am a Marxist-Leninist, and I will continue to be a Marxist-Leninist until the last day of my life." Most historians do not believe that Castro was a Communist in the 1950s, although his compatriots included his brother Raúl Castro and the Argentine, Ernesto "Ché" Guevara, both committed radicals. The Cuban Communist party did not initially embrace Castro's anti-Batista movement; the party only began to support Castro fervently after he took power. Castro gradually concluded that communism provided answers to Cuba's problems and that the communist concept of the "dictatorship of the proletariat" would enhance his drive for personal domination of Cuba. As Castro reaped the animosity of the United States, he predictably turned to the Soviet Union. In February 1960, Castro hosted a Soviet trade fair in Cuba and signed a commercial agreement. The Soviets agreed to purchase one million tons of Cuban sugar over each of the next five years and to provide the Cubans with a $100 million credit to purchase Soviet equipment.

By the end of 1959, U.S. officials spoke of overthrowing Castro. The Central Intelligence Agency (CIA) official responsible for the Western Hemisphere, Colonel J. C. King, suggestively recommended that "thorough consideration be given to the elimination of Fidel Castro." On 17 March 1960, President Eisenhower gave formal approval to a "program of covert action against the Castro regime." The plan included launching a propaganda offensive, creating anti-Castro forces within Cuba, and training a paramilitary force outside of Cuba for future action. Through the rest of 1960, the administration attacked Cuba. The CIA broadcast anti-Castro diatribes from a radio station on Swan Island, a dot of land off the coast of Honduras. The administration tried to strangle the Cuban economy, cutting off the sugar quota and banning U.S. exports to the island. The CIA began to train Cuban exiles in Guatemala with the mission of carrying out an amphibious invasion of Cuba. The CIA also contacted the criminal underworld of the United States, "the Mafia," urging members of organized crime to carry out a "gangland-style killing" of Castro and his chief associates. The CIA reasoned that the Mafia resented Castro for having driven gambling interests out of Havana. On 3 January 1961, Eisenhower broke diplomatic relations with Cuba.

John Kennedy's attitude toward Cuba evolved rapidly. As a senator, he denounced the Eisenhower administration for supporting the Batista regime, suggesting that Castro might have taken a rational course if the administration had "not backed the dictator so long and so uncritically." But in 1960, he seized on the mounting tension with Castro and transformed it into a major campaign issue. The radicalization of the Cuban Revolution and the growing relationship between Cuba and the Soviet Union lent credence to his basic campaign issue—the United States was losing the Cold War. On 27 November, the president-elect received an extensive briefing from CIA Director Allen Dulles on the covert campaign. Eisenhower repeatedly told aides that he hoped Kennedy would go forward with the invasion plans, and in two meetings with Kennedy, on 6 December and 19 January, he emphasized the importance of ousting Castro.

The U.S.-backed invasion took place at the Bay of Pigs on the southwestern shores of Cuba on 17–19 April 1961, less than three months after Kennedy took office. Castro's forces quickly routed the 1,400-man invasion force known as "Brigade 2506," killing 149 and capturing 1,189 of the Cuban exiles. Castro took personal command of the Cuban military, directed the counterattack, and garnered enormous prestige both at home and abroad for having defeated the United States. Indeed, he became an international hero and a leading actor on the world stage. The calamity at the Bay of Pigs represented a signal policy failure in the history of U.S. foreign relations. Why President Kennedy authorized the invasion and how he acted during the crisis have been controversial questions.[8]

The new president surely could have reasoned that he had no choice but to go forward with the invasion. If he had cancelled the invasion, he would have been rejecting the plans of the nation's most trusted military leader, General Dwight Eisenhower. He would also have what CIA officials dubbed a "disposal" problem. The Cuban exiles training in Guatemala would have returned to the United States and loudly complained to journalists and politicians that President Kennedy lacked resolve. The president would further have found it politically embarrassing to distance himself from his exaggerated campaign rhetoric on supporting "fighters for freedom." But aborting the invasion would have averted disaster. As a CIA internal postmortem concluded, the Bay of Pigs debacle "brought even more embarrassment, carried death and misery to hundreds . . . and seriously damaged U.S. prestige." Indeed, the president received strong advice to cancel Eisenhower's plan. Congressional leaders and State Department officials raised philosophical, diplomatic, and practical objections to the unprovoked invasion of a sovereign country. Presidential aide Arthur Schlesinger warned Kennedy that "Cuba will become our Hungary," referring to the ugly Soviet invasion of Hungary in 1956. Latin Americans would view an invasion "as a reversion to economic imperialism of the pre–World War I, Platt Amendment, big-stick, gun-boat diplomacy kind." Although the opponents of the Bay of Pigs invasion did not propose it, there was a politically expedient way for Kennedy to escape his dilemma. Newspapers and journals, including the *New York Times,* reported about the Cuban exiles training in Guatemala. Kennedy conceivably could have lamented this exposure and terminated the training. Instead, he asked editors to suppress the news.

Kennedy authorized the Bay of Pigs operation because he liked what he heard about the invasion plans and because he embraced the mass delusion that existed about political life in Cuba. CIA officials, especially Deputy Director for Plans Richard M. Bissell Jr., assured Kennedy that he could keep the U.S. hand hidden in the operation, although Schlesinger and others correctly pointed out that everyone in the world would blame the United States. Kennedy seems to have been impressed by the upbeat assessments he received about the fighting abilities of the brigade training in Guatemala. He also mistakenly believed that the brigade could disappear into the mountains and become a guerrilla force if the Cuban exiles did not achieve complete success at the beachhead. In fact, marshy areas surrounded the Bay of Pigs, and the Escambray Mountains were eighty miles away. Beyond these logistical realities, President Kennedy, like so many U.S. citizens, professed that Cubans suffered under Castro and prayed for their deliverance. The invasion supposedly would produce a "shock" in Cuba, triggering a mass uprising. As Inspector General of the CIA Lyman Kirkpatrick noted in his postmortem report, "we can confidently assert that the Agency [CIA] had no intelligence evidence that

Cubans in significant numbers could or would join the invaders or that there was any kind of effective and cohesive resistance movement under anybody's control." Castro enjoyed widespread popular support, which only intensified after his victory at the Bay of Pigs.

Critics have lambasted President Kennedy for undermining Brigade 2506 by refusing to provide adequate air and naval support on the day of the invasion. Implicit in this criticism is the idea that the brigade of exiles and the United States could have readily conquered Cuba. Castro and his forces were well prepared for an invasion. Fidel and Raúl Castro had built an army of twenty-five thousand and a loyal, self-defense force of over two hundred thousand Cubans who were armed with weapons obtained from the Soviet Union and Communist Eastern Europe. In April 1961, at least one battalion of troops patrolled every beach in Cuba. Castro's intelligence officers anticipated an invasion because they had read about the Guatemalan training base in U.S. newspapers. They presumably had also penetrated the exile community residing in Miami, Florida. Cubans further remembered that the United States had used an exile army to overthrow the government of Jacobo Arbenz Guzmán (1950–1954) in Guatemala in 1954. Ché Guevara had actually been in Guatemala in 1954. Finally, in Castro, the Cubans had an experienced military commander who had fought for three hard years in the Cuban mountains. The Bay of Pigs should be viewed as a Cuban victory.

Kennedy's critical decision during the Bay of Pigs was to cancel an air strike on Cuban airfields scheduled for the invasion day, or "D-Day." An air strike had taken place on April 15 that had some success, destroying five Cuban airplanes. But the second air strike would have likely hit empty airfields, since, after April 15, Castro's pilots were prepared to take off at a moment's notice. The president also rejected requests to directly introduce U.S. military forces to the battle. During the invasion, President Kennedy acted much as he would during the Berlin and Cuban missile crises. Once having blundered into a crisis, the president proved steady and cautious, rejecting options that could lead to wholesale conflict. An invasion of Cuba that included U.S. forces might have led to sustained, bloody war.

One feature of the Bay of Pigs invasion plan that was not disclosed in mid-April 1961 was the CIA's efforts to assassinate Castro. In mid-March and again in early April 1961, the CIA's underworld contacts managed to pass poison pills to anti-Castro Cubans in Havana. One plot failed when the pills, hidden in an icebox at Castro's favorite restaurant, froze to the coils. The plan was to place the lethal pills in Castro's ice cream dessert. What knowledge President Kennedy had of these and subsequent conspiracies to assassinate Castro cannot be precisely ascertained. Shortly after taking office, Special Assistant for National Security Affairs McGeorge Bundy received a briefing from the CIA on ZR Rifle, the code name for the CIA's assassination capabilities. In mid-May 1962, Attorney General Robert Kennedy received a thorough briefing from CIA Director of Security Sheffield Edwards about the CIA's contacts with gambling syndicate figures John Rosselli and Sam Giancana. (One of Giancana's girlfriends was Judith Campbell, who was also President Kennedy's mistress during his White House years.) No documentary record has appeared that would prove that either of Kennedy's closest advisors informed the president about assassination plots. But the president broached the subject in conversations with his good friend, Senator George Smathers (D-Fla.), and with a *New York Times* journalist, Tad Szulc. Both men later said that Kennedy expressed his distaste for the idea. Admirers, like Arthur Schlesinger, have also claimed that, as a Roman Catholic, Kennedy could not countenance assassination. On the other hand, these same admirers emphasize that John Kennedy was a leader who dominated the foreign policymaking process. The plots to murder Castro continued after the Bay of Pigs. No one has found a document to show that the president ordered the CIA to cease its efforts to assassinate Castro.

After the fiasco at the Bay of Pigs, Kennedy certainly gave no thought to reassessing U.S. policy toward Castro's Cuba. On 5 May 1961, he presided over a NSC meeting and ruled that U.S. policy would continue to "aim at the downfall of Castro." Kennedy foreclosed, however, an immediate U.S. military intervention in Cuba. The president awaited the report of a special board of inquiry on the Bay of Pigs chaired by General Maxwell Taylor and Robert Kennedy. President Kennedy would accept a key recommendation of the Taylor Report, establishing a new committee to oversee counterinsurgency efforts. Taylor and Attorney General Kennedy would direct the new "Special Group (CI)," overseeing military aid, counterinsurgency, and police training. Robert Kennedy would also become the president's point man on Cuba. He roughly informed U.S. military and intelligence officials that "the Cuban problem" was the top priority of the government and that "no time, money, efforts, or manpower is to be spared." Quoting his brother, Robert Kennedy noted in early 1962 that "the final chapter on Cuba has not been written."

While awaiting new ideas and plans for waging war against Cuba, President Kennedy brushed aside a Cuban peace offer. On 17 August 1961, Ché Guevara spoke late into the night with presidential aide Richard Goodwin. Both men were attending the inter-American conference on the Alliance for Progress held at Punta del Este, Uruguay. Guevara had previously sent Goodwin a handsomely designed box filled with the finest cigars from Havana. Guevara suggested that by discussing issues such as the U.S.-expropriated properties, trade, and Cuba's role in Latin America that the two countries could reach a modus vivendi—a way of living together. Goodwin personally informed Kennedy of his conversation and circulated a memorandum to national security officials. Nothing developed from the Goodwin-Guevara exchange. The president's only tangible gesture was to smoke one of the cigars.

In early November 1961, the president authorized a new campaign against Castro, "Operation Mongoose," under the direction of General Edward G. Lansdale, a supposed expert on counterinsurgency warfare. Operation Mongoose would, in Kennedy's words, "help Cuba overthrow the Communist regime." General Lansdale, drawing on a $50 million annual budget, assembled a team of terrorists and saboteurs that included four hundred CIA agents and thousands of Cuban exiles. Attack teams made their way to Cuba from Florida via speedboats and then burned sugar cane fields and blew up factories and oil storage tanks. Lansdale hoped that these attacks, combined with the organization of a resistance movement within Cuba, would spark a massive popular revolt. The United States could then openly support the revolt, perhaps with a military invasion. Like the Bay of Pigs planners, Lansdale refused to accept the reality of Castro's political strength. The U.S. Board of National Estimates, which was composed of intelligence analysts who conducted sober, scholarly studies and did not participate in "cloak and dagger" operations, repeatedly concluded in 1961–1962 that "the Castro regime has sufficient popular support and repressive capabilities to cope with any internal threat." The "great bulk" of the population accepted the regime and a "substantial number" supported it with "enthusiasm." Lansdale answered that Castro could be overthrown if the Operation Mongoose team "put the American genius to work."

The Kennedy administration applied other pressures on Cuba. It imposed a near total trade embargo on the island. It insisted that Latin American nations drive Cuba out of the inter-American community, the Organization of American States. The Department of Defense drew up extensive plans to attack Cuba with air strikes, parachute drops, and an amphibious assault. In April and May 1962, U.S. Marines trained for an amphibious assault by invading a small island off the coast of Puerto Rico. The military exercise carried the unoriginal code name "ORTSAC," which was "Castro" spelled backward. U.S. officials, including members of the Joint Chiefs of Staff and the attorney general, actually proposed staging an incident reminiscent of the "Remember the Maine" episode of 1898, sinking a U.S. ship anchored at the U.S. base in Guantánamo Bay, Cuba. The sinking could serve as a justification for an invasion. In a memorandum of 13 March 1962, the Joint Chiefs, in a detailed plan dubbed "Operation Northwoods," further suggested sinking a boatload of Cuban refugees sailing for Florida or shooting and wounding Cuban refugees in the United States. Cuban Communists would again be blamed.

Scholars and journalists have speculated about what led the Kennedy administration to engage in such bizarre and extreme behavior. Some, like the journalist Seymour Hersh, have suggested that the Kennedy brothers had a personal vendetta against Castro, taking a blood oath to make Castro and his Communist friends pay for staining the family's honor at the Bay of Pigs.[9] Evidence for such judgments exists, for example, in the diaries of Undersecretary of State Chester Bowles, who observed the Kennedys' conduct at NSC and cabinet meetings in the immediate aftermath of the Bay of Pigs. Bowles recorded that the president "was really quite shattered," for "his public career had been a long series of successes without any noteworthy setbacks." The Kennedy brothers had been "personally humiliated" and were demonstrating a "great lack of moral integrity" in demanding action against Castro. Former CIA operatives have also alleged that the Kennedys were, for personal reasons, obsessed with getting rid of Castro. Although personal animus toward Castro may have indeed informed the administration's policies, no document or taped conversation has yet appeared in which the president or attorney general vows revenge against Castro. Both in private conversations with U.S. officials and foreign leaders and in confidential memorandums, President Kennedy insisted that communism in the Western Hemisphere threatened the United States, impeded the U.S. ability to act in other areas of the world, and threatened to become a divisive domestic political issue. The president had learned the lessons of Munich, accepted the doctrine of containment, believed in the verities of NSC 68, and dreaded Khrushchev's "wars of national liberation" speech.

President Kennedy's fears about Cuba came true on 16 October 1962, when Bundy informed him that the Soviets were developing sites in Cuba for medium- and intermediate-range ballistic missiles equipped to carry nuclear weapons. U-2 spy planes photographed the Soviet activity. The revelation marked the onset of the most dangerous crisis of the Cold War. One historian has labeled the Cuban Missile Crisis as "the two most important weeks in human history," pointing to the potential for a nuclear holocaust and the destruction of civilization. Nikita Khrushchev and Fidel Castro bear significant responsibility for the crisis. President Kennedy had publicly warned that "the gravest issues would arise" if the Soviets sent "ground to ground missiles" to Cuba. Soviet and Cuban officials repeatedly assured the United States that the Soviet Union would not base offensive weapon systems in Cuba. But the Kennedy administration also caused the confrontation. The United States had undertaken a massive buildup of nuclear weapons and boasted of its nuclear superiority over the Soviet Union. The administration had also committed acts of war against Castro's Cuba. The president did not think about the consequences of his anti-Cuban policies. In fact, at the beginning of the crisis, Kennedy conceded he did not understand the motives behind missiles in Cuba, blurting out that "it's a goddamn mystery to me." From the Soviet and Cuban perspective, all evidence—assassination plots, the rejection of Ché Guevara's peace offering, Operation Mongoose, the trade embargo, military training exercises in the Caribbean—pointed to the conclusion that the United States wanted to invade Cuba and murder its leader. Desperate leaders and nations conceive of desperate policies.

Over the past four decades, scholars have learned about the course and conduct of the Cuban missile crisis. Participants have published memoirs, and U.S., Soviet, and Cuban officials have attended conferences in Havana and exchanged "war stories" about the confrontation. Scholars have gained access to some official Soviet and U.S. documents.[10] Most important, President Kennedy secretly taped many of the confidential deliberations he and his advisors carried out during the thirteen days of crisis. The president met regularly, almost continually, with a special group known as the Executive Committee of the National Security Council or "ExComm." These conversations have been declassified and transcribed.[11]

The basic outline of the Cuban missile crisis can be readily summarized. After extensive discussions in Moscow in mid-1962 with Cuban leaders Raúl Castro and Ché Guevara, the Soviets received permission from the Cubans in early September 1962 to install nuclear weapons in Cuba. The Soviets planned to send forty-eight medium-range missiles, thirty-two intermediate-range missiles, forty-eight light IL-28 bombers, and approximately one hundred tactical nuclear weapons. The Soviets could hit cities in the United States with the missiles and bombers, and the tactical nuclear weapons could be used to repel an invasion of the island. After the discovery, President Kennedy met secretly with the ExComm for almost a week. The president immediately vowed that "we're going to take out those missiles." Initial discussions focused on a military response, perhaps an air strike on the missile sites. The president decided, however, to postpone the military solution advocated strenuously by the Joint Chiefs of Staff and instead to accept the recommendation of his brother, among others, to impose a naval blockade, labeled a "quarantine," around Cuba. Robert Kennedy feared that a surprise attack on Cuba would remind the international community of Japan's sneak attack on Pearl Harbor. In a televised address on the evening of 22 October, a somber president informed the nation of the crisis, announced the quarantine, and demanded that the Soviets remove the missiles. Over the next week, tensions mounted between the two superpowers. On 24 October, as Soviet ships approached the quarantine line, Robert Kennedy thought that "we were on the edge of a precipice with no way off." On Saturday, 27 October, Secretary of Defense Robert McNamara wondered whether he would live to see another Saturday. But on 28 October, the president and Soviet Chairman Khrushchev struck a deal. The Soviets would remove the missiles, and, in turn, the United States would pledge not to invade Cuba. The United States also confidentially promised to dismantle Jupiter missile sites in Turkey. By 20 November, Kennedy announced the end of the crisis, with the Soviets having withdrawn the missiles and bombers from Cuba. The fifteen Jupiter missiles in Turkey were also removed the next year.

President Kennedy enjoyed immense international and domestic prestige after his diplomatic triumph in the fall of 1962. He had forced the Soviet missiles out of Cuba, while simultaneously avoiding a violent, potentially catastrophic clash. As Secretary of State Dean Rusk famously rejoiced, the Kennedy administration had gone "eyeball to eyeball" with the Soviets, and the Soviets had "blinked." The president now seemed the natural, gifted leader of the Western alliance. Kennedy's victory over Cuba would have also served him well in his reelection campaign. But over the past four decades, reviews of the president's management of the crisis have been more mixed; the criticism and the praise Kennedy has received are not mutually exclusive.

Scholarly questions about Kennedy's performance have centered on his decision to issue a public ultimatum to the Soviets instead of trying to resolve the crisis quietly and diplomatically. In addition, the president failed to make explicit the terms of settlement in his ultimatum. In a meeting with the ExComm on 20 October, Ambassador to the United Nations Adlai E. Stevenson argued that the president should tie his demand to remove the missiles to a public pledge not to invade Cuba, promising further to dismantle U.S. missile sites in Italy and Turkey and give up the U.S. naval base at Guantánamo. ExComm members, including the president, brusquely dismissed the plan, implying that Stevenson lacked fortitude and courage. In fact, Stevenson's proposal, which emphasized negotiation and diplomacy, served as the basis of the settlement. ExComm members knew that the Jupiter missiles in Italy and Turkey were redundant because the United States was in the process of introducing nuclear-powered submarines equipped with Polaris nuclear missiles into the Mediterranean region. The United States actually dismantled its missile sites in Italy, along with those in Turkey, after the crisis. The suggestion to return the Guantánamo base to the Cubans was too much for either Kennedy or the U.S. Congress, neither was interested in addressing the legacy of U.S. imperialism or improving relations with Fidel Castro.

For Kennedy to give diplomacy a first chance would not have jeopardized national security because the missiles in Cuba did not alter the nuclear balance of power. On 16 October, the first day of the crisis, Secretary McNamara directly and unequivocally informed the ExComm that the Cuban missiles did not alter the strategic balance. In terms of intercontinental ballistic missiles, the United States still retained about a seven-to-one advantage over the Soviets. In any case, in an era of thermonuclear weapons, counting missiles, bombers, and warheads was a ludicrous exercise. Both the United States and the Soviet Union had the means to destroy the world. Chairman Khrushchev was not exaggerating when he told his colleagues in Moscow on 28 October that "in order to save the world, we must retreat." To be sure, missiles in Cuba might give the perception of a Soviet advantage, but Cuban missiles would soon also be redundant. ExComm members could anticipate that the Soviets would have submarines equipped with nuclear missiles along the Atlantic and Pacific seaboards and in the Gulf of Mexico. Prime Minister Harold Macmillan of the United

Kingdom made that point when he wrote to Kennedy on 22 October, the day of the ultimatum, noting that "many of us in Europe have lived so long in close proximity to the enemy's nuclear weapons of the most devastating kind that we have got accustomed to it."

The problem in international relations with choosing a public confrontation over quiet diplomacy is that whereas a leader can initiate the course of events, the leader can also easily lose command over them. The Cuban missile crisis had the potential to spin out of control. Both on the U.S. and Soviet sides, subordinates made decisions that shocked their leaders. U.S. military leaders resisted being controlled by civilian officials. Chief of Naval Operations Admiral George Anderson flaunted U.S. constitutional principles, telling Secretary of Defense McNamara that the navy would run the naval quarantine its own way. The navy forced Soviet submarines patrolling near the quarantine line to surface. In one case, the navy chose the high-risk option of using light depth charges to force a submarine to the surface. The U.S. Air Force, readying its forces for nuclear war, issued alert instructions in the clear, rather than in code, because it wanted to impress the Soviets with the awesome nature of U.S. power. A U-2 plane based in Alaska became lost and wandered into Soviet airspace; Soviet fighters scrambled to intercept it. The president assumed that such surveillance flights had been postponed. Attorney General Kennedy worried that Operation Mongoose attack teams in Cuba would inflame the situation with a spectacular raid or an attack on Castro.

Khrushchev suffered similar command and control problems. On 27 October, at the height of the crisis, the Soviet leader was surprised to learn that a Soviet surface-to-air missile had brought down a U-2 plane over Cuba. Khrushchev was further unnerved by a letter he received from Fidel Castro shortly thereafter. Warning that an attack on the island was imminent, Castro urged Khrushchev not to "allow the circumstances in which imperialists could launch the first nuclear strike." Alarmed that Castro wanted the Soviet Union to launch a preemptive nuclear strike, Khrushchev took the unusual step of going on Radio Moscow to announce the end of the crisis.

Historians can also find much to praise in Kennedy's leadership during the missile crisis. His establishment of the ExComm demonstrated that he had learned from the haphazard way he had approached planning for Bay of Pigs to have his key advisors meet together and debate options in front of him. The prolonged discussions and debates gave proponents of the naval quarantine time to counter the arguments of those who called for an immediate air strike on Cuba. Kennedy deserved further credit for standing up to the Joint Chiefs of Staff. Their constant advice can be crudely but accurately put as: "Bomb now; ask questions later." Air Force General Curtis E. LeMay insulted Kennedy, saying to him in the cabinet room that, if he did not order direct military action, it would be "almost as bad as the appeasement at Munich." President Kennedy remained steady throughout, especially during the last days. He responded calmly to the news of the loss of the U-2 over Cuba. By 27 October, discussions in Ex-Comm were becoming unfocused and disorganized; the advisors, exhausted and under extreme stress, rambled and expressed incomplete thoughts. As revealed in the tapes and transcripts of the meetings, Kennedy remained poised, lucid, and capable of analytic thinking.

Kennedy chose a peaceful path out of the crisis. Disastrous consequences might have ensued if he had authorized air strikes or an invasion. U.S. intelligence analysts had underestimated the number of Soviet combat units in Cuba and their ability to defend themselves with tactical nuclear weapons. As the more than forty thousand Soviet military personnel on the island took casualties, pressures would have mounted on Khrushchev and local commanders to fire those tactical nuclear weapons. Khrushchev also grasped that shooting between the superpowers posed, in his words, "the danger of war and of nuclear catastrophe, with the possible result of destroying the human race." His decision to accept U.S. terms helped Kennedy keep the Joint Chiefs of Staff and others at bay. Both leaders had precipitated the Cuban missile crisis, and both Kennedy and Khrushchev, using separate methods, found a way out of it.

Whereas Soviet-American relations improved in the aftermath of the crisis, U.S. relations with Castro's Cuba stayed bad. In the year after the missile crisis, the Kennedy administration continued to pursue an aggressive, belligerent policy toward Cuba. In his 27 October letter to Chairman Khrushchev, Kennedy directly and concisely offered a noninvasion pledge for the removal of missiles from Cuba. But as British historian Mark J. White, a perceptive student of the missile crisis, has pointed out, Kennedy indicated in the ExComm debates that he disliked guaranteeing Communist Cuba's independence.[12] After 27 October, the administration always conditioned its noninvasion pledge with the provisos that Cuba must cease being a source of Communist aggression, that the United States reserved the right to halt subversion from Cuba, and that the United States intended for the Cuban people to gain their freedom one day. Because it judged that Castro's Cuba would never conform to U.S. standards, the administration considered itself free to attack Cuba, foreswearing only an unprovoked military invasion of the island. At his 20 November news conference announcing the lifting of the naval quarantine, Kennedy declined to give an unequivocal public pledge not to invade the island. The next day he told the NSC that the United States must "preserve our right to invade Cuba" in case of a civil war, if there were guerrilla activities emanating from Cuba, or if offensive weapons were again introduced into the island. He added: "We do not want to build up Castro by means of a non-invasion pledge."

Between December 1962 and November 1963, the administration renewed its war against Castro on all fronts. At the president's request, the Department of Agriculture and State Department investigated whether the United States could hurt the Cuban economy by manipulating the price of sugar on world markets. The State Department pressured U.S. friends in the North Atlantic world to curtail trade with Cuba. The administration also began the process of ejecting Cuba from the International Monetary Fund. The president coupled economic warfare with new military preparations. In April 1963, he urged his national security team to prepare for an invasion of Cuba, asking "are we keeping our Cuban contingency plans up to date." Kennedy wanted to send troops to Cuba quickly in the case of a general uprising, informing military officials that he wanted them to shorten the eighteen-day preparation period from alert to full-scale invasion.

The administration's fury against Castro mounted when the Cuban spent the entire month of May 1963 in the Soviet Union, frequently meeting with Chairman Khrushchev. The Communist leaders healed the wound that had developed in their relationship after Khrushchev withdrew the missiles without Castro's acquiescence. In April, Kennedy had personally approved the sabotage of cargoes on Cuban ships and the crippling of ships. He also authorized inciting Cubans to harass, attack, and sabotage Soviet military personnel in Cuba "provided every precaution is taken to prevent attribution." After Castro's trip, the president demanded and received an integrated program of propaganda, economic denial, and sabotage against Cuba. On 19 June, Kennedy, dubbed "Higher Authority" in CIA parlance, approved a sabotage program against Cuba, expressing "a particular interest" in external sabotage operations. The CIA was subsequently authorized to carry out thirteen major sabotage operations in

Cuba, including attacks on an electric power plant, an oil refinery, and a sugar mill. On 12 November, Higher Authority conducted a major review of his anti-Castro program and received an upbeat assessment from CIA Director John A. McCone. The president was also informed that the CIA would launch new attacks, including the underwater demolition of docks and ships. The memorandums of record state that "Higher Authority" rather than President Kennedy attended these meetings. This was to give the president, again in CIA language, the option of "plausible denial." U.S. officials wanted the president of the United States to be able to deny that he had authorized terrorism and sabotage.

Soviet officials, including Nikita Khrushchev, protested these attacks on Cuba, averring that the United States had reneged on the agreement that ended the missile crisis. President Kennedy deflected the complaints, charging that the Cubans were fomenting revolution throughout the Western Hemisphere. In fact, the United States lacked hard evidence to sustain those charges. Havana certainly exhorted revolutionaries throughout the region and invited political radicals to come to Cuba to study and train. But Cuba did not supply arms or troops to insurgent groups, and U.S. intelligence analysts knew that Khrushchev had made clear to Castro in May 1963 that the Soviet Union would not support armed insurrection in Latin America. Intelligence analysts also reported that Castro had repeatedly suggested, through a variety of intermediaries, that he was interested in relaxing U.S.-Cuban tensions.

The evidence the United States wanted was found on a Venezuelan beach in early November 1963, when Venezuela announced that it had discovered a cache of Cuban arms, allegedly left for leftist radicals determined to disrupt upcoming elections. This substantiation of the purported Cuban intervention raised many questions. The Venezuelan president, Rómulo Betancourt, was a close friend of Kennedy and fierce foe of Castro. In February 1963, President Kennedy had asked CIA Director McCone to find evidence of Cuban meddling in Venezuela. Former CIA agents have subsequently written that they believed that their colleagues planted the arms in Venezuela. In May 1963, the CIA sent an anti-Cuba plan to the NSC that included the idea of placing caches of arms from communist countries in selected regions of Latin America, "ostensibly proving the arms were smuggled from Cuba." The CIA played a similar trick against Guatemala in 1954. Nonetheless, the new Lyndon Johnson administration would use the discovery as proof that Cuba should be driven out of the Organization of American States.

Assassination plots against Castro also continued after the missile crisis. On 22 November 1963, the day of the president's death in Dallas, CIA agents rendezvoused in Paris with a traitorous Cuban official, Rolando Cubela Secades, code-named "AM/LASH." The agents passed to Cubela a ballpoint pen rigged with a poisonous hypodermic needle intended to produce Castro's instant death. In the previous month, Desmond Fitzgerald of the CIA's Directorate of Plans had assured Cubela that the CIA operated with the approval of Attorney General Kennedy. Former CIA operatives have also alleged that the president signaled encouragement to AM/LASH. On 18 November in Miami, in what turned out to be his last speech on inter-American affairs, Kennedy referred to Castro as a "barrier" to be removed. Kennedy loyalists, like Arthur Schlesinger, have denied any nefarious intent, but on 19 December 1963, McGeorge Bundy informed President Johnson that the Kennedy speech "was designed to encourage anti-Castro elements within Cuba to revolt," especially those in the armed forces.

Some scholars have suggested that Kennedy showed interest, during his last months in office, in improving relations with Castro. He responded to Castro's peace overtures, opening indirect lines of communication. Intermediaries were authorized to speak with Cuban officials. However, the Kennedy administration attached stringent conditions to these preliminary discussions, insisting that Cuba would have to break ties with the Soviet Union, expel Soviet troops from the island, and end subversion in Latin America. Speaking for the president, Bundy noted that even if the Cubans fulfilled those conditions it "may or may not be sufficient to produce a change in the policy of the United States." The United States also wanted Castro to renounce his faith in communism. In short, President Kennedy was prepared only to accept Castro's surrender. His administration never renounced its policy of either overthrowing Castro or plotting his death. It had constructed a policy of unremitting hostility toward Castro's Cuba that has persisted for four decades. Notwithstanding the palpable failures of Castro's brand of communism, that policy has contributed to misery and malnutrition in Cuba.

LATIN AMERICA AND THE ALLIANCE FOR PROGRESS

President Kennedy once remarked to an aide that "Latin America's not like Asia or Africa. We can really accomplish something there." In the context of the Cold War the president focused on relations with the Soviet Union, the arms and space races, and the confrontations over Berlin and Cuba. But he probably hoped that he would be remembered for what he had done for the hemispheric neighbors. The crowning achievement of the Truman administration was rebuilding Western Europe with the Marshall Plan. President Kennedy similarly hoped that he could modernize and transform Latin America with his Alliance for Progress.

In a stirring address on 13 March 1961, which was broadcast throughout the hemisphere, the new president demonstrated that he cared about the poor of Latin America and vowed to fulfill their yearnings for economic progress, social change, and democracy. He pledged that the United States would join in a "vast cooperative effort, unparalleled in magnitude and nobility of purpose, to satisfy the basic needs of Latin American people for homes, work and land, health and schools—*techo, trabajo y tierra, salud y escuela.*" Dubbed the Alliance for Progress—*Alianza para el Progreso*—the new program ostensibly represented a Marshall Plan for Latin America.[13]

The president and his advisors subsequently provided substance to the soaring rhetoric. At an inter-American conference held in August 1961 at Punta del Este, Uruguay, Secretary of the Treasury C. Douglas Dillon assured Latin American delegates that they could count on receiving $20 billion in public and private capital over the next ten years. With this influx of foreign money combined with an additional $80 billion from internal investment, Latin American nations could expect to achieve a real economic growth rate of at least 2.5 percent per year. Administration officials privately believed that growth might reach 5 percent per year. With this growth and the development programs of the Alliance, Latin Americans would witness a five-year increase in life expectancy, a halving of the infant mortality rate, the elimination of adult illiteracy, and the provision of six years of primary education to every school-age child. During the 1960s, "the decade of development," the Kennedy administration confidently predicted that it would build democratic, prosperous, socially just societies throughout the region.

The Kennedy administration launched the Alliance for both humanitarian and national security reasons. Latin America suffered from an ancient heritage of poverty, widespread illiteracy, and grave social injustice. In several countries—Bolivia, the Dominican Republic, El Salvador, Guatemala, and Haiti—malnutrition was widespread, with an inadequate daily caloric consumption of two thousand calories or less per capita and a daily intake of fifteen grams of animal protein. By comparison, North Americans daily consumed over three thousand calories and sixty-six grams of animal protein. Hungry people predictably had poor health records, with life expectancies of less than fifty years and 10 percent of newborns dying during their first year of life. The poor of Latin America also lacked education and skills. Even in relatively prosperous nations such as Brazil and Venezuela, adult illiteracy rates ranged from 35 to 40 percent. This misery was concentrated in the countryside, with *campesinos* working tiny plots of land and a rural oligarchy operating vast estates. In Colombia, 1.3 percent of the landowners controlled over 50 percent of the land. Desperate rural people were fleeing to urban areas, moving into dreadful shanty-towns that surrounded cities like Bogotá, Caracas, and Rio de Janeiro.

The Kennedy administration believed that Latin Americans were now ready to build progressive societies. In the postwar period, military dictators, who ruled on behalf of socioeconomic elites, dominated the region. But in a series of popular upheavals, ten military dictators fell from power between 1956 and 1960. Middle-class reformers, like Rómulo Betancourt of Venezuela, who vowed to rule democratically and to reform the archaic social structures, replaced the military men. They pleaded for U.S. economic assistance, noting that the United States had virtually ignored Latin America since 1945 while providing billions of dollars in assistance to Asian and European allies. These new leaders also sharply criticized the Eisenhower administration for having conducted cordial relations with the military tyrants because they had professed to be anticommunist. Latin Americans visibly expressed their anger with U.S. policies in 1958, when Vice President Richard M. Nixon toured South America. Angry South Americans hounded Nixon in Argentina, Peru, and Uruguay, and, in Caracas, Venezuela, a howling mob tried to assault the vice president.

Although sensitive to Latin America's appalling socioeconomic conditions and desiring to repair inter-American relations, Kennedy and his advisors especially worried that a Castro-style revolution would engulf the region. Latin America's poverty and injustice seemed the perfect breeding ground for the communist contagion to fester and spread. Ché Guevara, who actually attended the conference at Punta del Este, boasted that Latin America's "new age" would be under "the star of Cuba," not the Alliance for Progress. Kennedy's advisors interpreted Khrushchev's "wars of national liberation" pronouncement to mean that the Soviet leader intended to use Cuba as a base for military and intelligence activities against the United

States and for the conquest of Latin America. In an address to the nation in mid-1961, Kennedy warned U.S. citizens that it was "the Communist theory" that "a small group of disciplined Communists could exploit discontent and misery in a country where the average income may be $60 or $70 a year and seize control, therefore, of an entire country without Communist troops ever crossing any international border."

As identified by biographer Arthur Schlesinger, it became his boss's "absolute determination" to prevent a second communist outpost in the Western Hemisphere. The president repeatedly opined to U.S. officials and foreign dignitaries that communist expansion in the Western Hemisphere would threaten the United States, would impede the U.S. ability to act elsewhere in the world, and would set off a divisive domestic political debate. Indeed, Kennedy often suggested that his entire presidency depended on checking the communist menace in the hemisphere. As he remarked to an aide, "the whole place could blow up on us." The president once told Prime Minister Harold Macmillan of the United Kingdom that Latin America was "the most dangerous area in the world." Fighting and winning the Cold War in Latin America was Kennedy's paramount concern. The Alliance for Progress was his administration's weapon of choice because it would build sturdy, progressive societies that would reject the blandishments of Castro and his fellow travelers.

Although Cold War fears dominated Kennedy's approach to Latin America, he directed his Latin American initiatives with enthusiasm and vigor. During his one thousand days in office, he toured Colombia, Venezuela, Mexico, and Costa Rica and received tumultuous welcomes. The massive crowds that greeted him understood that he genuinely wanted to help Latin America's poor. He opened his office door to Latin American presidents; former presidents; foreign, finance, and labor ministers; ambassadors; generals; trade unionists; and economists. The memorandums of these conversations with Latin Americans reveal an articulate, educated, refined man who had studied his briefing papers. Kennedy was unfailingly polite with his Latin American visitors, with no hint of the patronizing, condescending attitude that had characterized some of his presidential predecessors. He enjoyed their company, especially friends like Venezuela's Betancourt. Latin American officials left the Oval Office both amazed at the depth of the president's understanding of their countries' problems and gratified by his eagerness to help.

Enthusiasm and empathy could not, however, overcome Latin America's daunting political and social problems. Even if President Kennedy had been granted a full eight years in office, it is unlikely he could have made the Alliance for Progress work. The Alliance proved to be a notable U.S. policy failure of the Cold War, superseded only by the U.S. debacle in Vietnam. During the 1960s, extraconstitutional changes of government constantly rocked Latin America. During the Kennedy years alone, military men overthrew six popularly elected Latin American presidents. Latin American economies performed poorly, registering an unimpressive annual growth rate of about 2 percent. Most of the economic growth took place at the very end of the decade. The number of unemployed Latin Americans actually grew from eighteen million to twenty-five million, and agricultural production per person declined. The Alliance also made imperceptible progress in achieving its numerical goals in health, education, and welfare.

The United States found it could not replay the success of the Marshall Plan years. Latin America was not Europe. Western European countries had been devastated by war, but they had financial and technical expertise, institutionalized political parties, skillful politicians, strong national identities, and, except for Germany, a democratic tradition. The United States had helped to rebuild counties whose social fabrics, political traditions, and economic institutions were notably similar to those of North Americans. On the other hand, the Iberian and Amerindian political heritage of Latin America, characterized by planned economies, strong central governments, and the organization of society into corporate groups, was virtually nonexistent in the United States. In his last address on inter-American affairs, President Kennedy conceded that the Alliance for Progress should not be compared to the Marshall Plan, for "then we helped to rebuild a shattered economy whose human and social foundation remained. Today we are trying to create a basic new foundation, capable of reshaping the centuries-old societies and economies of half a hemisphere." Yet Kennedy assured his audience that idealism, energy, and optimism would bridge the vast cultural gap and bring about the "modernization" of Latin America.

Kennedy also regretfully informed Latin Americans in private that the United States "could not give aid to Latin American countries in the same way that it had helped to rebuild Europe with the Marshall Plan." Through his eloquence and spectacularly successful trips to Latin America, he had galvanized public and congressional support for the Alliance. This represented a significant political and diplomatic triumph for the president. But with its global containment policy the United States had shouldered massive financial burdens, curbing U.S. generosity. Most Marshall Plan aid was in the form of grants, whereas the Alliance offered loans to Latin America. The region received about $14 to $15 billion of the promised $20 billion. Even then, with Latin American nations having to repay principal and interest on pre-1961 and Alliance loans, this meant that the actual net capital flow to Latin America during the 1960s averaged about $920 million per year. The annual net transfer of resources from the United States and international financial institutions amounted to about $4 per Latin American. By comparison, Marshall Plan money amounted to $109 annually in assistance for every person in the Netherlands.

The Alliance for Progress did some good, providing numerous low-cost homes, schools, and hospital beds. But because of an increasing population, the results seemed negligible. For example, Alliance programs helped cut the percentage of children not attending school from 52 to 43 percent, but the actual number of children not attending school increased during the 1960s. With a 2.9 percent annual growth rate, Latin America experienced the most rapid population increase in the world in the 1960s. President Kennedy took no interest in population control, apparently believing it to be politically and medically impractical and morally dubious. He in fact disputed what proved to be the accurate prediction that the world's population of three billion in 1960 would double to six billion by 2000. In truth, no Latin American leader raised population issues with the president.

Latin American leaders bore additional responsibility for the Alliance's failures. Their governments often proved incapable of designing the long-range plans needed to put their countries on the path of sustainable growth. They wasted U.S. money on short-term, politically expedient projects or directed the spending toward enhancing the living standards of the middle class, rather than the poor. In their defense, Latin American leaders pointed to the declining terms of trade. In order to generate the $80 billion in domestic investment called for in the Alliance, Latin Americans needed to export their primary products—coffee, sugar, bananas, copper, tin, lead, zinc, and oil. But the prices of these tropical foods and raw materials remained painfully low during the 1960s. The price of coffee, Latin America's chief export, fell from 90 cents per pound in the 1950s to 36 cents per pound in the early 1960s.

The failure of the Alliance for Progress cannot be explained, however, solely by these structural problems. If so, historians could limit their analyses to testifying that President John Kennedy nobly but unsuccessfully tried to end poverty and injustice in the hemisphere. But the president's Cold War initiatives also undermined the Alliance for Progress. He judged hemispheric governments on whether they accepted the U.S. conviction that Castro's Cuba represented the focus of evil. Leaders such as Arturo Frondizi in Argentina, João Goulart in Brazil, Juan José Arévalo in Guatemala, and Cheddi Jagan in British Guiana (a British colony in South America) failed this Cold War test, and the administration successfully worked to undermine their authority. These leaders respected constitutional processes and praised the Alliance for Progress, but the Kennedy administration would not trust any progressive leader or group deemed suspect on the issues of Castro and international communism. Such policies produced ironic results, for the authoritarian, anticommunist successors who gained power in Argentina, Brazil, Guatemala, and British Guiana opposed free elections and disdained the idea of social reform, the very essence of the Alliance for Progress. President Kennedy signaled his views early in his tenure when he listed U.S. policy options after the assassination of the Dominican Republic's vicious, right wing dictator, Rafael Trujillo (1930–1961). The president said: "There are three possibilities in descending order of preference: a decent, democratic regime, a continuation of the Trujillo regime, or a Castro regime. We ought to aim at the first, but we really can't renounce the second until we are sure that we can avoid the third."

The president's remark about the possibilities in the post-Trujillo Dominican Republic proved to be a reliable guide to what choices the administration would make throughout the hemisphere. In Venezuela, the president vigorously supported the decent, democratic regime established by Rómulo Betancourt (1959–1964), a social reformer and ardent anticommunist. Although rich in oil resources, Venezuela had deep social inequities and an authoritarian political past. During the early 1960s, Venezuela received over $200 million in loans and grants from the United States to finance public housing and public works projects. The administration backed Venezuela's requests for an additional $200 million in loans from international agencies. The president invited Venezuelan political and military leaders to the White House and urged them to respect democratic principles. To help keep the Venezuelan military loyal to President Betancourt, the administration authorized over $60 million in credits and grants for military equipment and training. Kennedy frequently consulted with Betancourt on inter-American issues and established a direct telephone line between the White House and Miraflores, the Venezuelan presidential palace. Venezuela could be considered one of the few success stories of the Alliance for Progress. Although Venezuela did not achieve significant economic growth in the 1960s, Betancourt and his successor Raúl Leoni (1964–1969) improved the lives of Venezuela's poor and helped establish democratic traditions.

President Kennedy admired President Betancourt's courage and commitment to the goals of the Alliance for Progress, but he especially appreciated Betancourt's anticommunism. Betancourt reportedly knew of and supported the Bay of Pigs invasion. He broke relations with Cuba in 1961 and supported the U.S. crusade to drive Cuba out of the OAS. He used U.S. military assistance to crush Venezuelan radicals who admired the Cuban Revolution. During the missile crisis, Venezuela held a seat on the UN Security Council. Its representative firmly defended the military quarantine of Cuba, and Betancourt sent two destroyers to assist the U.S. Navy in enforcing it. Betancourt also permitted Cuban exiles to operate in Venezuela. And he allegedly discussed with U.S. officials ways to arrange the assassination of Fidel Castro. President Kennedy always had time and found money for decent Latin American democrats who shared the president's loathing of Castro.

By comparison, the president disdained Brazilian leaders, such as Jânio Quadros (1961) and his successor João Goulart (1961–1964), men who supported the Alliance for Progress. Latin America's largest and most populous nation angered the Kennedy administration because it refused to break diplomatic relations with Cuba and it established commercial ties with the Soviet Union. Many in the southern cone countries of Argentina, Brazil, Chile, and Uruguay opposed a showdown with Cuba, judging Castro to be little threat. He ruled a small island country of impoverished sugar cane workers thousands of miles away from the glittering, European-like metropolises of Buenos Aires, Montevideo, Santiago, and Rio de Janeiro. South Americans called for patience, predicting that the Communist system in Cuba would ultimately, in President Goulart's words, "deteriorate under its own weight." Southern cone leaders worried, however, that a Cold War confrontation with Cuba would exacerbate political tensions in their countries, exciting extremists on both sides of the political spectrum. Both Brazil and Argentina offered to mediate between the United States and Cuba, warning that U.S. pressure on Cuba was pushing Castro into the hands of the Soviets. But the Kennedy administration dismissed such overtures, believing that the South Americans were naïve about the Communist threat. U.S. officials further speculated that the Soviet Union would use commercial links to subvert Latin American governments. Brazilian leaders responded that they understood strategic threats, pointing out that they condemned Cuba during the missile crisis. They also noted that trade with the Soviet Union represented only 3 percent of Brazil's international commerce. The balance of trade favored Brazil, because the Soviets offered goods of poor quality.

The Kennedy administration first tried to buy Brazil's support for its anti-Castro campaigns. In March 1961, it offered the new Quadros administration a $100 million gift to help it import capital goods and then asked for Brazilian support for the impending Bay of Pigs invasion. As outgoing Ambassador to Brazil John Moors Cabot recalled in disgust: "It was obvious it was just a bribe. I mean that's what it amounted to. And Quadros, with increasing irritation, said no." In May 1961, President Kennedy made his pitch. Meeting with the Brazilian finance minister, Kennedy observed that the United States had just agreed, together with the International Monetary Fund, to give Brazil $335 million in credits. In negotiating the loan, the United States "had completely avoided mention of political factors," but the Brazilians had to understand that the United States considered Castro an agent of international communism and a peril to the hemisphere. It would be impossible for the United States to drive Cuba out of the OAS unless the major Latin American nations agreed "on the basic analysis of the situation in Cuba." Quadros again refused to change Brazil's foreign policy.

In August 1961, Quadros suddenly resigned and his vice president, Goulart, assumed power. Goulart quickly earned U.S. enmity both because he continued his predecessor's independent foreign policy and because he worked with leftist groups in Brazil. Goulart explained that he needed the support of the political left because he correctly feared that conservative elements, including military officers, plotted against him. U.S. officials rejected these arguments, telling themselves that Goulart either favored Communists or that he did not understand the true intentions of Communists. As Kennedy remarked, the situation in Brazil "worried him more than that in Cuba."

The administration launched a series of initiatives to undermine Goulart. The president dispatched Robert Kennedy to Brazil to confront Goulart over his "putting those leftists and Communists in positions of power." Beyond lecturing Goulart, the administration manipulated the

Brazilian political scene. In 1962 the CIA spent $5 million funding the campaigns of candidates for 15 federal Senate seats, 8 state governorships, 250 federal deputy seats, and some 600 seats for state legislatures. The agency also covertly funded trade union groups and encouraged them to organize strikes and demonstrations against Goulart. In addition, the administration focused its Alliance for Progress funds in Brazilian states whose governors opposed Goulart. More ominously, it dispatched Colonel Vernon Walters, who knew Brazilian officers, to Brazil to maintain close contacts with military leaders, especially General Humberto Alencar Castello Branco.

On 2 April 1964, Brazilian generals, led by Castello Branco, disposed of Goulart and established a military regime that would last until 1985. The United States approved of the military conspiracy and pre-positioned war matériel and readied a naval task force for duty off the coast of Brazil, in case the generals encountered stiff resistance from Goulart's supporters. Although the overthrow came during the Johnson administration, the attack fulfilled the Kennedy administration's policy against Goulart. Robert Kennedy, for example, expressed satisfaction, alleging that "Brazil would have gone Communist" if Goulart had not been overthrown. Over the next twenty years, the generals gave Brazil economic growth but not the socioeconomic reform called for in the Alliance for Progress. They also committed wholesale violations of basic human rights, torturing and murdering Brazilians who clamored for freedom and justice. President Kennedy would undoubtedly have been appalled at the course of Brazilian military rule. But his opposition to the constitutional, civilian governments of Brazil underscored his readiness, in the context of the Cold War, to accept "Trujillo-style" regimes throughout the hemisphere.

President Kennedy brought high ideals and noble purposes to his Latin American policy. Ironically, however, his unwavering determination to wage Cold War in "the most dangerous area in the world" ultimately led him and his administration to compromise and even mutilate those grand goals for the Western Hemisphere.

VIETNAM

Any fair examination of the Kennedy presidency must inevitably assess John F. Kennedy's role in precipitating the U.S. disaster in Vietnam. The twenty-year effort to build and secure an independent, noncommunist South Vietnam represents the striking U.S. policy failure of the Cold War and one of the most deplorable episodes in U.S. history. During the Vietnam era, U.S. soldiers and marines used the ironic term "wasted" to depict the combat death of one of their buddies. The war in Vietnam did indeed represent a "waste" of precious blood and treasure. Between 1961 and 1973, the United States suffered over 350,000 physical casualties in Vietnam, with approximately 58,000 servicemen and women dying. The mental toll on Vietnam veterans has also been high. The Veterans Administration has estimated that up to 400,000 Vietnam veterans have experienced some form of post-traumatic–stress disorder. The United States spent about $120 billion in Vietnam and incurred massive future costs: veteran-related expenses and repayment of principal and interest on the money borrowed to fight the war.

The war had horrific consequences for the people of Vietnam. Perhaps as many as 2 million Vietnamese, civilian and military, died and another 4.5 million were physically wounded. There are still over 200,000 Vietnamese who are missing and unaccounted for. The fighting and violence created a wasteland in Vietnam. With bombing campaigns like "Rolling Thunder," the United States dropped over fifteen million tons of high explosives on Vietnam, the equivalent of four hundred Hiroshima bombs. During the two-week "Christmas bombing" of 1972, U.S. bombers dropped more tonnage on Hanoi, the capital of North Vietnam, than Nazi Germany did on London between 1940 and 1945. U.S. planes also sprayed Vietnam with nineteen million gallons of defoliants—Agents Orange, White, and Blue—destroying 35 percent of South Vietnam's hardwood forests.

The conflict in Vietnam seems a tragedy of epic proportions, considering the evolution of U.S. relations with Vietnam, which, at the beginning of the twenty-first century, is now a unified country under Communist rule. In 1994, the United States abandoned its trade embargo against Vietnam and the next year normalized diplomatic relations. In 1996, Douglas Peterson, a former prisoner of war in Vietnam, became the first U.S. ambassador to Hanoi. Thereafter, the United States began the process of extending special trade privileges to Vietnam. Old warriors, such as Secretary of Defense Robert McNamara, attended scholarly conferences in Vietnam and traded war stories with former adversaries, such as General Vo Nguyen Giap. And, as one of the last acts of his presidency, Bill Clinton visited Vietnam in late 2000. Clinton's visit sparked popular enthusiasm throughout Vietnam and favorable commentary in the United States. In 2001, Colin Powell, a Vietnam veteran and the new secretary of state for the George W. Bush administration, had a similarly pleasant visit to Vietnam. That the United States and Communist Vietnam have developed a peaceful and potentially prosperous relationship gave further meaning to the term "wasted" as a metaphor for death in Vietnam.

John Kennedy did not cause this death and destruction. The Johnson and Nixon administrations bear primary responsibility for the U.S. war in Vietnam. But most historians believe that the decisions Kennedy and his advisors made between 1961 and 1963 made it more likely that Johnson would seek military solutions in Vietnam. Johnson's and Nixon's Vietnam policies followed logically, albeit not inevitably, from Kennedy's actions. As Fredrik Logevall, a historian who has written sympathetically about Kennedy's Vietnam dilemma, has noted, the Vietnam problem that Kennedy left behind "was much larger than the one he inherited."[14]

President Kennedy certainly inherited a Vietnam problem from Eisenhower. Since 1954 the United States had committed itself to building, fortifying, and preserving an independent, noncommunist South Vietnam. Eisenhower's decisions, in turn, flowed from those of his predecessor, President Harry S. Truman. Almost since the end of World War II, the United States had been opposing the revolutionary movement in Vietnam led by the nationalist and Communist Ho Chi Minh.[15]

The people of Vietnam had lived under French colonial rulers since the mid-nineteenth century. The Vietnamese, who had a two-thousand-year history of resistance to Chinese domination of their culture, would ultimately turn to Ho Chi Minh and his Communist supporters for their liberation from the French. Ho, who came from a traditional, patriotic Vietnamese family, left his country around 1912 and did not return for three decades. Traveling the world, including in the United States, he listened to a variety of doctrines that addressed contemporary questions of socioeconomic inequality, both on the domestic and international levels. During the period of World War I, Ho, then in Paris, joined the French Socialist Party and became enthusiastic about Woodrow Wilson and his Fourteen Points (1918), which seemed to promise national self-determination and the end of colonialism. But Ho eventually decided that his fellow Socialists and Wilson had only a theoretical interest in the liberation of the Vietnamese people. A founding member of the French Communist Party, he went to Moscow in the 1920s to study communism, convinced that the international communist movement led by Vladimir Lenin and Leon Trotsky was unequivocally committed to an anticolonial policy. He also embraced the doctrine that communism provided answers to Vietnam's socioeconomic problems. In exile, often in China, Ho organized the Vietnamese Communist party and in 1940 slipped back into his homeland.

During World War II, Ho organized the Vietminh movement to end Japanese and French domination of Vietnam. As part of its imperial drive throughout Asia, the Japanese militarists had pushed the French colonialists aside and taken control of the country. Ho appealed to Vietnamese of all political stripes to join the Vietminh in a broad based political and military effort to secure liberation. During the war, the United States actually assisted the Vietminh with arms, munitions, and training. U.S. military and intelligence officers met Ho, were favorably impressed, and sent back positive reports about the Vietminh and its anti-Japanese activities. In the aftermath of the U.S. military defeat of Japan and with the French colonialists discredited, Ho declared Vietnam's independence on 2 September 1945. U.S. officers were guests of honor at the independence ceremony in Hanoi, and Ho borrowed directly from Thomas Jefferson's famous declaration.

The French refused to accept their loss and waged a pitiless, colonial war against the Vietminh from 1946 to 1954. As a matter of principle, the United States opposed colonialism, but the Truman administration eventually supported the French. France was a Cold War ally and the leaders of the Vietminh were Communists. The Truman administration ignored various communications between 1945 and 1949 from Ho, who pleaded for U.S. aid and insisted that, albeit a Communist, he was an independent nationalist not beholden to the Soviet Union. After 1949, Ho accepted military aid from the Soviet Union and Communist China. The Truman administration was establishing a precedent that its presidential successors would follow, placing Vietnam, a regional issue, within the global context of the Soviet-American confrontation. Between 1950 and 1954, the United States sent $2 billion in military aid to the French, paying for 75 percent of the cost of the war. The Vietminh, however, gradually exhausted the French with their guerrilla war tactics and then administered a severe conventional defeat in May 1954 at the battle of Dien Bien Phu. Thereafter, at a conference in Geneva, the great powers—the United States, the

Soviet Union, the People's Republic of China, and the United Kingdom—liquidated the French folly. Under the terms of the Geneva Accords (1954), all foreign forces would withdraw from Vietnam, the country would be temporarily divided at the seventeenth parallel, the Vietminh would withdraw its troops to the northern half of the country, and a unification election would be held under international auspices within two years. Most international observers assumed that the Communist-led Vietminh movement would win that forthcoming national election.

The United States declined to sign the Geneva Accords, which represented a triumph for the Communists, and worked to salvage something from the French defeat. The Eisenhower administration backed the installation of Ngo Dinh Diem (1954–1963) first as prime minister and then as chief of state in South Vietnam. Diem was an anticommunist nationalist who had opposed the French but also refused to join the Vietminh. He spent much of the colonial war in exile, living in a seminary in the United States. A devout Catholic, Diem won the friendship of influential churchmen and prominent politicians including his fellow Catholic, Senator John Kennedy. Kennedy saw in Diem a leader who could release and harness "the latent power of nationalism to create an independent, anti-Communist Vietnam." With the acquiescence of the Eisenhower administration, Diem rigged his own election, ignored the Geneva Accords' call for a unification election, and launched a military campaign against South Vietnamese loyal to Ho, to communism, and to the concept of national unification. Between 1954 and 1960, the Eisenhower administration supported Diem with $2 billion in aid, principally military assistance. By January 1961, there were approximately seven hundred U.S. military advisors in South Vietnam, working with Diem's troops. The Eisenhower administration had fully committed the United States to the preservation of an independent, noncommunist South Vietnam under the leadership of President Diem.

Beyond creating a new U.S. responsibility, Eisenhower left Kennedy with an alarming problem. Diem commanded little popular support in his country. He had not carried out the type of land and tax reform that might have built a base of popular support among South Vietnamese peasants, the majority of the population. Diem coddled Vietnamese landlords, including those who had sided with the French in the anticolonial struggle. His policies seemed to favor urban areas, like Saigon, over the countryside. Diem also staffed his government with Vietnamese Catholics, a minority of the southern population. Two Catholics, Diem's brother and his sister-in-law, would foster discrimination against Buddhists and, in 1963, authorize attacks on Buddhist pagodas.

Diem and Kennedy also faced a growing Communist insurgency in Vietnamese villages. In 1959, Hanoi authorized its allies in the south to initiate armed resistance to the Diem regime. South Vietnamese Communists, pejoratively known as the "Vietcong," had pleaded for Hanoi's backing, fearing that Diem's U.S.-equipped army would annihilate them. Southerners who had trained in North Vietnam began to infiltrate back into their native villages. In 1960, Hanoi further ordered its southern brethren to form a political coalition with noncommunist opponents of the Diem regime. Thereafter, the power of the Vietcong and its political arm, the National Liberation Front, would steadily increase among both impoverished, landless peasants and nationalists who resented the growing U.S. presence in their country.

Kennedy had supported Eisenhower's containment policy in South Vietnam. In 1956, Senator Kennedy declared that South Vietnam represented "the cornerstone of the Free World in Southeast Asia, the keystone to the arch, the finger in the dike," and he predicted that many Asian nations would be endangered if "the Red tide of communism" flowed into Vietnam. Kennedy approached Vietnam, of course, with his firmly held judgments about the global communist threat. Vietnam seemed like a classic case in which the Soviet Union masked its imperial designs behind the doctrine of "wars of national liberation." But the president characteristically believed that the United States could find a "third" or "middle" way between colonialism and communism through the nation-building process.

Kennedy had not made the defense of South Vietnam a focal point of his campaign, and the issue was not covered in his postelection briefings with Eisenhower. But after reading reports from the field of the expanding armed insurgency, he quickly realized that the United States had serious political and military problems in South Vietnam. In May 1961, he reaffirmed Eisenhower's policy of preventing Communist domination of Vietnam by approving National Security Action Memorandum (NSAM) 52. He also sent Vice President Johnson to Saigon to signal U.S. solidarity with the Diem government. The first of Kennedy's two fateful decisions on the U.S. role in Vietnam would come, however, in November 1961, when he endorsed NSAM 111. The United States would begin a direct military effort in Vietnam.

The policy paper, NSAM 111, flowed from the recommendations submitted to the president by General Maxwell Taylor, Kennedy's personal military aide, and presidential aide Walt Rostow. Kennedy had dispatched the men to Vietnam to assess the validity of the pessimistic field reports he had been reading. Taylor and Rostow confirmed that the insurgency was spreading and the Diem government seemed unable to cope. But Taylor and Rostow optimistically reaffirmed the U.S. ability to arrest the deterioration and build a sturdy, self-reliant nation by offering a significant increase in aid and advice. U.S. advisory groups, placed within the South Vietnamese bureaucracy, could identify and solve critical domestic problems, and U.S. military officers could teach the South Vietnamese army how to take the war to the enemy. Taylor and Rostow further recommended that the United States transfer sophisticated military equipment to South Vietnam. Most important, Taylor and Rostow called for assigning eight thousand troops to the embattled Mekong Delta, a fertile region in the southern part of the country, ostensibly to assist in flood relief. Once on the ground, U.S. forces would serve as a tangible signal of U.S. support and would be available for combat.

Both the Taylor/Rostow report and the continuing success of the Vietcong and the National Liberation Front prompted hard thinking and furious debate within the Kennedy administration. The Joint Chiefs of Staff, Secretary of State Rusk, Secretary of Defense McNamara, and NSC advisor Bundy all called for building on the Taylor/Rostow report by publicly guaranteeing South Vietnam's survival and by preparing to send U.S. combat forces to the region. Rusk and McNamara also foresaw the day when U.S. forces might strike at North Vietnam. Undersecretary of State Chester Bowles and Averell Harriman, a respected, experienced diplomat, opposed such militaristic policies. Both Harriman and Bowles argued that the United States should not tie its credibility and prestige to the unpopular and repressive Diem regime. Harriman, who was negotiating with the Soviet Union over the status of Laos, Vietnam's neighbor, proposed seeking a comprehensive solution based on the 1954 Geneva Accords.

President Kennedy did not like the options presented to him by his warring advisors and tried to split the differences between them. But the seemingly cautious decisions he made on 22 November 1961 dramatically expanded the U.S. role in the region. Kennedy considered combat troops a "last resort" and he warned that the introduction of some U.S. troops would inevitably lead to calls for more troops. It was, in Kennedy's words, "like taking a drink. The effect wears off, and you have to take another." The president further told the NSC "that he could make a rather strong case against intervening in an area ten thousand miles away against sixteen thousand guerillas with a native army of two hundred thousand, where millions have been spent for years and with no success." Despite his clairvoyance about the quagmire in Vietnam, Kennedy rejected the idea of a negotiated solution. Kennedy interpreted regional events through the global prism of the Soviet-American confrontation. The Soviet Union would be emboldened in Berlin, Cuba, and elsewhere if the United States permitted Communist aggression to go unchecked in South Vietnam. Kennedy further upheld the "domino theory," arguing that Asian Communists would run rampant throughout Southeast Asia if the United States failed to preserve a noncommunist South Vietnam. Although he rejected the idea of dispatching a massive combat force, Kennedy authorized a significant expansion of U.S. advisors and aid to South Vietnam. His decision violated the Geneva Accords, which had called for the withdrawal of foreign forces from Vietnam.

Over the next two years, the U.S. military presence in South Vietnam grew measurably. The administration established a formal military command in the country and gave the military commander, General Paul D. Harkins, equal status with the U.S. ambassador in Saigon. The number of military advisors reached thirty-two hundred by the end of 1961, grew to nine thousand by the end of 1962, and reached over sixteen thousand by 1963. Because these advisors operated advanced equipment, such as helicopters, they became directly involved in combat operations. During the Kennedy years, 186 U.S. personnel died in Vietnam. U.S. advisors taught South Vietnamese troops the tactics of helicopter envelopment and assisted them in carrying out covert raids against North Vietnam. The president authorized the use of defoliants to deny the guerrillas ground cover and herbicides to destroy the food supplies of the enemy. General Harkins asserted that he could terrify the Communists by bombing them with napalm.

The battle of Ap Bac revealed, however, that the U.S. military had been unable to transform the South Vietnamese army into a fighting machine. The battle took place on 2 January 1963 in a village in the Mekong Delta, forty miles from Saigon. Government forces, numbering approximately 1,400 men, took on about 350 Vietcong fighters. U.S. helicopter pilots ferried South Vietnamese units to the battlefield. Artillery, armored personnel carriers, helicopter gunships, and jet fighters supported the infantry. By comparison, the Vietcong were lightly equipped with handheld weapons. Nonetheless, the Vietcong stood their ground and demonstrated that they had learned how to counter modern military technology. They shot down five helicopters, killing three U.S. advisors and wounding eight other Americans. The Vietcong attacked the armored personnel carriers on foot, throwing hand grenades. In the face of such boldness, the South Vietnamese forces refused to engage the enemy aggressively. The U.S. military advisor, Lt. Colonel John Paul Vann, became so distressed at what he was witnessing from his spotter plane that he actually asked a U.S. advisor on the ground to shoot the South Vietnamese commander. Vann labeled the South Vietnamese effort as "a miserable damn performance." The Vietcong, who had the support of the local villagers, withdrew from the battlefield in good order, having inflicted approximately two hundred casualties. The Vietcong suffered only about sixty casualties.

The pathetic South Vietnamese military leadership on display at Ap Bac reflected the political weakness of the government in Saigon. President Kennedy and his advisors thought that they could combine the stepped-up military effort with a reform of the Diem regime. They understood that Saigon's inefficiency, repression, and lack of political support within the countryside would undermine efforts to strengthen the army. In November 1961, the administration informed President Diem that it wanted a role in decision making. However, Diem, a nationalist, adamantly refused to allow his country to become a "protectorate." The administration retreated since, as the president knowingly observed, "Diem is Diem and the best we've got." But the "best" U.S. man in Saigon proved unable to contain the insurgency. By the end of 1962, perhaps three hundred thousand South Vietnamese associated with the National Liberation Force. By the end of 1963, Vietcong forces controlled up to 30 percent of the countryside.

With the Communists gaining strength, Kennedy made his second fateful decision on Vietnam—to acquiesce in the removal of President Ngo Dinh Diem from power. The Buddhist crisis of 1963 prompted the Kennedy administration to move against the Diem regime. In May 1963, South Vietnamese troops attacked Buddhist marchers who were celebrating the birth of Buddha. In protest, several Buddhist monks immolated themselves. Americans saw a horrifying photograph of an elderly monk, in a flowing orange robe, burning to death. Their shock grew upon hearing Diem's sister-in-law, a fanatical Catholic, refer to these public suicides as "barbecues" and then contemptuously offer to provide matches and gasoline for other monks. After promising to resolve the situation, Diem further infuriated U.S. officials when, on 21 August, forces under his brother's command raided pagodas and arrested fourteen hundred Buddhist dissidents.

On 24 August 1963, while on vacation at the family retreat in Hyannis Port, Massachusetts, President Kennedy casually approved a memorandum that gave wide latitude to his representatives in Saigon to support a coup d'état. South Vietnamese generals had made secret contacts with U.S. officials, inquiring about the U.S. attitude if they overthrew Diem and his brother. In the memorandum, the new ambassador, Henry Cabot Lodge Jr., was instructed to insist that Diem remove his brother from power. If Diem refused, the United States "must face the possibility that Diem himself cannot be preserved." Lodge was further authorized to inform the generals that if Diem declined to reform his government the United States would provide them with "direct support in any interim period of breakdown of central government mechanism."

Although Kennedy quickly regretted not consulting more fully with his advisors about the new policy and never actually issued a direct order to encourage the South Vietnamese generals to strike, he also never repudiated the 24 August memorandum. The president had a man in Saigon, Ambassador Lodge, who made it clear that Diem must go. In Lodge's words, "we are launched on a course from which there is no respectable turning back." Trying to pressure Diem to reform, the president cut back on military and economic aid to the regime. The generals took that as a signal that the administration no longer had faith in Diem. A CIA agent kept in regular contact with the generals. On 1 November the generals moved against the government and shortly thereafter captured and then murdered Diem and his brother. Kennedy was deeply distressed to hear of Diem's assassination.

Kennedy and his advisors probably hoped that a new government in Saigon would build a base of popular support and wage war effectively against the Vietcong, thereby hastening the day when U.S. military advisors could go home. But the overthrow of Diem further entangled the United States in the region. The new president, General Duong Van "Big" Minh lasted only a few months in power. Political chaos ensued, with South Vietnam having four governments in 1964 alone. The Communists predictably increased their strength in the countryside. The overthrow of Diem also eliminated whatever chances existed for a settlement negotiated by the Vietnamese. In 1963, Hanoi and Saigon began secret contacts, with tentative talks about a coalition government headed by Diem in the South and the withdrawal of foreign forces from Vietnam. In the aftermath of the overthrow of Diem and the refusal of the South Vietnamese generals to continue the contacts, Hanoi decided in December 1963 to pursue its "sacred war" to achieve a unified, Communist Vietnam. North Vietnam instructed its followers in the South to take the offensive against the government and army of South Vietnam, and it resolved to assist them with an increased flow of men and matériel across the seventeenth parallel. If he had lived and continued to serve in office, President Kennedy would have faced the same crisis that President Johnson encountered in 1964–1965. Communist forces would win the war in South Vietnam if the United States did not use its military might to stop them.

Kennedy partisans have ventured that President Kennedy would not have chosen full-scale military intervention. They have pointed to various remarks he made in 1963. One aide, Kenneth O'Donnell, claimed that Kennedy privately assured a worried Senator Mike Mansfield (D-Minn.), that he intended to withdraw from Vietnam after the 1964 election. In a television interview with CBS News broadcaster Walter Cronkite on 2 September, Kennedy observed that the United States could help the South Vietnamese, but "in the final analysis, it is their war. They are the ones who have to win it or lose it." On the other hand, at a news conference in July, Kennedy vowed "we are not going to withdraw from this effort." In an interview on 9 September with NBC News broadcaster Chet Huntley, he professed his belief in the domino theory for Southeast Asia. And, in his undelivered speech of 22 November at the Dallas Trade Mart, Kennedy intended to reiterate the U.S. commitment in Southeast Asia. Assistance to Vietnam, Kennedy planned to say, could be "painful, risky, and costly," but "we dare not weary of the task." Kennedy did indeed authorize in October a withdrawal of one thousand men from South Vietnam, but nothing in the declassified documents suggests that this represented a major policy initiative. The limited withdrawal was part of the selective pressure the administration was applying to the Diem regime in late 1963. If President Kennedy had a secret plan for peace, he apparently never discussed it in detail with any of his aides, including his most trusted advisor, Attorney General Robert Kennedy.

Perhaps the strongest argument to support the view that Kennedy would not have dramatically intensified the war effort is that he had rejected advice, most notably in the late 1961 debate over the Taylor/Rostow report, to Americanize the war through a massive influx of combat troops. He also understood the critical political weakness of the Saigon regime. A historian cannot, however, predict what President Kennedy would have done when it became apparent in 1964–1965 that the overthrow of Diem had not resolved South Vietnam's political and military problems and that the Communist insurgency was spreading. Kennedy certainly did not seek a major war in Southeast Asia, but he wanted an independent, noncommunist South Vietnam. In pursuing that goal, he made decisions that had heightened and deepened the U.S. presence in the region. Lyndon Johnson was not bound to wage war in Vietnam as a result of Kennedy's decisions, but he could reasonably believe that he was continuing his predecessor's policies.

CONCLUSION

Many scholars would accept the critical analysis presented here of President John F. Kennedy as a dogmatic anticommunist who willfully waged Cold War. Some historians have tried, however, to modify that harsh judgment. Although conceding that President Kennedy had been impetuous and confrontational, they have suggested that during the last year of his life the president was beginning to display a mature concern about the ultimate issues of war and peace in the nuclear age. In the words of Professor Robert A. Divine of the University of Texas at Austin, the first two years in office served as "the education of John F. Kennedy." The Cuban missile crisis had been a sobering turning point in the president's intellectual journey. Having come to the brink of a nuclear holocaust, the president now resolved to work to reduce international tensions. Kennedy had learned that he could not resolve international dilemmas simply by flaunting U.S. power. Divine and others pointed to the president's speech at American University in June 1963 and his subsequent negotiation of the Limited Test Ban Treaty as evidence of a leader now prepared "to put his hard-won education to work."[16]

Kennedy emerged from the Cuban missile crisis in a powerful political position. His job approval rating soared to 75 percent in December 1962. In part, the president and his advisors helped generate popular enthusiasm by providing friendly journalists with insider accounts of the crisis. All emphasized that the president had acted boldly and decisively, minimizing the confusion and mistakes that had actually dominated the crisis. With the president's consent, aides also "leaked" negative accounts about U.N. Ambassador Adlai Stevenson's role, suggesting that he favored the appeasement of the Soviet Union. In truth, Stevenson's proposals provided the basis for the settlement of the crisis. Nonetheless, the president took up the cause of a nuclear test ban, which had been championed by President Eisenhower. He began a personal correspondence with Chairman Khrushchev and used Norman Cousins, a notable literary figure, as an intermediary between himself and Khrushchev. Kennedy sensed that the U.S. public would welcome a test ban. The resumption of open-air nuclear testing in 1961 meant that the United States and the Soviet Union were again poisoning the atmosphere with radioactive fallout. Indeed, since 1945 the two superpowers had conducted over four hundred nuclear tests in the atmosphere. Babies and children drank milk laced with radioactive contaminants.

The president was at his most eloquent on 10 June 1963, when he delivered the commencement address at American University in Washington, D.C. According to speechwriter Theodore Sorensen, Kennedy wanted "the usual threats of destruction, boasts of nuclear stockpiles, and lectures on Soviet treachery" left out of this speech. The United States, Kennedy told the university graduates, wanted a "genuine peace" and not "a Pax Americana enforced on the world by American weapons of war." He observed that U.S. and Soviet citizens abhorred war, adding that no nation had ever suffered more than the Soviet Union did during World War II. Nazi Germany had turned one-third of the Soviet territory into wasteland, "a loss equivalent to the devastation of this country east of Chicago." He called upon Americans to reexamine their attitude toward the Soviet Union. Mutual fear fueled the Cold War, with both sides "caught in a vicious and dangerous cycle in which suspicion on one side breeds suspicion on the other, and new weapons beget counterweapons." Kennedy conceded that fundamental differences over politics and economics separated the two societies, but he pointed out that their common humanity also linked them. Kennedy reminded his audience that "we all inhabit this small planet. We all breathe the same air. We all cherish our children's future. And we are all mortal." Calling for a "fresh start," Kennedy pledged, at the end of his address, that the United States would not test nuclear weapons in the atmosphere "so long as other states do not do so."

Kennedy's elegant, lyrical address and generous pledge produced substantive results. Chairman Khrushchev responded positively, calling it "the best speech by any President since [Franklin] Roosevelt." The Soviet leader further agreed to negotiations, and, by late July 1963, the two sides had struck a deal to ban the testing of weapons in the atmosphere. Kennedy then gave an effective televised address, urging the U.S. Senate to ratify the treaty. Republican senators and U.S. military officers had questioned whether the Soviets could be trusted to abide by any treaty. By September 1963, 81 percent of the U.S. public supported the treaty, and the Senate ratified the treaty by an overwhelming vote of eighty to nineteen.

President Kennedy's handiwork, the Limited Test Ban Treaty, remains in effect. Since 1963, neither the United States nor the Soviet Union/Russia has exploded a nuclear weapon in the atmosphere. The atmospheric test ban has helped preserve the environment and the health of global citizens. The treaty also set a precedent for future Soviet-American arms control treaties, such as the Nuclear Non-Proliferation Treaty (1969) and SALT I (1972), which prohibited either side from building an antiballistic missile system. The Kennedy administration helped stabilize the forbidding nuclear arms race. The president had exercised leadership.

The peaceful benefits of the atmospheric test ban should not, however, be magnified. President Kennedy did not achieve a comprehensive test ban treaty, which would have prohibited the underground testing of nuclear warheads. The Joint Chiefs of Staff opposed such a measure, and the Soviets showed little interest. Khrushchev opposed the on-site inspections thought necessary to insure compliance with a comprehensive test ban. The Soviet leader alleged that the CIA would use on-site inspections as a way to spy on his country. Between 1963 and 1990, the United States and the Soviet Union conducted nearly eleven hundred underground nuclear tests. The development of nuclear weapons continued apace and arguably even accelerated because the public took little notice of the underground tests. Moreover, the Kennedy administration's test ban initiatives took place simultaneously with its massive buildup of nuclear delivery vehicles like ICBMs and Polaris submarines. The Kennedy-era buildup stimulated the Soviet arms buildup of the late 1960s. Professor Divine has conceded that the huge nuclear buildup of the 1960s became "Kennedy's grimmest legacy."

President Kennedy did not always stick to the conciliatory sentiments expressed in the American University speech. To be sure, the president gave another gracious address about peace in the nuclear age when he visited Salt Lake City in the fall of 1963. Perhaps he wanted to make amends for his aggressive speech in the Utah capital during the 1960 campaign when he had depicted the Cold War as an ultimate struggle for supremacy—God and America versus the devil and the Soviet Union. Such divisive language reappeared, however, in Kennedy's speeches during the last months of his life. Kennedy's triumphal appearance and speech in Berlin, coming less than three weeks after his American University speech, left Khrushchev uncertain whether the president wanted a relaxation of tensions, a détente, or further conflicts. Kennedy attacked communism and Fidel Castro in Miami on 18 November in his last speech on inter-American affairs. And, in his undelivered speech in Dallas, the president again intended to boast about U.S. nuclear and military prowess.

Whereas President Kennedy's views on Soviet-American relations may have been gradually and unevenly evolving, it is the historical record that he compiled during his one thousand days in office that must be evaluated. Kennedy merits high praise for being steady and restrained during the Bay of Pigs invasion, the Berlin crisis, and the Cuban missile crisis. In each case, he rejected the recommendations of advisors, especially high ranking military officers, to resolve the crises with risky military responses. Kennedy had no appetite for thermonuclear exchanges. But applause for his crisis-management skills must be balanced by hard questions about why the president found himself in these superpower showdowns. The president's overblown rhetoric, nuclear arms buildup, and reckless behavior toward Castro's Cuba helped precipitate these confrontations. During the presidential campaign of 1960, Kennedy had offered U.S. voters a misleading analysis of the global balance of power, warning them that the Soviet Union might soon be in a position to rob them of their freedom. In fact, President Eisenhower's quiet confidence in the political, socioeconomic, and intellectual health of the United States proved accurate. Despite their tiresome rhetoric about the inevitable triumph of socialism, Communist leaders such as Nikita Khrushchev implicitly understood the strengths of U.S. society. Kennedy's harsh words and provocative deeds alarmed them, leading them to consider ill-advised policies such as placing nuclear missiles in Cuba.

Finally, scholars have exaggerated when they conclude that the Kennedy administration left the world in a more peaceful state than it was in January 1961.[17] As a result of the waning of the Berlin crisis, the resolution of the Cuban missile crisis, and the Limited Test Ban Treaty, Soviet-American relations probably improved during the Kennedy years. At the same time, each superpower rapidly expanded its nuclear arsenal and gained the power to destroy civilization. The administration avoided some pitfalls, declining, for example, to intervene militarily in Laos. But Kennedy bequeathed a terrible legacy in Vietnam. The president and his advisors bear responsibility for the disastrous intervention in Vietnam and the waste of millions of U.S. and Asian lives. The president hoped that his Alliance for Progress would accomplish in Latin America what the Marshall Plan had done in Western Europe. The goal proved too ambitious. But the president undermined his good intentions by destabilizing constitutional regimes in Latin America because they did not share his analysis of the perils of communism. These covert interventions helped create bloody military dictatorships that dominated the region through the 1980s. In the twenty-first century, international observers judge the continued U.S. political and economic isolation of Cuba to be vindictive and unproductive. The United States continues to pursue policies established by John and Robert Kennedy. Unlike the Kennedy administration, recent U.S. governments have not, however, sanctioned sabotage and terrorism against Cuba or tried to assassinate Cuban leaders.

NOTES

1. Arthur M. Schlesinger Jr., *A Thousand Days: John F. Kennedy in the White House* (Boston: Houghton Mifflin, 1965), 1030–31; Theodore C. Sorensen, *Kennedy* (New York: Harper & Row, 1965), 5–7; Roger Hilsman, *To Move a Nation: The Politics of Foreign Policy in the Administration of John F. Kennedy* (Garden City, N.Y.: Doubleday, 1967), 582.

2. James N. Giglio, *The Presidency of John F. Kennedy* (Lawrence: University Press of Kansas, 1991), 281–87.

3. Alan Brinkley, *Liberalism and Its Discontents* (Cambridge, Mass.: Harvard University Press, 1998), 210–21.

4. Philip Caputo, *A Rumor of War* (New York: Ballantine Books, 1978), xiii–xv.

5. A copy and analysis of NSC 68 can be found in Ernest R. May, ed., *American Cold War Strategy: Interpreting NSC 68* (Boston: Bedford Books, 1993).

6. For nuclear policies during the Eisenhower and Kennedy administrations see Ronald E. Powaski, *March to Armageddon: The United States and the Nuclear Arms Race, 1939 to the Present* (New York: Oxford University Press, 1987), 60–112.

7. A good analysis of the Berlin crisis can be found in Michael R. Beschloss, *The Crisis Years: Kennedy and Khrushchev, 1960–1963* (New York: Edward Burlingame Books, 1991), 211–90.

8. An important analysis of the Bay of Pigs incident can be found in Peter Kornbluh, ed., *Bay of Pigs Declassified: The Secret CIA Report on the Invasion of Cuba* (New York: Free Press, 1998).

9. Seymour M. Hersh, *The Dark Side of Camelot* (Boston: Little, Brown, 1997), 220.

10. A useful account of the missile crisis can be found in Alexsandr Fursenko and Timothy Naftali, *"One Hell of a Gamble": Khrushchev, Castro, and Kennedy, 1958–1964* (New York: W.W. Norton, 1997).

11. Ernest R. May and Philip D. Zelikow, eds., *The Kennedy Tapes: Inside the White House during the Cuban Missile Crisis* (Cambridge, Mass.: Belknap Press of Harvard University Press, 1997).

12. Mark J. White, "The Cuban Imbroglio: From the Bay of Pigs to the Missile Crisis and Beyond" in *Kennedy: The New Frontier Revisited*, ed. Mark J. White (New York: New York University Press, 1998), 83. See also Stephen G. Rabe, "After the Missiles of October: John F. Kennedy and Cuba, November 1962 to November 1963," *Presidential Studies Quarterly* 30 (December 2000): 714–26.

13. For an analysis of the Alliance for Progress see Stephen G. Rabe, *The Most Dangerous Area in the World: John F. Kennedy Confronts Communist Revolution in Latin America* (Chapel Hill: University of North Carolina Press, 1999).

14. Fredrik Logevall, "Vietnam and the Question of What Might Have Been" in *Kennedy: The New Frontier Revisited*, ed. White, 19–62.

15. A standard account of the U.S. role in Vietnam is George C. Herring, *America's Longest War: The United States and Vietnam, 1950–1975*, 4th ed. (New York, McGraw Hill, 2002).

16. Robert A. Divine, "The Education of John F. Kennedy" in *Makers of American Diplomacy: From Theodore Roosevelt to Henry Kissinger*, ed. Frank J. Merli and Theodore A. Wilson (New York: Charles Scribner's Sons, 1974), 317–44.

17. Lawrence Freedman, *Kennedy's Wars: Berlin, Cuba, Laos, and Vietnam* (New York: Oxford University Press, 2000), 415–19.

Documents

1

PREAMBLE TO NATIONAL SECURITY COUNCIL MEMORANDUM NO. 68 (NSC 68) 7 APRIL 1950

I. BACKGROUND OF THE PRESENT CRISIS

Within the past thirty-five years the world has experienced two global wars of tremendous violence. It has witnessed two revolutions—the Russian and the Chinese—of extreme scope and intensity. It has also seen the collapse of five empires—the Ottoman, the Austro-Hungarian, German, Italian and Japanese—and the drastic decline of two major imperial systems, the British and the French. During the span of one generation, the international distribution of power has been fundamentally altered. For several centuries it had proved impossible for any one nation to gain such preponderant strength that a coalition of other nations could not in time face it with greater strength. The international scene was marked by recurring periods of violence and war, but a system of sovereign and independent states was maintained, over which no state was able to achieve hegemony.

Two complex sets of factors have now basically altered this historical distribution of power. First, the defeat of Germany and Japan and the decline of the British and French Empires have interacted with the

Source: Excerpted from U.S. Department of State, *Foreign Relations of the United States, 1950*, Vol. I: *National Security Policy*. Washington: Government Printing Office, 1977.

development of the United States and the Soviet Union in such a way that power has increasingly gravitated to these two centers. Second, the Soviet Union, unlike previous aspirants to hegemony, is animated by a new fanatic faith, antithetical to our own, and seeks to impose its absolute authority over the rest of the world. Conflict has, therefore, become endemic and is waged, on the part of the Soviet Union, by violent or non-violent methods in accordance with the dictates of expediency. With the development of increasingly terrifying weapons of mass destruction, every individual faces the ever-present possibility of annihilation should the conflict enter the phase of total war.

On the one hand, the people of the world yearn for relief from the anxiety arising from the risk of atomic war. On the other hand, any substantial further extension of the area under the domination of the Kremlin would raise the possibility that no coalition adequate to confront the Kremlin with greater strength could be assembled. It is in this context that this Republic and its citizens in the ascendancy of their strength stand in their deepest peril.

The issues that face us are momentous, involving the fulfillment or destruction not only of this Republic but of civilization itself. They are issues which will not await our deliberations. With conscience and resolution this Government and the people it represents must now take new and fateful decisions.

II. FUNDAMENTAL PURPOSE OF THE UNITED STATES

The fundamental purpose of the United States is laid down in the Preamble to the Constitution: ". . . to form a more perfect Union, establish Justice, insure domestic Tranquility, provide for the common defense, promote the general Welfare, and secure the Blessings of Liberty to ourselves and our Posterity." In essence, the fundamental purpose is to assure the integrity and vitality of our free society, which is founded upon the dignity and worth of the individual.

Three realities emerge as a consequence of this purpose: Our determination to maintain the essential elements of individual freedom, as set forth in the Constitution and Bill of Rights; our determination to create conditions under which our free and democratic system can live and prosper; and our determination to fight if necessary to defend our way of life, for which as in the Declaration of independence, "with a firm reliance on the protection of Divine Providence, we mutually pledge to each other our lives, our Fortunes and our sacred Honor."

III. FUNDAMENTAL DESIGN OF THE KREMLIN

The fundamental design of those who control the Soviet Union and the international communist movement is to retain and solidify their absolute power, first in the Soviet Union and second in the areas now under their control. In the minds of the Soviet leaders, however, achievement of this design requires the dynamic extension of their authority and the ultimate elimination of any effective opposition to their authority.

The design, therefore, calls for the complete subversion or forcible destruction of the machinery of government and structure of society in the countries of the non-Soviet world and their replacement by an apparatus and structure subservient to and controlled from the Kremlin. To that end Soviet efforts are now directed toward the domination of the Eurasian land mass. The United States, as the principal center of power in the non-Soviet world and the bulwark of opposition to Soviet expansion, is the principal enemy whose integrity and vitality must be subverted or destroyed by one means of another if the Kremlin is to achieve its fundamental design.

2

PRESIDENT KENNEDY
AND CHAIRMAN KHRUSHCHEV
DEBATE THE FATE OF BERLIN
AT THE VIENNA SUMMIT
4 JUNE 1961

Vienna, June, 4, 1961, 3:15 p.m.

SUBJECT

Vienna Meeting Between The President And Chairman Khrushchev

PARTICIPANTS

The President
D—Mr. Akalovsky (interpreting)

Chairman Khrushchev
Mr. Sukhodrev, Interpreter, USSR
Ministry of Foreign Affairs

After lunch, the President said he wanted to have a few words with the Chairman in private.

The President opened the conversation by saying that he recognized the importance of Berlin and that he hoped that in the interests of the relations between our two countries, which he wanted to improve, Mr. Khrushchev would not present him with a situation so deeply involving our national interest. Of course, he recognized that the decision on East Germany, as far as the USSR was concerned, was with the Chairman. The Pres-

Source: Excerpted from U.S. Department of State, *Foreign Relations of the United States, 1961–1963*, Vol. 14: *Berlin Crisis, 1961–1962*. Washington: Government Printing Office, 1993.

ident continued by saying that evolution is taking place in many areas of the world and no one can predict which course it would take. Therefore, it is most important that decisions be carefully considered. Obviously the Chairman will make his judgment in the light of what he understands to be the best interests of his country. However, the President said, he did want to stress the difference between a peace treaty and the rights of access to Berlin. He reiterated his hope that the relations between the two countries would develop in a way that would avoid direct contact or confrontation between them.

Mr. Khrushchev said he appreciated the frankness of the President's remarks but said that if the President insisted on US rights after the signing of a peace treaty and that if the borders of the GDR—land, air, or sea borders—were violated, they would be defended. The US position is not based on juridical grounds. The US wants to humiliate the USSR and this cannot be accepted. He said that he would not shirk his responsibility and would take any action that he is duty bound to take as Prime Minister. He would be glad if the US were to agree to an interim agreement on Germany and Berlin with a time limit so that the prestige and the interests of the two countries would not be involved or prejudiced. However, he said, he must warn the President that if he envisages any action that might bring about unhappy consequences, force would be met by force. The US should prepare itself for that and the Soviet Union will do the same.

The President inquired whether under an interim arrangement forces in Berlin would remain and access would be free. Mr. Khrushchev replied that would be so for six months. In reply to the President's query whether the forces would then have to be withdrawn, the Chairman replied in the affirmative.

The President then said that either Mr. Khrushchev did not believe that the US was serious or the situation in that area was so unsatisfactory to the Soviet Union that it had to take this drastic action. The President referred to his forthcoming meeting with Macmillan and said the latter would ask what had happened. The President said that he would have to say that he had gained the impression that the USSR was presenting him with the alternative of accepting the Soviet act on Berlin or having a face to face confrontation. He had come here to prevent a confrontation between our two countries and he regretted to leave Vienna with this impression.

Mr. Khrushchev replied that in order to save prestige we could agree that token contingents of troops, including Soviet troops, could be maintained in West Berlin. However, this would be not on the basis of some occupation rights, but on the basis of an agreement registered with the UN. Of course, access would be subject to GDR's control because this is its prerogative. Mr. Khrushchev continued by saying that he wanted peace and that if the US wanted war, that was its problem. It is not the USSR that threatens with war, it is the US.

The President stressed that it was the Chairman, not he, who wanted to force a change.

Mr. Khrushchev replied that a peace treaty would not involve any change in boundaries. In any event, the USSR will have no choice other than to accept the challenge; it must respond and it will respond. The calamities of a war will be shared equally. War will take place only if the US imposes it on the USSR. It is up to the US to decide whether there will be war or peace. This, he said, can be told Macmillan, De Gaulle and Adenauer. The decision to sign a peace treaty is firm and irrevocable and the Soviet Union will sign it in December if the US refuses an interim agreement.

The President concluded the conversation by observing that it would be a cold winter.

3

PRESIDENT KENNEDY URGES CITIZENS TO PREPARE FOR NUCLEAR WAR 25 JULY 1961

RADIO AND TELEVISION REPORT TO THE AMERICAN PEOPLE ON THE BERLIN CRISIS

We have another sober responsibility. To recognize the possibilities of nuclear war in the missile age, without our citizens knowing what they should do and where they should go if bombs begin to fall. In May, I pledged a new start on Civil Defense. Last week, I assigned, on the recommendation of the Civil Defense Director, basic responsibility for this program to the Secretary of Defense, to make certain it is administered and coordinated with our continental defense efforts at the highest civilian level. Tomorrow, I am requesting of the Congress new funds for the following immediate objectives: to identify and mark space in existing structures—public and private—that could be used for fall-out shelters in case of attack; to stock those shelters with food, water, first-aid kits and other minimum essentials for survival; to increase their capacity; to improve our air-raid warning and fall-out detection systems, including a new household warning system which is now under development; and

Source: Excerpted from U.S. General Services Administration, *Public Papers of the President: John F. Kennedy, 1961*. Washington: Government Printing Office, 1962.

to take other measures that will be effective at an early date to save millions of lives if needed.

In the event of an attack, the lives of those families which are not hit in a nuclear blast and fire can still be saved—if they can be warned to take shelter and if that shelter is available. We owe that kind of insurance to our families—and to our country. In contrast to our friends in Europe, the need for this kind of protection is new to our shores. But the time to start is now. In the coming months, I hope to let every citizen know what steps he can take without delay to protect his family in case of attack. I know that you will want to do no less.

V.

The addition of $207 million in Civil Defense appropriations brings our total new defense budget requests to $3.454 billion, and a total of $47.5 billion for the year. This is an increase in the defense budget of $6 billion since January, and has resulted in official estimates of a budget deficit of over $5 billion. The Secretary of the Treasury and other economic advisers assure me, however, that our economy has the capacity to bear this new request.

4

PRESIDENT KENNEDY EXPLAINS HIS DECISION NOT TO LAUNCH AN AIR STRIKE AGAINST CUBA 22 OCTOBER 1962

Portion of the NSC Meeting Minutes, Monday, October 22, 1962

The President discussed the reasons why he had decided against an air strike now. First, there was no certainty that an air strike would destroy all missiles now in Cuba. We would be able to get a large percentage of these missiles, but could not get them all.

In addition we would not know if any of these missiles were operationally ready with their nuclear warheads and we were not certain that our intelligence had discovered all the missiles in Cuba. Therefore, in attacking the ones we had located, we could not be certain that others unknown to us would not be launched against the United States. The President said an air strike would involve an action comparable to the Japanese attack on Pearl Harbor. Finally, an air strike would increase the danger of a worldwide nuclear war.

The President said he had given up the thought of making an air strike only yesterday morning. In summary, he said an air strike had all the disadvantages of Pearl Harbor. It would not insure the destruction

Source: Excerpted from U.S. Department of State, *Foreign Relations of the United States, 1961–1963*, Vol. 13: *Cuban Missile Crisis and Aftermath*. Washington: Government Printing Office, 1996.

of every strategic missile in Cuba, and would end up eventually in our having to invade.

Mr. Bundy added that we should not discuss the fact that we were not able to destroy all the missiles by means of an air strike because at some later time we might wish to make such an attack.

5

HIGHER AUTHORITY (PRESIDENT KENNEDY) APPROVES A SABOTAGE PROGRAM AGAINST CUBA 19 JUNE 1963

Washington, June 19, 1963

SUBJECT

Meeting at the White House concerning Proposed Covert Policy and Integrated Program of Action towards Cuba

PRESENT

Higher Authority
Secretary McNamara
Under Secretary Harriman
Mr. McCone
Mr. McGeorge Bundy
Mr. Thomas Parrott
Mr. Desmond FitzGerald
Air Force Vice Chief of Staff, General W.F. McKee

1. The program as recommended by the Standing Group of the NSC was presented briefly to Higher Authority who showed a particular interest in proposed external sabotage operations. He was shown charts indicating

---

Source: Excerpted from U.S. Department of State, *Foreign Relations of the United States, 1961–1963*, Vol. 13: *Cuban Missile Crisis and Aftermath*. Washington: Government Printing Office, 1996.

typical targets for this program and a discussion of the advantages and disadvantages ensued. It was well recognized that there would be failures and a considerable noise level. [*2 lines of source text not declassified*] Mr. Bundy described the integrated nature of the program presented and made the point that, having made the decision to go ahead, we be prepared to take the consequences of flaps and criticisms for a sufficient period to give the program a real chance. Mr. Harriman stated that the program would be "reviewed weekly" by the Special Group. (It is believed that an arrangement can be made with Mr. Bundy for less detailed control by the Special Group than was indicated by Mr. Harriman.)

2. Higher Authority asked how soon we could get into action with the external sabotage program and was told we should be able to conduct our first operation in the dark-of-the-moon period in July although he was informed that we would prefer to start the program with some caution selecting softer targets to begin with. Higher Authority said this was a matter for our judgement. Although at one stage in the discussion Higher Authority said that we should move ahead with the program "this summer" it is believed that Mr. Bundy will be able to convince him that his is not a sufficiently long trial period to demonstrate what the program can do.*

Desmond FitzGerald
Chief, Special Affairs Staff

*[CIA Director John] McCone added an addendum to this memorandum stating that he emphasized to the President "the importance and necessity for continuous operations," and he also pointed out that the activities "would create quite a high noise level." McCone also stated that the noise level "must be absorbed and not create a change in policy." He concluded that "no single event would be conclusive."

6

PRESIDENT KENNEDY EXPRESSES RESERVATIONS ABOUT INCREASED U.S. MILITARY INVOLVEMENT IN SOUTH VIETNAM 15 NOVEMBER 1961

NOTES ON THE NATIONAL SECURITY COUNCIL MEETING, WASHINGTON, NOVEMBER 15, 1961, 10 A.M.

Mr. Rusk explained the draft of Memorandum on South Viet Nam. He added the hope that, in spite of the magnitude of the proposal, any U.S. actions would not be hampered by lack of funds nor failure to pursue the program vigorously. The President expressed the fear of becoming involved simultaneously on two fronts on opposite sides of the world. He questioned the wisdom of involvement in Viet Nam since the basis thereof is not completely clear. By comparison he noted that Korea was a case of clear aggression which was opposed by the United States and other members of the U.N. The conflict in Viet Nam is more obscure and less flagrant. The President then expressed his strong feeling that in such a situation the United States needs even more the support of allies in such an endeavor as Viet Nam in order to avoid sharp domestic partisan criticism as well as strong objections from other nations of the world. The President said that he could even make a rather strong case against intervening in an area 10,000

Source: Excerpted from U.S. Department of State, *Foreign Relations of the United States, 1961–1963,* Vol. 1: *Vietnam, 1961.* Washington: Government Printing Office, 1988.

miles away against 16,000 guerrillas with a native army of 200,000 where millions have been spent for years with no success. The President repeated his apprehension concerning support, adding that none could be expected from the French, and Mr. Rusk interrupted to say that the British were tending more and more to take the French point of view. The President compared the obscurity of the issues in Viet Nam to the clarity of the positions in Berlin, the contrast of which could even make leading Democrats wary of proposed activities in the Far East.

Mr. Rusk suggested that firmness in Viet Nam in the manner and form of that in Berlin might achieve desired results in Viet Nam without resort to combat. The President disagreed with the suggestion on the basis that the issue was clearly defined in Berlin and opposing forces identified whereas in Viet Nam the issue is vague and action is by guerrillas, sometimes in a phantom-like fashion. Mr. McNamara expressed an opinion that action would become clear if U.S. forces were involved since this power would be applied against sources of Viet Cong power including those in North Viet Nam. The President observed that it was not clear to him just where these U.S. forces would base their operations other than from aircraft carriers which seemed to him to be quite vulnerable. General Lemnitzer confirmed that carriers would be involved to a considerable degree and stated that Taiwan and the Philippines would also become principal bases of action.

7

PRESIDENT KENNEDY COMMENTS ON SOUTH VIETNAM AND THE "DOMINO THEORY" 9 SEPTEMBER 1963

TRANSCRIPT OF BROADCAST ON NBC'S "HUNTLEY-BRINKLEY REPORT"

Mr. Huntley: Mr. President, in respect to our difficulties in South Viet-Nam, could it be that our Government tends occasionally to get locked into a policy or an attitude and then finds it difficult to alter or shift that policy?

THE PRESIDENT. Yes, that is true. I think in the case of South Viet-Nam we have been dealing with a government which is in control, has been in control for 10 years. In addition, we have felt for the last 2 years that the struggle against the Communists was going better. Since June, however, the difficulties with the Buddhists, we have been concerned about a deterioration, particularly in the Saigon area, which hasn't been felt greatly in the outlying areas but may spread. So we are faced with the problem of wanting to protect the area against the Communists. On the other hand, we have to deal with the government there. That produces a kind of ambivalence in our efforts which exposes us to some criticism. We are using our

Source: Excerpted from U.S. General Services Administration, *Public Papers of the President: John F. Kennedy, 1963*, Washington: Government Printing Office, 1964.

influence to persuade the government there to take those steps which will win back support. That takes some time and we must be patient, we must persist.

Mr. Huntley: Are we likely to reduce our aid to South Viet-Nam now?

THE PRESIDENT. I don't think we think that would be helpful at this time. If you reduce your aid, it is possible you could have some effect upon the government structure there. On the other hand, you might have a situation which could bring about a collapse. Strongly in our mind is what happened in the case of China at the end of World War II, where China was lost, a weak government became increasingly unable to control events. We don't want that.

Mr. Brinkley: Mr. President, have you had any reason to doubt this so-called "domino theory," that if South Viet-Nam falls, the rest of southeast Asia will go behind it?

THE PRESIDENT. No, I believe it. I believe it. I think that the struggle is close enough. China is so large, looms so high just beyond the frontiers, that if South Viet-Nam went, it would not only give them an improved geographical position for a guerrilla assault on Malaya, but would also give the impression that the wave of the future in southeast Asia was China and the Communists. So I believe it.

Mr. Brinkley: In the last 48 hours there have been a great many conflicting reports from there about what the CIA was up to. Can you give us any enlightenment on it?

THE PRESIDENT: No

Mr. Huntley: Does the CIA tend to make its own policy? That seems to be the debate here.

THE PRESIDENT. No, that is the frequent charge, but that isn't so. Mr. McCone, head of the CIA, sits in the National Security Council. We have had a number of meetings in the past few days about events in South Viet-Nam. Mr. McCone participated in every one, and the CIA coordinates its efforts with the State Department and the Defense Department

Mr. Brinkley: With so much of our prestige, money, so on, committed in South Viet-Nam, why can't we exercise a little more influence there, Mr. President?

THE PRESIDENT. We have some influence. We have some influence, and we are attempting to carry it out. I think we don't—we can't expect these countries to do every thing the way we want to do them. They have their own interest, their own personalities, their own tradition. We can't make everyone in our image, and there are a good many people who don't want to go in our image. In addition, we have ancient struggles between countries. In the case of India and Pakistan, we would like to have them settle Kashmir. That is our view of the best way to defend the subcontinent against communism. But that struggle between India and Pakistan is more important to a good many people in that area than the struggle against the Communists. We would like to have Cambodia, Thailand, and South Viet-Nam all in harmony, but there are ancient differences there. We can't make the world over, but we can influence the world. The fact of the matter is that with the assistance of the United States, SEATO, southeast Asia and indeed all of Asia has been maintained independent against a powerful force, the Chinese Communists. What I am concerned about is that Americans will get impatient and say because they don't like events in southeast Asia or they don't like the government in Saigon, that we should withdraw. That only makes it easy for the Communists. I think we should stay. We should use our influence in as effective a way as we can, but we should not withdraw.

8

PRESIDENT KENNEDY'S UNDELIVERED REMARKS AT THE TRADE MART IN DALLAS 22 NOVEMBER 1963

I want to discuss with you today the status of our strength and our security because this question clearly calls for the most responsible qualities of leadership and the most enlightened products of scholarship. For this Nation's strength and security are not easily or cheaply obtained, nor are they quickly and simply explained. There are many kinds of strength and no one kind will suffice. Overwhelming nuclear strength cannot stop a guerrilla war. Formal pacts of alliance cannot stop internal subversion. Displays of material wealth cannot stop the disillusionment of diplomats subjected to discrimination.

Above all, words alone are not enough. The United States is a peaceful nation. And where our strength and determination are clear, our words need merely to convey conviction, not belligerence. If we are strong, our strength will speak for itself. If we are weak, words will be of no help.

I realize that this Nation often tends to identify turning-points in world affairs with the major addresses which preceded them. But it was not the Monroe Doctrine that kept all Europe away from this hemisphere—it was the strength of the British fleet and the width of the Atlantic Ocean. It

Source: Excerpted from U.S. General Services Administration, *Public Papers of the President: John F. Kennedy, 1963*, Washington: Government Printing Office, 1964.

was not General Marshall's speech at Harvard which kept communism out of Western Europe—it was the strength and stability made possible by our military and economic assistance.

In this administration also it has been necessary at times to issue specific warnings—warnings that we could not stand by and watch the Communists conquer Laos by force, or intervene in the Congo, or swallow West Berlin, or maintain offensive missiles on Cuba. But while our goals were at least temporarily obtained in these and other instances, our successful defense of freedom was due not to the words we used, but to the strength we stood ready to use on behalf of the principles we stand ready to defend.

This strength is composed of many different elements, ranging from the most massive deterrents to the most subtle influences. And all types of strength are needed—no one kind could do the job alone. Let us take a moment, therefore, to review this Nation's progress in each major area of strength.

First, as Secretary McNamara made clear in his address last Monday, the strategic nuclear power of the United States has been greatly modernized and expanded in the last 1,000 days, by the rapid production and deployment of the most modern missile systems, that any and all potential aggressors are clearly confronted now with the impossibility of strategic victory—and the certainty of total destruction—if by reckless attack they should ever force upon us the necessity of a strategic reply.

In less than 3 years, we have increased by 50 percent the number of Polaris submarines scheduled to be in force by the next fiscal year, increased by more than 70 percent our total Polaris purchase program, increased by more than 75 percent our Minuteman purchase program, increased by 50 percent the portion of our strategic bombers on 15-minute alert, and increased by 100 percent the total number of nuclear weapons available in our strategic alert forces. Our security is further enhanced by the steps we have taken regarding these weapons to improve the speed and certainty of their response, their readiness at all times to respond, their ability to survive an attack, and their ability to be carefully controlled and directed through secure command operations.

But the lessons of the last decade have taught us that freedom cannot be defended by strategic nuclear power alone. We have, therefore, in the last 3 years accelerated the development and deployment of tactical nuclear weapons, and increased by 60 percent the tactical nuclear forces deployed in Western Europe.

Nor can Europe or any other continent rely on nuclear forces along, whether they are strategic or tactical. We have radically improved the readiness of our conventional forces—increased by 45 percent the number of combat ready Army divisions, increased by 100 percent the procurement of modern Army weapons and equipment, increased by 100 percent our ship construction, conversion, and modernization program, increased by 100 percent our procurement of tactical aircraft, increased by 30 percent the number of tactical air squadrons, and increased the strength of the Marines. As last month's "Operation Big Lift"—which originated here in Texas—showed so clearly, this Nation is prepared as never before to move substantial numbers of men in surprisingly little time to advanced positions anywhere in the world. We have increased by 175 percent the procurement of airlift aircraft, and we have already achieved a 75 percent increase in our existing strategic airlift capability. Finally, moving beyond the traditional roles of our military forces, we have achieved an increase of nearly 600 percent in our special forces—those forces that are prepared to work with our allies and friends against the guerrillas, saboteurs, insurgents and assassins who threaten freedom in a less direct but equally dangerous manner.

But American military might should not and need not stand alone against the ambitions of international communism. Our security and strength, in the last analysis, directly depend on the security and strength of others, and that is why our military and economic assistance plays such a key role in enabling those who live on the periphery of the Communist world to maintain their independence of choice. Our assistance to these nations can be painful, risky and costly, as is true in Southeast Asia today. But we dare not weary of the task. For our assistance makes possible the stationing of 3.5 million allied troops along the Communist frontier at one-tenth the cost of maintaining a comparable number of American soldiers. A successful Communist breakthrough in these areas, necessitating direct United States intervention, would cost us several times as much as our entire foreign aid program, and might cost us heavily in American lives as well.

About 70 percent of our military assistance goes to nine key countries located on or near the borders of the Communist bloc—nine countries confronted directly or indirectly with the threat of Communist aggression—Viet-Nam, Free China, Korea, India, Pakistan, Thailand, Greece, Turkey, and Iran. No one of these countries possesses on its own the resources to maintain the forces which our own Chiefs of Staff think needed in the common interest. Reducing our efforts to train, equip, and assist their armies can only encourage Communist penetration and require in time the increased overseas deployment of American combat forces. And reducing the economic help needed to bolster these nations that undertake to help defend freedom can have the same disastrous result. In short, the $50 billion we spend each year on our own defense could well be ineffective without the $4 billion required for military and economic assistance.

Our foreign aid program is not growing in size, it is, on the contrary, smaller now than in previous years. It has had its weaknesses, but we have undertaken to correct them. And the proper way of treating weaknesses is to replace them with strength, not to increase whose weaknesses by emasculating essential programs. Dollar for dollar, in or out of government, there is no better form of investment in our national security than our much-abused foreign aid program. We cannot afford to lose it. We can afford to maintain it. We can surely afford, for example, to do as much for our 19 needy neighbors of Latin America as the Communist bloc is sending to the island of Cuba alone.

JOHN F. KENNEDY AND THE NATION

James N. Giglio

In entering the twenty-first century, the image of John Fitzgerald Kennedy continues to evoke adoration among ordinary Americans. This is reflected in recent public opinion polls in which Kennedy is still acclaimed our favorite president. Americans can also view favorable cinematic images of his presidency, from *JFK* in 1991 to *Thirteen Days* ten years later. They can read sympathetic cover stories in news magazines about him and family whenever Kennedy books are published or Kennedy family tragedies occur, both taking place with considerable frequency over the last decade of the twentieth century.[1]

John Kennedy's assassination on 22 November 1963, of course, contributed much to the romantic notions that Americans have had of him and his presidency. His youthful image, much more Hollywood than Washington, remains frozen in our national memory, as do his glamorous wife and two attractive children who bore his tragic death with remarkable grace. Kennedy reached his ultimate potential as president as a consequence of his death. People remembered his perceived idealism and vision in the wake of an unraveling social fabric that included the Vietnam escalation, the student protest movement, more assassinations, and the urban riots of the late 1960s, which were then followed by Watergate and the transgressions of the 1970s and 1980s. Consequently, many Americans have reasoned that if Kennedy had lived then none of those bad things would have happened and he instead would have fulfilled our democratic ideals.

Scholars have had less exalted views of Kennedy and his presidency. In fact, there is arguably a greater divergence between the general public and historians in their assessment of JFK than of any other president. This is reflected in various polls in which scholars have rated presidents from the greatness of Lincoln to the failure of James Buchanan. There has been a gradual descent in Kennedy's appraisal in recent years. His current position: in the middle of the pack, bordered by John Quincy Adams, George Bush, and Jimmy Carter—eighteenth among thirty-eight presidents evaluated, according to one recent poll.[2]

Unquestionably, Kennedy's scant 1,033 days in the White House have always handicapped him because he was not afforded the luxury of a full term, leaving many of his initiatives unfulfilled. Beyond that, his association with excessive presidential activism in places such as Vietnam and Cuba and the perceived limitations of the welfare state have also weakened his standing among scholars, as have Bill Clinton's sexual indiscretions, which cast Kennedy's similar activities in a darker light even though no evidence exists that Kennedy's White House trysts affected public policy.

Similarly, scholars specializing in the Kennedy presidency have altered their assessments since the Camelot School of the 1960s. Spearheaded by *Kennedy*, which was crafted by Theodore Sorensen, Kennedy's chief counsel and speechwriter, and *A Thousand Days*, by Arthur M. Schlesinger Jr., special assistant to the president and court historian, the Camelot school saw Kennedy in terms of presidential greatness, a predominant view of the time. Their canonizing of Kennedy led to the inevitable backlash of historical revisionism in the 1970s, featuring Bruce Miroff's *Pragmatic Illusions* (1976) and Henry Fairlie's *The Kennedy Promise* (1973). Early revisionists, relying mostly on published sources, viewed Kennedy as a cold warrior in foreign affairs and an ineffectual and overly pragmatic leader in domestic matters. Although no longer nearly as dominant, revisionism continued through the 1990s with the publication of such critical studies as Thomas Reeves's *A Question of Character* and Seymour Hersh's *The Dark Side of Camelot*.[3]

By the 1980s, however, Kennedy revisionism had given way to more balanced approaches. Most of these works, grounded in the rich primary sources of the John Fitzgerald Kennedy Library in Boston, were less concerned with challenging Kennedy's reputation as a bold and progressive leader. They recognized the constraints Kennedy faced from the ideological right and a recalcitrant Congress. At the same time, they were more sensitive to the intrusion of foreign crises, many of which Kennedy inherited and sometimes resolved. Several postrevisionists recognized that while all too often his appeal rested on style and inflated rhetoric, it nevertheless had enormous impact. Kennedy had in fact energized young Americans to embrace politics and government service as honored professions, motivating them to serve as Peace Corps volunteers in Third World countries and as Special Forces advisers in South Vietnam. Indeed, many Democratic political figures in our own time—including William Jefferson Clinton—had heeded Kennedy's clarion call to enter public service. To them Kennedy remains a hero. Among the most representative of these postrevisionist studies are Herbert Parmet's *Jack* and *JFK,* Richard Reeves's *President Kennedy: Profile of Power,* and my *The Presidency of John F. Kennedy.* Although virtually all Kennedy studies give much greater focus to foreign-policy issues, which dominated the Cold War years of the 1960s, this essay will evaluate Kennedy primarily on domestic matters, leaving an analysis of foreign policy to Stephen Rabe.

Kennedy had always possessed a deeper interest in international affairs. Early in his senate career he had confided to Sorensen that secretary of state or secretary of defense were the cabinet posts that appealed to him. Nonetheless, Kennedy understood that to achieve presidential greatness, he needed to advance domestic Democratic goals evolving from Franklin D. Roosevelt's New Deal and economic bill of rights address of January 1944, the latter setting the agenda for the welfare state in postwar America.

When beginning his quest for the presidency in the mid-1950s, Kennedy had consequently moved even further away from the conservatism of his father, Joseph P. Kennedy, a former Wall Street entrepreneur. Kennedy explained his gradual drift leftward by suggesting that "some people have their liberalism 'made' by the time they reach their late twenties. I didn't. I was caught in the crosscurrents and eddies. It was only later that I got into the stream of thought." Kennedy's moderation placed him in the mainstream of the party. Even though he embraced the liberal agenda of recent Democratic presidents, he nevertheless remained a fiscal conservative until at least 1963. He also rejected self-labeling; when pressed he called himself a "realist" or an "idealist without illusions."

Kennedy comprehended the relationship between domestic and foreign policy, that the success of one depended upon the promotion of the other. He knew, for example, that an orderly development of civil rights at home could win the neutrality—if not the allegiance—of the newly emerging nations of Africa. That sensitivity to national policy, involving the incorporation of the domestic with the foreign, enabled him to broaden his "New Frontier" to include initiatives as far reaching as the space program, the Peace Corps, women's rights, and civil rights. No other presidential rubric, whether it be the Square Deal, the New Deal, or the Fair Deal, was as inclusive or as expansive.

ASSUMING THE PRESIDENCY

Kennedy took the presidential oath of office on a sunny, frigid, snow-covered 20 January in front of the Capitol where Chief Justice Earl Warren swore in the hatless and coatless forty-three year old. Kennedy's inaugural address, crafted mostly by Sorensen, remains one of the most inspiring and eloquent speeches of that genre even though scholars have noted its militancy and globalism. No passage has been more quoted than the following: "let every nation know whether it wishes us well or ill, that we shall pay any price, bear any burden, meet any hardship, support any friend, oppose any foe to assure the survival and success of liberty. This much we pledge—and more." With another memorable phrase calling for sacrifice, Kennedy concluded, "Ask not what your country can do for you—ask what you can do for your country." Cold War challenges obviously consumed a president who inherited crises in Berlin, Southeast Asia, and Africa and soon created them elsewhere particularly in Cuba where Fidel Castro had forged a communist state that Kennedy perceived as a national security threat. As a result, domestic issues were ignored in his inaugural address. It would not be until his first weeks in office that Kennedy quietly presented a legislative program to Congress.

He did so with several strikes against him. First of all, he barely carried the popular vote, winning the 1960 election with a plurality of less than 120,000 of 66 million ballots cast and allegations of voting fraud in at least two states. The lack of a convincing victory made it impossible for him to claim any mandate for such controversial matters as civil rights or medical insurance for the aged, particularly since public opinion polls reflected a rather conservative society satisfied to keep things much as they were. Congress was no different; twenty-one Democrats lost House seats in 1960. While the Democrats retained a commanding majority, 108 Democrats in the House and 81 in the Senate came from the conservative South. They often consorted with Republicans on social issues, a tradition begun during Roosevelt's 1937 court-packing fight.

The antiprogressive coalition remained an imposing force for Kennedy at a time when, as a consequence of the razor-thin presidential election, Republican congressional partisanship was intense. At this critical juncture the Democrats lacked effective leadership in Congress. In the Senate the powerful authority of the majority leader, Lyndon Johnson, no longer held sway now that he was Kennedy's vice president. Power reverted to several "feudal lords" who chaired key standing committees, while Mike Mansfield (D-Mont.) proved too mild mannered as majority leader to bring them together behind Kennedy's program. In the House the once powerful Democratic Speaker of the House Sam Rayburn (Tex.) was a shadow of his former self; before cancer claimed him that fall, he had barely succeeded in enlarging the powerful House Rules Committee from twelve to fifteen members, giving the administration a slight edge in determining which bills went to the floor for a vote. The House Rules fight not only exposed the weaknesses in Rayburn's leadership, but also exacerbated partisan differences. Rayburn's replacement, the vacuous-looking John McCormack (D-Mass.), who often opposed Kennedy in intraparty squabbles in Massachusetts, proved even less effective than a dying Rayburn.

Kennedy's own shortcomings in the legislative arena contributed to the administration's difficulties. Despite his fourteen years in Congress, he had failed to penetrate the inner circle. Legislative leaders such as Richard Russell (D-Ga.) and Lyndon Johnson (Tex.) had viewed him as too detached, independent, overrated, and overly ambitious. Other critics claimed that he was unwilling to fight or work harder for his programs and instead depended too much on his staff and the congressional leadership. Larry O'Brien, special assistant to the president for congressional relations, concurred that Kennedy "rarely asked a member for his vote. . . . That was not his style. If there were arms to be twisted, that was our job." Instead of cajoling Congress, Kennedy relied on reason; if that failed he surmised that the time was not ripe. He was reluctant to push Congress too hard, not wanting to jeopardize other administration proposals. Even Schlesinger conceded that working with Congress "was [not] the part of the Presidency which gave him the greatest pleasure or satisfaction." His penchant for compromising on programs too soon compounded the problem. Congressmen, according to one administrative assistant, consequently looked on Kennedy as a "nice boy who could [not] get what he wanted." Senator Allen Ellender (D-La.) knew no president "less aggressive," and House Ways and Means Chairman Wilbur Mills (D-Ark.) referred to his "timid approach."

Yet such personal criticism seems harsh given the difficulties of Roosevelt and Harry S. Truman with a similar coalition of conservative Democrats and Republicans that had dominated Congress since the late 1930s. Arguably, neither president would have performed much better in the Kennedy era. Given the constraints of the time, it is surprising that Kennedy did as well as he did. In fact, by responding successfully to a number of domestic problems, Kennedy unquestionably left the nation better off than he found it. And partly as a result of Kennedy's martyred death in 1963, the country—and hence the Congress—finally became momentarily receptive to the adoption of the remaining Democratic agenda under the skillful leadership of President Lyndon Johnson.

President Kennedy had first focused on domestic considerations in his State of the Union address on 30 January 1961. The sagging economy, reflected by a seven-month recession and seven years of diminished growth, represented his most disturbing concern because it furthered the impression of a declining superpower. Typical of a president who saw domestic issues in foreign-policy terms, Kennedy argued that "we must show the world what a free country can do—to reduce unemployment, to put unused capacity to work, to spur new productivity, and to foster higher economic growth." Likewise, in a special message to Congress on 2 February, he warned that the United States "cannot afford, in this time of national need and world crisis, to dissipate its opportunities for economic growth. . . . Our programs must aim at expanding American productive capacity at a rate that shows the world the vigor and vitality of a free economy." Kennedy's statements came at the apex of the Cold War, one month after Nikita Khrushchev's national liberation speech, which proclaimed the ultimate triumph of communism.

Kennedy's economic goals included a balanced budget that would somehow elevate the growth rate of about 2.5 percent annually over the prior three and one-half years to 5 percent, causing the nearly 7 percent unemployment rate to decrease substantially. One of our most fiscally conservative presidents of the modern era, partly because of political considerations and his father's lingering influence, he also became concerned about the balance of payment deficit. This deficit resulted in more dollars leaving the country than entering because of increased American imports and rising investments and expenditures abroad, the U.S. military buildup in Europe contributing to the latter. Trade revenues were never enough to overcome the imbalance. By 1960 the problem worsened when foreign nations exchanged dollars for gold, draining U.S. gold reserves. To Kennedy, a country was only as strong as its currency.

Because of the balance of payment problem, Kennedy could not respond to the depressed economy by imposing monetary solutions. Reducing interest rates would fuel inflation and worsen the imbalance of payments by forcing U.S. dollars into foreign markets. Nor could he appreciably increase the budget deficit because it would cause foreign bankers to doubt the strength of the dollar, leading to the withdrawal of more gold. To deal with these problems, Kennedy relied on the advice of the Republican secretary of the treasury, Douglas Dillon, as well as the more liberal Council of Economic Advisers (CEA), especially its chairman, Walter Heller, a Keynesian economist who, unlike Dillon, favored stimulating a floundering economy through tax cuts and self-instituted deficits, as was done in the Great Depression. Given the imbalance of payments, the former solution seemed more appealing to Heller.

THE DOMESTIC LEGISLATIVE AGENDA

Early in his presidency Kennedy submitted to Congress five major bills that Democrats had favored since Roosevelt's economic bill of rights address. Those legislative proposals reflected the postwar liberalism of Truman, Adlai Stevenson, Kennedy, and others who sought to update Roosevelt's New Deal by strengthening existing programs and extending government assistance into new areas such as national health insurance. This would be accomplished not by redistributing wealth and income but by promoting economic growth to appease corporate interests as well as to improve the lot of middle- and lower-income Americans. In that way liberalism sought to orchestrate class harmony. Democratic liberals, believing that hardcore poverty had been eradicated, thought more in terms of improving the quality of life for all Americans. But by 1960 poverty-stricken areas such as Appalachia revealed to a campaigning Kennedy the extent to which economic distress still existed. Even he underestimated a problem that sociologist

Michael Harrington soon revealed in *The Other America* (1962). As the 1960s unfolded, Kennedy's liberalism faced even greater challenges with an emerging civil rights movement that threatened to shatter the New Deal coalition of which the white South remained an integral part.

Kennedy's initial bills dealt with an increase in the minimum wage, federal assistance to public schools, hospital insurance for the aged, housing assistance, and aid to depressed areas, all of which were designed to provide economic stimulus. Absent at first was civil rights legislation, which party officials thought too controversial for immediate submission. Largely because of Republicans and conservative Democrats, Kennedy faced opposition at almost every turn. He won a nominal victory in raising the minimum wage to $1.25 an hour, his stated goal, but at the expense of excluding previously uncovered employees who needed a minimum wage the most, including laundry workers, who were mostly black women, and 350,000 others in menial jobs. Democrat Carl Vinson (Ga.), who introduced in the House of Representatives the amendment to exclude laundry workers, joked, amid considerable laughter, that he had "wash[ed] laundry workers clear out of the picture." It had not helped that the Kennedy forces mismanaged the floor fight in the House by appearing too willing to compromise too early. Moreover, several potential supporters had missed the roll call, causing the passage of a vastly inferior nonadministration bill that excluded workers who were not employed in interstate firms. As frustrating as this might have been to Kennedy, it bore no comparison to the Bay of Pigs fiasco that soon followed, one of several foreign-policy crises that occupied his attention that spring and summer. To Republican Richard Nixon, he confided, "It is really true that foreign affairs is the only important issue for a President to handle, isn't it? I mean who gives a shit if the minimum wage is $1.15 or $1.25 in comparison to something like this?"

Kennedy faced a greater roadblock in extending federal assistance to America's schools, despite the need to elevate education in impoverished areas. Resistance came from several northern Democrats who normally supported progressive legislation. They represented Catholic constituents who resented Kennedy's opposing aid to parochial schools based on the strict constitutional grounds of separation of church and state. For that reason the National Catholic Welfare Conference and Francis Cardinal Spellman of New York both opposed Kennedy's legislation. Meanwhile, Republicans rejected the bill because of ideology and cost while southern

Democrats feared that federal funds might be withheld from racially seg-regated schools.

The school-assistance bill requested $2.3 billion in federal aid to the states over a three-year period for the construction, operation, and main-tenance of public schools, for teachers' salaries, or for both. The amount of grant money each state received would be based on its per capita income. To win Catholic support Kennedy championed the inclusion of special-purpose loans for parochial schools for the construction of college class-rooms or the purchase of science equipment. The National Defense Edu-cation Act (NDEA) of 1958 had provided for such loans to private schools. Special-purpose loans, Kennedy suggested, could be included in supple-mental legislation.

While the Senate passed the bill, the legislation failed to make it out of the House Rules Committee by an eight-to-seven vote. The key vote came from James J. Dulaney, representing a Catholic district in New York City, who thought the bill discriminatory. The NDEA bill providing special-purpose loans for parochial schools, he believed, had no chance of surviving a Rules Committee vote. Following the committee defeat, the administration adopted a parliamentary maneuver on a watered-down bill to bypass the Rules com-mittee. It failed by a 170 to 242 floor vote with only six Republicans voting affirmatively, and eighty-two Democrats, mostly from the South, voting against it. While the religious issue played a part in its defeat, partisan and southern Democratic opposition proved more crucial. Critics also blamed ad-ministration officials, including the president, who might have worked harder for its passage.

By 1963, however, Congress became somewhat more responsive to Kennedy's education agenda by appropriating construction funds and stu-dent loans to medical, dental, and related professional schools. It approved Kennedy's mental health and retardation program by authorizing $329 million in grants for the construction of facilities for research and the treat-ment of the mentally ill and retarded and by extending funds for training teachers for all handicapped children. Nearly $300 million went to the states and communities for the prevention and treatment of mental retar-dation. Congress also provided assistance to existing and proposed voca-tional programs and authorized nearly $1.2 billion in grants and loans for construction or improvement of public and private facilities for higher ed-ucation. At least on the college level and in a limited way, assistance to pri-vate schools was worked out, leading to its further resolution during the

Johnson presidency, which not only secured the core of Kennedy's educational program but went well beyond it. Kennedy domestic adviser Myer Feldman later claimed that Kennedy had no deep personal commitment to public education except for mental retardation, an affliction of the president's sister, Rosemary. Historian Hugh Graham, who has written the most definitive work on Kennedy and education, asserts further that Kennedy's partial victory represented more "a political determination to meet the expectations of the Democratic coalition that would be needed to re-elect him, and a resentment at the political embarrassment of repeated legislative defeats."

In 1961, Kennedy faced a more crushing defeat on medical insurance for the aged. His February proposal would have imposed an additional quarter-percent increase in Social Security payroll taxes to pay the hospital and nursing bills of persons eligible for old-age benefits. According to public opinion polls, most Americans favored it because the elderly and their families found it difficult to meet rising health costs. Kennedy explained that this was "not a program of socialized medicine" because "every person will choose his own doctor and hospital." The American Medical Association, the bill's biggest critic, responded that it would introduce "compulsion, regulation and control into a system of freely practiced medicine." Moreover, the cost to taxpayers would be prohibitive.

In July the House Ways and Means Committee finally began hearings on the bill. Chairman Wilbur Mills (D-Ark.), a longtime opponent of health benefits tied to Social Security, joined other Southern Democrats and Republicans to curb action. Kennedy refused to pressure Mills unduly, so as not to jeopardize other pending legislation. The administration decided instead to introduce in the Senate a medicare amendment to the public welfare bill, which had passed in the House. To encourage bipartisan support, twenty-one Democrats and five Republicans sponsored the compromise amendment. Before a national television audience, Kennedy addressed a Madison Square Garden gathering of senior citizens to dramatize the issue and increase public pressure. He spoke passionately of the need for such assistance and condemned the AMA for its opposition, but to no avail.

The Senate tabled the amendment by a vote of fifty-two to forty-eight. Aside from its five sponsors, no Republican voted for it, and twenty-seven Democrats, mostly from the South, also turned their backs on the administration. The key vote came from Democratic Senator Jennings

Randolph (W.Va.), who rejected medicare after sitting on the fence for most of the deliberations. The impact of Senator Robert Kerr (D-Okla.) as a power broker apparently exceeded that of Kennedy and administration spokesmen. Kerr had campaigned for Randolph in 1960 and had promised to amend the welfare bill to eradicate West Virginia's indebtedness. Had Randolph voted favorably, Kennedy would have held Senator Carl Hayden (D-Ariz.), despite in state opposition, and Vice President Johnson would have then cast the tie-breaking vote. Even if the bill had passed the Senate, however, it would have faced major problems in the House.

No defeat angered Kennedy more. His complaint that "he couldn't get a Mother's Day resolution through that goddam Congress" poignantly expressed his feelings at the time. The education and medicare bills, more than any others, symbolized Kennedy's domestic frustration in 1961, regardless of other legislative successes. He eventually abandoned medicare for the aged, later writing to new Secretary of Health and Welfare Anthony Celebrezze that "events will not permit legislative action in 1963," but that "we should proceed on the assumption that we are attempting to secure it."

Kennedy fared better on his other key 1961 proposals. Congress passed his "depressed areas" bill in April, providing for a four-year $394 million redevelopment program for areas plagued by chronic unemployment. The act funded commercial and industrial development, technical assistance in community planning, and the retraining of unemployed workers. It created the Area Redevelopment Administration (ARA) under the auspices of the Commerce Department. The bill received the support of southern Democrats after administration spokesmen promised that federal money would be channeled into depressed areas of the South. Kennedy had first committed himself to the program in 1960, after viewing firsthand the poverty of West Virginia. In Charleston that September he pledged that within sixty days of his election he would submit a program to bring new jobs and industry to neglected areas of the country. The Area Redevelopment program had limited success. By late 1962, 662 areas participated, twenty-six thousand jobs were created, and training programs emerged for nearly fifteen thousand people. It suffered a major setback in 1963 when the House failed to provide the ARA with $455.5 million in new funds. By 1965 the operation ended after having spread itself too thin.

The Manpower Development and Training Act (MDTA) of 1962 would continue ARA's training activities. Kennedy labeled it "perhaps the most significant legislation in the area of employment since the historic

Employment Act of 1946." It established programs to retrain workers who had inadequate or obsolete skills. Administered by the Department of Labor, MDTA soon became the administration's primary tool against structural unemployment. Kennedy officials discovered, however, that job training created no jobs in the tight labor market of the early '60s. It only raised the educational level of the unemployed. Moreover, later studies reveal that the training was for low-level jobs and that only twenty-seven thousand people had participated by early 1963. Yet even critic Allen Matusow concedes that graduates of the manpower program had "an advantage over other disadvantaged workers competing for the same jobs," and they earned higher wages.

Housing legislation constituted Kennedy's final major legislative proposal, which passed Congress in 1961 despite considerable Republican opposition. He called the Housing Act "the most important and far-reaching housing legislation since 1949." It broadened and extended existing programs such as urban renewal, public housing, and housing for the elderly and college students. It established the first middle income housing program, authorizing low-interest, thirty-five-year loans with a required 3 percent down payment. The loans, to be used on new construction, were available to those whose income was too high to qualify for public housing. The act also provided funds for the development of mass transportation and for open-space land in the cities. Overall, Congress appropriated $4.88 billion to fund the omnibus housing venture, partly because of the 1960–1961 recession.

Yet Congress refused to provide Kennedy with a Department of Urban Affairs to better address housing and other urban problems. He had promised in 1960 to launch a comprehensive program for cities to be administered by a new department with cabinet level status. He chose Robert Weaver, potentially the first black cabinet appointee, for department secretary. The Urban Affairs bill failed to make it out of committee in 1961 largely because of the appointment of Weaver. Southerners resented his strong support for racially integrated housing. One southern senator even charged him with having "a pro-Communist background." Rural congressmen saw nothing in the bill for them, and Republicans opposed the expansion of the federal bureaucracy. In January 1962 the bill met its first defeat in the Rules Committee by a vote of six to nine, with two southern Democrats breaking ranks—largely because of how such a racially charged vote would affect their upcoming elections. The Kennedy forces then circumvented the Rules Committee by bringing the bill to the House floor as a reorganization measure, which did not require the approval of the Rules Committee. The House overwhelmingly disapproved the plan; the vast majority of southern Democrats abandoned the administration along with most Republicans.

In the Senate, Democratic majority leader Mike Mansfield, acting on Kennedy's apparent approval, forced the bill out of committee prematurely on a discharge motion. This only hardened the opposition. On 20 February 1962 the Senate convincingly voted against the motion, thereby killing the bill. Kennedy acknowledged that he had "played it too cute," while Mansfield accepted responsibility for "jumping the gun." Another Democratic Senate leader also believed the bill had been handled badly, faulting Larry O'Brien the most. Certainly, enough blame existed to go around, but even if the administration had moved faultlessly, the House would still have balked because of Weaver's race and liberalism and the House's rural orientation. By 1962 Kennedy had lost luster, particularly with liberals. The Americans for Democratic Action, in its October newsletter, complained about the "failure of leadership" on the executive side.

Still, the administration achieved some legislative successes in other areas of importance. The Trade Expansion Act of 1962—the first major trade bill since Roosevelt's Trade Agreements Act of 1934—gave the president a five-year authority to cut tariff duties by 50 percent, eliminate tariffs altogether on certain goods, and take retaliatory action against "unreasonable" trade policies. It enabled Americans to sell on more equal terms with the European Common Market, a customs union that employed discriminatory tariffs to protect the markets of its six nations, as both sides now sought to negotiate lower tariffs. Increased trade with Europe, moreover, would improve the unfavorable balance of trade. The bill also provided economic incentives for Common Market countries to approve Great Britain's entry, an objective Kennedy pursued mostly for political reasons. Even though Britain's rejection slowed down the move toward Western unity, the Common Market tariff wall was gradually lowered in 1963, and U.S. exports soon increased appreciably. Even so, Kennedy's short-term successes failed to prevent America's relative decline in world trade later in the 1960s in the face of an economically rising Western Europe.[4]

AGRICULTURAL POLICY

Kennedy had much less interest in agricultural policy because of its minimal impact on national security and because he came from a state with few commercial farmers. As a senator from Massachusetts he had pragmatically supported the Eisenhower administration's reduced, flexible price supports that included lax restrictions on production and marketing. All of this fueled the huge commodity surpluses in federal storage facilities and low farm prices characterizing the 1950s. Regardless, Kennedy told Harvard economist John Kenneth Galbraith, "I don't want to hear about agricultural policy from anyone except you and I don't want to hear about it from you." His lack of interest may have contributed to his defeat for the Democratic vice presidential nomination in 1956. Consequently, as he began his presidential quest he called the agricultural decline the "number 1 domestic problem." He proposed a new program for beleaguered farmers based on supply management in which they would receive full income parity with nonfarm producers if they accepted mandatory production or marketing controls. Besides wanting to elevate farm income, he sought to reduce surpluses and cut United States Department of Agriculture (USDA) expenditures. More immediately, he hoped to make political inroads in midwestern and southern agricultural communities as a result of his proposed program. He admitted as much when he told an aide following a 1960 campaign speech at the South Dakota state fair, "Well, that's over. Fuck the farmers after November."

That response belied Kennedy's intent to honor his promise to institute a new farm program despite carrying few farm states in 1960. As on so many other domestic matters, however, he turned it over completely to his staff, who worked closely with Secretary of Agriculture Orville Freeman, the former governor of Minnesota. Only rarely did Freeman deal directly with the president, who said that he did not understand anything about agriculture and that it was entirely Freeman's responsibility. Kennedy saw agriculture in terms of potential political achievements. When success was not always forthcoming, he became frustrated and lost interest. Moreover, foreign crises continued to occupy his attention, leaving even less time for a problem his brother Robert thought insoluble.

The Kennedy farm program initially emphasized mandatory controls. Its approach, in terms of permanency and stringency, went beyond even President Roosevelt's efforts in the 1930s. It reflected Kennedy's urban, fiscally conservative nature, which demanded that farmers heed the sacrificial call of the New Frontier in return for a guaranteed parity of income with nonfarmers. With the resulting reduced commodity surpluses, the federal government's expenditures for crop storage would also likely lessen substantially. In April 1961, the administration submitted a comprehensive farm bill to Congress, which included mandatory acreage and marketing restrictions. Because the bill required Congress to surrender some of its legislative powers to the executive branch, it never made it out of committee.

Moreover, by the following year, the administration had suffered several defeats in attempting to impose permanent mandatory controls on feed grains (corn, barley, oats), wheat, and dairy products in exchange for higher price supports. The conservative American Farm Bureau, the largest and most powerful farm organization, led the opposition in blaming farmers' woes on the continued interference of the federal government since the 1930s. In Congress the bureau had the support of virtually every Republican, because of both ideology and a partisan response to the rigorous Democratic attack against the GOP farm program of the 1950s.

Amid considerable arm-twisting from White House lobbyists, the Kennedy administration had to adopt voluntary controls in extending higher price supports—and stringent enforcement—to limit production. Noncooperating farmers could grow as much as they wanted but only at the lower market price. Beginning with the Emergency Feed Grains Bill of 1961, the Kennedy administration achieved some success with voluntary control programs. The former contributed to a production drop of 13 million tons in feed grains, leading to a decrease of 280 million bushels in surplus stock, the first meaningful reduction since 1952. More important, net farm income rose to $1 billion, an eight-year high, in large part the result of the feed grain bill. Its major weakness, the administration acknowledged, was its cost. The government paid $786 million for land diversion, some of which it recovered through storage-cost reductions.

In the next two years, in spite of strong Republican resistance, the administration extended voluntary programs to wheat, while failing to secure the necessary legislation for cotton and dairy products. By March 1963 Freeman reported a combined reduction of feed grains and wheat holdings totaling over one billion bushels. Per capita farm income, even though rising, stood at only 60 percent of nonfarm income, however, a far cry from the parity Kennedy had proposed. Moreover, much to Kennedy's dismay, USDA commodity expenditures remained high, partly because of the costly voluntary programs. The feed grain expenditure in 1963, for example, was over $1 billion, minus storage cost reductions as surpluses dropped further. Compared to the Eisenhower period the Kennedy administration had made some advances in the commodity area. Given the political realities, it did all that it could do.

It also sought to address farm problems in other ways. Kennedy's give-away programs reduced farm surpluses while fulfilling a Democratic commitment to the downtrodden. Additionally, food assistance efforts might have won over urban congressmen to commodity programs. That commitment began on 21 January 1961 when Kennedy's first executive order increased food assistance to the needy. He soon announced a pilot food-stamp program embracing six areas, the first such commitment since the late 1930s. In 1962 the administration expanded the program to eighteen areas, feeding 240,000 people at an annual cost of about $22 million. Kennedy also invigorated the school lunch and milk programs begun under the Eisenhower administration, enabling 700,000 more children to enjoy a hot school lunch and eighty-five thousand more schools, child care centers, and camps to receive fresh milk.

The administration also sought to use American agricultural abundance abroad, a greater concern to Kennedy. Increasing farm exports would reduce surpluses and world hunger and promote American foreign policy. Secretary Freeman frequently publicized that Soviet consumers spent 56 percent of their income on food in comparison to 20 percent for U.S. consumers. Moreover, American agricultural efficiency enabled 8 percent of the population to produce more than enough to feed the nation, while the Soviet system required a farm population of over 50 percent and supplementary imports. Freeman employed various world food conferences to propagandize the "superiority of 'free' American agriculture." In 1962 he used the Soviet minister of agriculture's visit to the United States "to dramatize . . . to the rest of the world how far American agriculture is ahead of the Soviet[s]." Telling the president what he most wanted to hear, Freeman also alluded to the newly emerging nations in Africa and the Middle East that were moving away from Soviet collectivism "in light of the smashing success of American agriculture and the well advertized failure of Communist agriculture." Further confirmation of this failure came in 1963 when Kennedy authorized the sale of surplus wheat to the Soviet Union, a major propaganda victory for Freeman.

Food could indeed win over have-not nations, and the Food for Peace program became the major vehicle for this. The effort had originated in 1954 with the passage of the Agricultural Trade Development and Assistance Act (Public Law 480), which permitted the donation, barter, and sale of governmental surpluses. It initially focused solely on the removal of agricultural surpluses, but by the late 1950s liberal senators, led by Hubert Humphrey (D-Minn.), wanted to go beyond the original objectives of the law. They sought a major assistance program that took into consideration the long-range needs of newly developing nations. In 1960 Humphrey recommended hiring a Food for Peace administrator who would also serve as a special assistant to the president, which the Eisenhower administration rejected.

In 1960 Kennedy embraced the idea of Food for Peace and established the White Office of Food for Peace. He suggested that "American agricultural abundance offers a great opportunity for the United States to promote the interests of peace and to play an important role in helping to provide a more adequate diet for peoples all around the world." Meanwhile, the United States would also be resolving a domestic farm problem.

Under George McGovern, its first director, Food for Peace became more of an economic development program, as the government appreciably increased food donations to the newly emerging nations while reducing surplus sales under PL 480. Total commitments of Food for Peace remained comparable with those of the late Eisenhower presidency, however, with the amount rarely exceeding $2 billion annually. During the Kennedy years Congress continued to cut appropriation requests and generally opposed the expansion of the program. Differences also developed between Freeman and McGovern, with the former opposing McGovern's efforts to expand Food for Peace above the $2 billion annual level. Freeman instead sought to improve distribution and protect the normal commercial relations of recipient countries. More important, he feared that considerable expansion would provide a "convenient hook for any commodity leader to use in resisting supply management programs on the grounds that all we have to do is ship it abroad."

Following McGovern's resignation in July 1962 to run for the Senate in South Dakota, his replacement, Richard Reuter of Cooperation for American Relief Everywhere (CARE), a U.S. based and privately funded international agency to help needy people, worked more closely with Freeman. By 1963

Food for Peace surpluses fed some ninety-two million a day, including thirty-two million school children in impoverished countries in the Third World. In some instances the food served as wages to finance economic development projects such as hospitals, schools, and road construction. Yet Kennedy himself admitted in an 2 April 1963 message to Congress that "the relative burden of our assistance programs has been steadily reduced—from some two percent of our national product at the beginning of the Marshall Plan [1947] to seven-tenths of one percent today—from 11.5 percent of the Federal Budget in 1949 to 4 percent today." When a reporter asked him why, Kennedy alluded to the "limitation of available funds."

THE ENVIRONMENT AND NATIVE AMERICANS

Kennedy devoted even less attention to the environment and Native Americans, subjects that have only recently come to the attention of scholars.[5] He relied on Secretary of the Interior Stewart Udall, a former Arizona congressman known for his defense of natural resources and other liberal causes, to deal with those two issues. Not an outdoorsman, the urbane Kennedy had little appreciation for conservation, but his love of the sea drove him to protect the seashores at Cape Cod, Massachusetts; Point Reyes, California; and Padre Island, Texas, through legislative action. He also undertook western tours in 1962 and 1963 to highlight conservation policies. Under Udall's prodding, Kennedy committed to several legislative measures, particularly the Wilderness and Conservation Fund bill, most of which passed Congress in the year after Kennedy's death. This included the creation of Canyonlands National Park, Fire Island National Seashore, and the Ozark National Scenic Riverways. Even though Kennedy and Udall sometimes remained insensitive to the new thrusts of environmentalism, which emphasized preservation over resource use, "they were, with the exception of Lyndon Johnson's Great Society," according to one recent study, "the most conservation minded administration in the postwar era." Given the paucity of activity from other administrations, this hardly reflects a ringing endorsement.

Meanwhile, on Indian policy, Kennedy promised a "sharp break with the Republican party," a shift Udall's task report called traversing a "new trail." The Kennedy administration provided job training, infrastructure improvement, better housing, and higher wages through the ARA and other federal projects. But in the end it remained rooted to the policies of the past as it quietly acquiesced to a conservative Congress on issues relating to tribal treaty rights and sovereignty. And while it adhered to the goal of Indian self-sufficiency, it did little to effect it. Consequently, Udall's gradual termination policy, which meant the eventual withdrawal of federal services, proved nearly as much a threat to Indian well-being in the Kennedy presidency as it had been in the Eisenhower years. Beyond Kennedy's lack of knowledge of Indian affairs, Udall thought Kennedy "was so consumed with the goddamed Cold War" to make Indian affairs a higher priority.

Kennedy's most innovative approaches and arguably his most memorable domestic achievements center on the remaining issues of this essay. Kennedy paid particular attention to them because of their national security and political considerations. Moreover, they have elicited the greatest attention and differences of opinion among Kennedy scholars.

THE ECONOMY

Perhaps the foremost issue remained the economy. By mid-February 1961 the Eisenhower recession had suddenly ended, followed by a slow upswing thanks to the Kennedy administration's increase in expenditures, which spurred the economy. Expenditures included $3.7 billion for "urgent" national security needs, $3.5 billion in response to the Berlin crisis, and $2.3 billion for domestic programs, all of which Kennedy achieved with only a $3.3 billion budget deficit, an indication of his conservative financial approach.

The goals of 5 percent annual growth, lowering the unemployment rate to 4 percent, and ending the imbalance of payments proved more problematic, however. In addressing these matters, Kennedy initially listened more to Treasury Secretary Dillon, who had close ties with the financial community. Dillon urged focusing on the balance of payments problem, controlling expenditures in the interest of a balanced budget and instituting a business investment tax credit of 7 percent to stimulate economic growth. Dillon made even more sense to Kennedy politically. Kennedy feared being called a reckless spender, a label that had hung on practically every Democratic presidential candidate since Roosevelt. The influence of financial conservatives in the Congress caused him to proceed cautiously. Otherwise, "they would kick us in the balls," Kennedy warned. Consequently, he kept the federal budget under one hundred billion dollars and the annual deficits below those of the Eisenhower years. No wonder one economic liberal referred to the early Kennedy presidency as the "Third Eisenhower Administration."

Kennedy's economic views were far from static or rigid, however. As early as the late 1950s he had begun to explore Keynesian theories from Harvard and MIT economists John Kenneth Galbraith, Seymour Harris, and Paul Samuelson. He impressed them with his intelligent questions and his capacity to learn. Through their prodding he entered the presidency with a greater tolerance for deficits and increased expenditures during economic downturns. He realized, too, that he would have to spend more money on social and military programs. The challenge came in reconciling a liberal social philosophy with a conservative financial one.

Galbraith of Harvard, whom the president truly liked, had the least influence. An advocate of increased public expenditures to stimulate the economy, he wrote Kennedy at the height of the early 1961 recession, "I am a little appalled at the eloquence of the explanations as to why things, neither radical nor reactionary but only wise, cannot be done."[6] Galbraith recommended an omnibus measure to assist families of the unemployed, extend emergency grants and loans for towns with serious unemployment, provide a system of grants and/or deferred interest loans to unemployed families for the renovation of their houses, and create a youth conservation corps to help unemployed teenagers. "Should the foregoing be unacceptable," Galbraith concluded, "there is still clean living and regular prayer."

William McChesney Martin, the chairman of the Federal Reserve Board, particularly aroused Galbraith because his obsession with inflation kept interest rates high. As an antirecession measure, Galbraith recommended that Kennedy "set Bill Martin on his ass." Kennedy thought Galbraith was too audacious despite his delightful company and might better serve the country as ambassador to India. Nonetheless, whenever Galbraith returned from India, he invariably offered Kennedy unsolicited advice on economic policy. The president would then phone or send a memo to Dillon. After one call, Dillon responded, "Fine, Mr. President, I'll think about it but I just wonder if Ken Galbraith is in town?" The president laughed and said, "He's right here. Do you want to talk to him?"

Walter Heller, chairman of the Council of Economic Advisers, exerted more liberal influence on the president, who met frequently with the three-member council. Like Heller, James Tobin of Yale and Kermit Gordon of Williams College were Keynesians, respected in the profession and among the White House staff. Their Keynesian views differed from Galbraith's in that they favored a general tax cut, instead of deficit spending, to stimulate economic growth. Their efforts to educate the president in 1961 met with little success, however.

Their only victory occurred during the Berlin crisis of that summer when the president's brother, Attorney General Robert Kennedy, proposed a 1 percent increase in income and corporation taxes to finance the rise in military expenditures and to lay the basis for a balanced budget, as well as to provide a way to heed JFK's sacrificial call. This proposal had Dillon's and the president's enthusiastic approval until the CEA persuasively called it "bad economics" and warned that the tax increase might well "choke off" full recovery. The CEA also rejected the assertion that inflation threatened because of a growing deficit. Moreover, it questioned whether a tax measure would create a spirit of sacrifice since the hike was unsubstantial. From New Delhi, Galbraith echoed that the administration must cease promising a balanced budget. "Control you must make the *sine qua non* of financial responsibility, which indeed it is. If we have a deficit it is because we want it and accept the necessity. Far better to have a deficit that we expect and predict than one that comes as an admission of error—especially as we will have a deficit in either case." Thus the economic education of John Kennedy continued.

And so did slow economic growth. In the first quarter of 1962 the gross national product (GNP) inched upward only 1.1 percent from the preceding quarter. Heller called it an unusually small gain for a period of emerging growth. He consequently lowered the projected $570 billion annual GNP to $565 billion or lower; the economic forecast for 1962 became much less promising.

THE STEEL CRISIS

Other related problems surfaced that spring when President Kennedy sought to implement guideposts created by the CEA to keep prices and wages at a level not to exceed the productivity rate (output per worker) for any given industry. The administration was responding to wage-price spirals in key industries such as steel, automobile manufacturing, and construction, where powerful unions forced higher costs upon equally mighty corporations who then passed on the markup to consumers in the form of higher prices. Government intervention could hold inflation in check and improve the marketability of American goods abroad.

Kennedy's guideposts reflected a desire to work closely with big business in the common interest of an expanding economy, a theme begun in the 1960 campaign. He recognized that the anti–big business, trust-busting perception of the Democratic party must be overturned if he were to win the confidence of the business world. Yet Kennedy had sent mixed signals. He had courted corporate executives with budget balancing rhetoric, tax incentives, and conservative appointments such as Dillon. At other times, in presenting legislation to Congress, he had sounded like a New Dealer. He also had appointed Lee Loevinger, a Minnesota antitrust attorney and judge associated with Hubert Humphrey, as head of the Department of Justice's Antitrust Division. By 1962 that division had filed ninety-two cases, the most ever, many of them in the price-fixing category. Several other "suspicious" appointments filled key administrative posts.

Kennedy's clash with United States Steel in April 1962 heightened overall differences between Kennedy and corporate interests. His assault on big steel preceded the collapse of the stock market in May. While corporate leaders claimed that Kennedy's actions eroded business confidence, leading to the market decline, his backers cited a Securities and Exchange Commission report that stocks had been overpriced in relation to company earnings. Actually both probably contributed. A concurring May 1962 CEA report also mentioned the problem of gold outflow and higher interest rates at commercial banks and savings and loan institutions, which lured small investors away from the market. Regardless of the cause, the stockmarket collapse had a detrimental effect because it reduced capital investment necessary for economic growth.

Meanwhile, the conflict with steel had emerged over that bellwether industry's response to Kennedy's wage-price guideposts. Labor Secretary Arthur Goldberg, a former attorney for the United Steel Workers of America, had pressured the union to accept a contract that provided a 2.5 percent increase in benefits, well within the wage-price guidelines. The steel companies, of course, had benefited from the government's intercession and therefore were expected to hold the line on a price increase, especially since the companies had not indicated otherwise.

But on Tuesday 10 April 1962, the bespectacled, scholarly looking Roger Blough, U.S. Steel chairman, handed President Kennedy a mimeographed press release, indicating that the company, which accounted for more than 25 percent of American steel production, was raising prices to $6 a ton, a 3.5 percent increase that exceeded the guidepost limitations. This proved necessary, the memo explained, because of a price-cost squeeze. One day after Blough's announcement seven competitors, including Bethlehem and Republic Steel, followed with similar raises. On 10 April the press had quoted the president of Bethlehem as saying at a stockholders' meeting that "there shouldn't be any price rise. We shouldn't do anything to increase our costs if we are to survive." Had the powerful Blough engaged in collusion?

Blough, ignoring the conspiracy charge, insisted that he had often hinted at a possible increase and questioned the administration's contention that the industry could overcome the recent hike in labor costs without a substantial price rise. Steel profits, Blough claimed, were at an all-time low. He thought it unfair that no steel price increase had occurred since 1958, despite a substantial wage boost in January 1960, which Vice President Nixon had encouraged the industry to absorb—at least until after the election.

Blough might have succeeded had he only waited a decent interval before announcing selective price increases. In that way the administration's credibility and authority would have been less flagrantly challenged. Was Blough that insensitive? Just as puzzling, the general price hike could only make steel even less competitive with foreign producers. Europe already underpriced Americans by 30 percent. Had Kennedy not forced recision, steel might have had to reverse its price increase on some products out of economic necessity. At the time, however, Blough apparently counted on improved domestic demand, modernization, and a stronger, lighter steel to overcome the foreign competition. One wonders, however, whether Blough also attempted to challenge a supposedly unfriendly Democratic administration that had increased federal authority over the price sector— an allegation that Blough later bitterly denied. If that indeed were a motive, his effort backfired.

One thing is certain. Kennedy responded forcefully and resolutely to Blough's announcement. After Blough informed him of the price hike, a stunned Kennedy told him that he was making a mistake. Kennedy clearly understood the impact this would have on his presidency and on the country. He quickly called Goldberg, who arrived in less than five minutes. Goldberg expressed his anger to Blough for his alleged duplicity during the wage negotiations: "You kept silent and silence is consent. One thing you owe a President is candor." Immediately after Blough's departure, Kennedy phoned David McDonald, president of the Steelworkers Union, to say, "Dave, You've been screwed and I've been screwed." One aide, observing Kennedy's fury, recalled that "there should have been a speedometer on his rocking chair."

The president quickly consulted with Sorensen, the CEA, his brother Robert, Goldberg, Special Assistant Kenneth O'Donnell, and others. He then read a statement at a press conference the day following Blough's bombshell, charging that the steel price increase "constituted a wholly unjustifiable and irresponsible defiance of the public interest." He then recited how others—including servicemen in Vietnam—had heeded his call for sacrifice, before chiding the "tiny handful of steel executives whose pursuit of private power and profit exceeds their sense of public responsibility." He made it clear that he wanted the price increases rescinded.

Publicly Kennedy remained calm but determined; never before, however, had he been so critical and brusque at a press conference. Privately he expressed considerable anger. He asked Benjamin Bradlee of *Newsweek,* "Are we supposed to sit there and take a cold deliberate fucking?" He soon answered his own question by saying, "They fucked us, and we've got to fuck them." To staffers he raged that "my father always told me that all businessmen were sons of bitches, but I never believed it till now." The politically damaging comment leaked to *Newsweek,* causing Kennedy to deny that he damned all businessmen. His father had referred only to steel men, he protested. Despite loyalists like Sorensen, who echoed the president's explanation, there is little reason to question the reporting. Joe Kennedy, after all, had expressed contempt for businessmen after the 1929 crash. Unlike Eisenhower, according to journalist Charles Bartlett, Kennedy never had a high opinion of most businessmen.

Kennedy was prepared to throw the full power of the government against steel to force a recision. To do otherwise not only would have reflected badly on his economic policies but also on him personally. It would have also affected his standing abroad. Too, the last thing he wanted was the perception of being weak within his own party—particularly with organized labor, which had grudgingly supported his economic program.

Robert Kennedy, shortly after the president's death, revealed the extent to which they were willing to pressure steel; their plans included a grand jury investigation in which steel executives were to be subpoenaed. "We were going for broke," he admitted, "their expense accounts and where they'd been and what they were doing. I picked up all their records and I told the FBI to interview them all—march into their offices the next day. We weren't going to go slowly. I said to have them done all over the country. All of them were hit with meetings the next morning by agents. . . . I agree it was a tough way to operate. But under the circumstances we couldn't afford to lose." No wonder Republican opponents accused the administration of Gestapo-like tactics.

The attempt to disclose price-fixing led the FBI to question journalists who had reported that the president of Bethlehem Steel had opposed a steel increase but reversed himself after Blough's announced hike. FBI agents called on reporters in the middle of the night. Whether the attorney general had anything to do with these nocturnal intrusions is unclear. In any case, in addition to encouraging investigations of steel by the antitrust division of the Justice department, the Federal Trade Commission, and congressional committees, the administration applied pressure in other ways, much of it counterproductive, ineffectual, and unnecessary, inviting criticism from the press. Certainly, it did nothing to improve Kennedy's relations with congressional Republicans, who bitterly resented his forceful interference in the private sector.

Kennedy's most effective action included efforts to rally public opinion. Practically every major administration official became involved in coordinated press conferences and speeches. Some, like Heller, who had friends in the business world, made timely telephone calls. The administration also employed economic leverage effectively. Defense Secretary Robert McNamara, for example, ensured that a $5.5 million order for steel plate for Polaris submarines went to Lukens Steel, a company that did not raise prices. Such actions represented a strategy of divide and conquer, designed to prevent other companies from raising prices. The administration had other economic weapons, including its support of tax depreciation measures. No corporation wished to see these endangered. Consequently, three key companies—Inland Steel, Kaiser Steel, and Armco—soon decided not to raise prices. Even though the offending companies controlled about 85 percent of the market, they still became vulnerable to contract losses. Blough, at a news conference, admitted the difficulty his company faced. It worsened when Bethlehem rescinded its increase, starting a chain reaction until United States Steel followed suit on 12 April. Seventy-two hours after it began, the crisis ended. Kennedy was elated. Despite some negative criticism from the press, he came out of the crisis with his popularity intact. He received only a 22 percent disapproval rating in a 20 May Gallup Poll and secured a 73 percent presidential approval rating in another poll three days later.

Scholars have generally responded favorably to Kennedy's handling of the steel crisis. While recognizing that he might have overreacted, they acknowledge that a failure of leadership would have affected his ability to deal with the economy and issues relating to the Soviet Union. Arthur Schlesinger, in particular, views Kennedy's actions in the progressive tradition of strong presidents since Jackson who contended against the private sector. He easily could have compared Kennedy with the two Roosevelts in their efforts to elevate the national government over big business. Other scholars such as Bruce Miroff point out that Kennedy—like earlier "progressive" presidents—sought intervention in the economy not so much to check corporate power but to stabilize and rationalize it. Even the most critical scholarly appraisal, however, has few kind things to say about Roger Blough and his cohorts. At the same time, most historians note that steel companies won a belated victory with selected price increases in April and October 1963, amounting to an overall hike of about 3 percent, which Kennedy only mildly protested.

MENDING BUSINESS FENCES

Kennedy realized that he needed to mend fences with the business community following the steel crisis and the May stock market crash. Corporate executives, wearing buttons with "SOB" captions and purchasing bumper stickers stating "I miss Ike—hell, I even miss Harry," flaunted their hostility. Kennedy understood that a strained atmosphere would contribute to the economic woes. Lower business profits meant reduced government revenues and economic growth. In public statements he emphasized the need for business, labor, and government to work together, proclaiming himself no enemy of business.

Indeed, no previous Democratic administration proved as supportive of corporate interests. This approach sometimes perplexed old-line Democrats like Felix Frankfurter, the elderly and ill Supreme Court Justice whom Kennedy visited in July just prior to Frankfurter's retirement. Hardly a flaming liberal at this stage in his life, Frankfurter reminded Kennedy that Democratic presidents had a long-standing tradition of opposing the monied interests. This opposition developed from broader concerns and values that often conflicted with business interests. As a consequence, Democratic presidents should expect the resistance of corporate executives and think nothing of it, Frankfurter advised. Kennedy responded sympathetically, but his actions belied the lessons of the past provided by a ghost of the New Deal.

Kennedy was already appeasing business. Sorensen's recommendations that the administration publicize the ways in which it was probusiness soon involved most governmental departments in a concerted effort. Loevinger, for example, now argued that antitrust action was inherently probusiness because "its objective is to increase business freedom and maintain the free enterprise system." Assistant Attorney General Nicholas Katzenbach further pointed out that antitrust litigation generally stemmed from complaints from businessmen "who have been unfairly damaged by the illegal and predatory activity of the antitrust violators." By early 1963 the administration moved Loevinger, whom businessmen labeled a frustrated crusader, out of Justice, despite his supposed probusiness, antitrust approach. Businessmen perceived this action as yet another effort to improve the climate between the White House and the corporate boardroom. Ultimately, the Kennedy administration did no better than Eisenhower in enforcing the antitrust laws.

Kennedy also decided to lower corporate taxes to erase the antibusiness image and encourage capital accumulation. In July, through executive action, he instituted new depreciation allowances for machinery and equipment, which amounted to a tax cut for business. Business would gain $1.5 billion in lower taxes in the first year alone. In October Congress also passed Kennedy's investment tax credit bill, which gave business a 7 percent tax credit on new investment. First introduced in April 1961, these actions were expected to stimulate economic growth, promote modernization, and create trade opportunities abroad, thereby helping the payment imbalance; they would also establish Kennedy as a probusiness president. Heller emphasized the latter point in his meeting with corporate executives where he "made clear that there never was an administration so dedicated to the free market system, so devoted to private enterprise, profits, and investments, so determined to restrain government expenditures, so diligent in stimulating competition—as the Kennedy administration." Robert Kennedy later claimed, "I think more was done for business [by the Kennedy administration] than has ever been done. . . . When the story is eventually written it will be rather impressive."

TOWARD A GENERAL TAX CUT

The story must also include Kennedy's commitment to a general tax cut in 1962 (which served the corporate interest). He finally considered tax reduction in the summer, following difficulties with the steel industry and the stock market. While the economy continued its disappointing, gradual rise during this period, several weak spots stood out, including insignificant plant expansion and declining retail sales. In June the CEA, fearing a recession sometime in 1962, recommended an immediate tax cut of between $5 and $10 billion. On the advice of Dillon and others, Kennedy rejected a "quick fix" on the assumption that Congress and the American public would "piss all over" a 1962 tax cut measure.

The Republican leadership, concerned about a rising deficit, was even more negative. Also, as Heller admitted, 72 percent of the respondents in a recent Gallup Poll survey disapproved of a tax reduction (probably out of concern for the national debt). Besides, by August the economy seemed improved. In a nationwide address on the thirteenth Kennedy told the American people that since no clear and present danger to the economy existed, he was rejecting an immediate tax cut. He intended, however, to submit a bill to reduce personal and corporate taxes the next year, retroactive to January 1963. He explained that the current tax rate, originating in the World War II era, had retarded economic growth. The right kind of tax cut, he insisted, would eventually reduce deficits by increasing productivity, employment, and hence federal revenues.

Sometime in early 1962 Kennedy had become a convert to Keynesian economics. A remarkably educable president, he had grasped the logic of accepting temporarily larger deficits to achieve economic well-being. His frequent meetings with the CEA, along with Heller's superbly clear memos, had convinced him, as had his own studies on the greater growth rate of competing Western European countries.

The losers were liberals like Galbraith and Leon Keyserling, who, instead of a tax cut, favored the Keynesian alternative of vastly increased federal spending in the public sector to effect stimulation through improved parks, schools, hospitals, and welfare programs—all of which were badly needed, they argued. "I am not sure," Galbraith said, "what the advantage is in having a few more dollars to spend if the air is dirty, the water is too polluted to drink . . . the streets are filthy, and schools so bad that the young . . . stay away." Keyserling, dismayed by Kennedy's choice of Keynesian approaches, commented that he was "as bad as Eisenhower," a statement that angered the president.

Yet Heller underwent some disappointments too. He failed to obtain a quickie tax cut in 1962. Moreover, Dillon, who continued to have Kennedy's ear, advised adhering to the deficit ceiling of the Eisenhower period in order to sell a tax cut to Republicans. To keep the deficit down Kennedy would have to postpone some domestic programs. Dillon, more flexible than his Republican friends had anticipated, also convinced Kennedy to incorporate a reform provision in the tax bill to tighten loopholes and remove inequities. Tax reform could increase federal revenues by some $3 billion and win over congressmen who otherwise would oppose a tax cut. Dillon also pushed for the reduction of personal income rates at the upper level as well as the lowering of corporate taxes from 52 to 47 percent. This led Galbraith to argue that by nature tax cuts favored those who needed them least, unlike social expenditures, which worked on behalf of the disadvantaged.

Kennedy fought an uphill battle to sell Keynesian economics to the establishment despite its general acceptance by economists. One major effort to do so came in his widely publicized commencement address at Yale University on 11 June 1962. It revealed how far he had come since 1960, and it clearly represented one of his most thoughtful speeches. He gave the address after receiving an honorary doctor of laws degree, enabling him to quip that now "I have the best of both worlds, a Harvard education and a Yale degree."

Many of his remarks focused on dispelling mythology. "For the great enemy of truth," Kennedy asserted, "is very often not the lie—deliberate, contrived, and dishonest—but the myth—persistent, persuasive, and unrealistic." He first addressed the myth of a growing federal government, which, he contended, had grown less rapidly over the last fifteen years than the economy as a whole. He then challenged the belief that federal deficits caused inflation and budget surpluses prevented it. He reminded the audience that budget surpluses after the war had failed to prevent inflation and that the deficits of recent years had left price stability unaffected. He also said that deficits—and surpluses—were neither always dangerous nor beneficial. Furthermore, he strongly disputed that the national debt had grown enormously since World War II; in relation to a rising GNP, the debt had dropped considerably. In absolute terms the national debt had increased only 8 percent since 1945 at a time when private debt had risen 305 percent and that of state and local governments had jumped 378 percent. Borrowing also proved neither bad nor good, he maintained. It could lead to overextension and collapse as well as growth and strength. He resurrected the words of Jefferson, invoking the need for new phrases and approaches to fit changing times. In this way the nation could achieve full employment, increased productivity, stable prices, and a strong dollar.

Kennedy's public profession of Keynes might have pleased liberals, but it seemed heretical to a concerned business community, thus further explaining the administration's concerted efforts to win over business that summer. The reaction also caused Kennedy to fear even more the political repercussions of exorbitant deficits. Clearly all of this drew him closer to Dillon, the architect of the proposed tax cut measure as much as Heller.

The president's address before the Economic Club of New York on 14 December, which Galbraith exaggeratedly called the most "Republican speech since McKinley," reflected Dillon's influence. Kennedy spoke before an audience of mostly Republican businessmen whose approval he—and Dillon—thought essential. Consequently, according to one news magazine, he sounded more like an officer of the National Association of Manufacturers. After first praising the free enterprise system, he stressed the need to keep public expenditures down while encouraging private spending through incentives. He assured corporations and upper-income individuals that they would be treated favorably. Budget deficits, he insisted, "are not caused by wild-eyed spenders but by slow economic growth and periodic recessions, and any new recession would break all deficit records." His goals, he concluded, remained greater profits and a balanced budget, which could be achieved through a tax cut.

Kennedy's well received Economic Club address went a long way toward winning the approval of business. He had also won the endorsement of labor organizations, despite apprehension about the nature of the tax cuts and the desire for spending programs. The speech's reception also contributed to his own enthusiasm for a tax cut. On 24 January 1963, he presented a special message to Congress on tax reduction and reform.

The Kennedy tax proposal included reductions at every tax level. The personal income rates would change from a range of 20 (for annual incomes of $4,000 and under) to 91 percent ($400,000 and over) to a range of 14 to 65 percent. Corporate income taxes would drop from 52 percent to 47 percent, with special breaks given to small business. The total tax reduction came to $13.6 billion—$11 billion for individuals and $2.6 billion for corporations. It was adjusted to $10.2 billion after incorporating the anticipated $3.4 billion gain from tax reform. The latter tightened personal itemized deductions, capital gains, and dividend exclusion and tax allowances, and it also provided tax advantages for the aged and those with physical handicaps. Kennedy spread the tax cut over a three-year period to be fully effective by 1 January 1965. He balanced Heller's desire for a full tax cut in the first year to ignite economic growth with his own concerns that the annual deficit not exceed $12.8 billion, Eisenhower's 1958 performance level. In short, he did everything he possibly could to make the measure palatable to Congress.

Nevertheless, Republicans and some southern Democrats opposed the measure in Congress. They portrayed Kennedy as a spendthrift president carving out a legacy of increased expenditures, astronomical deficits, and emerging inflation. A tax cut, they argued, must accompany a promise to reduce expenditures. Despite 173 of 174 Republicans voting for recommital, their efforts in the House to recommit the bill failed, largely because the vast majority of southern Democrats stuck with the party leadership.

Primary attention now shifted to tax reform, with the administration caught in a crossfire between liberals and conservatives. Most of the fireworks came from the latter, representing vested interests who objected to the closing of various tax loopholes. As a result, the administration abandoned most of the revenue-saving reforms, including the provisions for tightening capital gains and personal deductions and raising taxes in the oil and gas industry. This invited liberal criticism that the administration showed "insufficient enthusiasm" for tax reform, yet neither Dillon nor Kennedy wished to jeopardize the tax cut in the face of mounting opposition. With major interest group support, the amended bill sailed through the House on 25 September 1963. It likely would have cleared the Senate in early 1964 had Kennedy lived. As it turned out President

Johnson provided the final touches in January 1964. To appease the Senate economic bloc he reduced the 1964 budget and also shifted more of the tax cut into 1964. This bill then passed the following month.

The Kennedy tax bill represents one of his most innovative and enduring initiatives. No other president had dared to impose a tax cut on top of a significant deficit or to ask for deficits to avert a possible recession. That the lagging economy had marginally improved from 1962 made his action more politically difficult. Yet Kennedy understood that growth had barely kept pace with an expanding labor force—one that would require twelve million new jobs over the next ten years. He faulted an antiquated tax structure, which caused an annual loss of $30 billion of potential output. As a newly converted Keynesian, Kennedy put his faith in the multiplier effect. A $10 billion tax cut, he reasoned, would create an additional $20 billion fiscal stimulus in the GNP, as business investment increased due to consumer demand. This in turn would generate full employment, which the CEA defined as 4 percent unemployment. Kennedy risked the political repercussions of short-term, near-record deficits on the assumption that a limping economy in November 1964 would be a greater liability.

Following Kennedy's death, the Revenue Act of 1964 did seem to have an impact on the economy. Unemployment dropped from 5.5 percent in December 1963 to 5 percent by the end of the following year. By the close of 1965 it had plummeted to 4.1 percent, close to the CEA's definition of full employment and a far cry from the 7 percent unemployment rate Kennedy had inherited. The annual growth rate rose from 2.5 percent in 1960 to over 6 percent by 1964, surpassing Kennedy's 5 percent goal of 1960. The GNP had jumped over $100 billion in that period. Profits also soared by 1964. And despite the lower tax rates, federal receipts increased in the years after the tax cut, as Kennedy had predicted. More remarkably, the inflation rate held at 1.3 percent, unlike during the later Johnson presidency when the economy overheated because of a guns-and-butter policy and a failure to raise taxes as U.S. involvement in Vietnam escalated. Nor did Kennedy have enormous budget deficits. Though his average yearly deficit exceeded that of Eisenhower, he avoided the double-digit annual deficit that afflicted both Eisenhower ($12.8 billion in 1958) and Johnson ($25.1 billion in 1968), all of which strengthened Sorensen's 1987 assertion that Kennedy was "more [fiscally] conservative than any president we've had since."

Kennedy also improved the balance of payments situation—especially the gold loss. The administration worked to make American goods competitive in foreign markets and persuaded other nations to buy more military goods from the United States. Moving against the so-called tourist gap, it wooed foreigners to this country and reduced the amounts that Americans could spend abroad without paying duties. The administration also nudged upward short-term interest rates to discourage the investment of capital abroad, at the same time keeping long-term interest rates on bonds and mortgages down so as not to retard domestic economic growth. It imposed a 1 percent tax on foreign securities purchased by Americans to encourage domestic investments. As a result, the crisis over gold outflow ended because of Kennedy's actions. The amount of gold leaving the country fell by more than one-third, an indication of increased confidence in U.S. currency by foreign nations. Kennedy, of course, saw all of this as a national security achievement as much as a domestic gain.

CONSIDERING AN ANTIPOVERTY PROGRAM

Critics who have called Kennedy's economic policy reactionary Keynesianism and corporate liberalism for its efforts to promote corporate prosperity ignore the fact that the tax cut produced jobs and that Kennedy intended to address economic inequities beyond the piecemeal approaches of earlier programs like Area Redevelopment. On Armistice Day 1963 Kennedy said to Heller, "First, we'll have your tax cut; then we'll have my expenditure program." Dwight Macdonald's lengthy review essay in the *New Yorker* of Michael Harrington's *The Other America* (1962) had further convinced Kennedy that widespread poverty remained hidden next to widespread affluence. Moreover, he anticipated possible criticism that his proposed tax cut provided no benefit to the poor. He also sensed a greater public concern because of recent studies on poverty—including a TV documentary—and a spiraling civil rights movement that exposed black deprivation. The country was obviously moving in a more liberal direction by 1963.

Once again Kennedy relied on Heller to analyze the extent of poverty and to recommend solutions. Heller brought into the study a deep belief that poverty was wrong on practical as well as moral grounds because it spawned crime, disease, and other social problems, leading to lower productivity. He was also politically aware enough to believe that an antipoverty program would benefit Kennedy. He consequently asked Robert J. Lampman, a full-time CEA staffer and an expert on wealth and income distribution, to begin an investigation. Lampman soon determined economic growth and full employment would have some impact on poverty. Because this approach would have minimal effect on the aged, disabled, and families headed by women, he recommended additional forms of federal assistance.

Like Harrington and other students of poverty, Lampman suspected a culture of poverty, whereby negative or defeatist attitudes and behavior perpetuated themselves from one generation to another, virtually guaranteeing its extension. To break the cycle Lampman and other administration economists emphasized the education of youth, retraining, and other rehabilitation programs, all requiring a considerable financial commitment. Neither he nor Heller favored income redistribution or transfers, which might invite political criticism. Above all they wanted a relatively modest, workable, and popular program. They favored one that promoted a sacrificial spirit, in which local well-to-do community members participated. Such proposals as a national service corps and a youth conservation corps would be natural components in any antipoverty program.

Yet no decision transpired by fall 1963 except that Kennedy had "tentatively decided that a major focus in the domestic legislative program in 1964 will be on a [commitment] variously described as 'Human Conservation and Development,' 'Access to Opportunity,' and 'Attack on Poverty.'" Three days before his assassination the president once again expressed an interest, provided that "we can get a good program." Whether Kennedy would have pushed hard for a concrete program in an election year when other legislative proposals were pending is uncertain. Nonetheless, he might have used congressional opposition as a major campaign issue, particularly if the Republicans nominated archconservative Barry Goldwater. Ideological lines would then be clearly drawn, with Kennedy running on an updated New Deal platform in a more liberal environment than in 1960. As it turned out, Lyndon Baines Johnson, in the spiritual aftermath of Kennedy's death, declared war on poverty, elevating it to a level probably unintended by his predecessor. Johnson profited from the planning and proposals on poverty and the concepts evolving from the Kennedy presidency. Many Kennedy people played an integral part in the new administration's efforts to eradicate poverty.

ECONOMIC RIGHTS TO WOMEN

Kennedy also played a key transitional role in extending economic rights to women, making him arguably the first president to do so. In 1960 more than one-third of all women worked for wages, an increase of 3.5 percent since 1950, and the number of wage-earning women who had children under the age of six virtually doubled in that ten-year period. Most female employees confronted an enormous differential in wages with male counterparts, discrimination in hiring practices, and a lack of day care facilities for children. Of equal concern to Kennedy, a sizable number of skilled and talented women had surrendered careers to become full-time homemakers, thereby denying Cold War America needed skills in such fields as science, education, and medicine.

By 1960 women's groups had grown more impatient with injustices. This reached greater intensity with the publication of Betty Friedan's *Feminine Mystique* in 1963, laying the foundation for the National Organization for Women (NOW), which called into question women's traditional roles along with a multitude of discriminatory practices. During the 1960 campaign Kennedy had responded to such practices by endorsing the Democratic party platform of equal pay for equal work and by calling for the adoption of the Equal Rights Amendment (ERA), guaranteeing women complete legal equality with men.

But Kennedy did remarkably little on behalf of women early in his administration because he was diverted by crises such as Berlin. Also, his background had provided him with little sensitivity to women or women's issues. In any case, he made only ten Senate-confirmed appointments of women, at least five fewer than Truman or Eisenhower. Unlike Eisenhower, he made none at the cabinet level. Only 2.4 percent of all Kennedy's appointive positions went to women, a percentage comparable to the two previous administrations. Furthermore, Kennedy failed to consult Margaret Price, the vice chair and director of women's activities for the Democratic National Committee, and other leading Democratic women when making appointments. Nor did he address the economic problems that working women faced. Not surprisingly, he came under fire, particularly from May Craig, a longtime White House reporter known for her tough-minded questions at press conferences. On 9 November 1961 she asked Kennedy what he had done for women in accordance with the party platform. Recognizing a loaded question,

Kennedy smilingly responded, "Well, I'm sure we haven't done enough, Mrs. Craig," amid considerable laughter.

Yet May Craig had made her point as Kennedy acknowledged on 12 February 1962, when he explained why he had created the President's Commission on the Status of Women: "One [reason] is for my own self-protection: every two or three weeks Mrs. May Craig asks me what I am doing for women!" Kennedy could have mentioned the criticism he had also received from Eleanor Roosevelt and several others. Politically, a response seemed appropriate; more importantly, he recognized the problems women faced in the workplace, particularly discrimination in wages and hiring. That same concern had motivated him to push for a stronger minimum wage law for all workers.

Kennedy charged the commission to "review progress and make recommendations as needed for constructive action" relating to virtually every aspect of female employment. For the first time, a study of the status of women received national focus. Kennedy chose Eleanor Roosevelt as chairperson to highlight its significance. Much of the work, however, fell to Esther Peterson, the new director of the Women's Bureau, whom Kennedy had also appointed as assistant secretary of labor. Peterson, enormously capable and well connected to organized labor, became the administration's key spokesperson on women.

Peterson reflected the viewpoint that the administration should concentrate less on appointing women to governmental offices and more on improving their economic status in society. She, more than anyone else, convinced Kennedy to create the twenty-six person presidential commission, undoubtedly hoping to control the direction of the women's movement through her involvement in the commission. Coming from a strong labor background, she represented traditional feminism, which feared that protective labor legislation, in existence since the Progressive era, was in jeopardy as a result of the ERA. She contended that the ERA would only benefit women in the professions and business, those who least needed assistance. Although the commission contained all points of view, Peterson's followers dominated it.

The commission issued its final report, "American Women," on 11 October 1963, the birthday of Eleanor Roosevelt, who had died that previous November. It emphasized that "equal opportunity for women in hiring, training, and promotion should be the governing principle in private employment." Yet the commission predictably hedged on the ERA in concluding that "a constitutional amendment need not now be sought in order to establish this principle." Most commission members contended that the Fifth and Fourteenth Amendments could ensure equality of opportunity, particularly if the Supreme Court validated that assertion through appropriate test cases.

Even before the final report, the administration had responded to the commission's concerns. In May 1963 Congress approved an administration bill that guaranteed equal pay to women doing work equal to that of men. First considered in Congress in 1945, the Equal Pay Act, an amendment to the Fair Labor Standards Act of 1938, applied only to those workers covered by the Fair Labor Standards Administration (approximately seven million women). It meant little to the many women engaged in sexually segregated occupations or in plants with fewer than twenty-five employees. Other critics asserted that the phrase "comparable" work instead of "equal" might have served women better. Despite the act's minimal practical impact, Cynthia Harrison, the leading scholar of this legislation, rightly argues that it "marks the entrance of the federal government into the field of safeguarding the right of women to hold employment on the same basis as men." In that respect it represented a milestone in antidiscrimination legislation, one that other administrations, beginning with Johnson's, further extended.

In July 1962 Kennedy also directed the chairman of the Civil Service Commission to ensure that employment in the federal service be based solely on individual merit and fitness. That same year Congress acted on Kennedy's recommendation to assist states in establishing day care facilities, in May appropriating $800,000 for that purpose, a far cry from the president's $5 million recommendation. Yet this represented the first day-care expenditure since World War II. The Kennedy administration also eliminated the quota system, which limited the number of women military officers. Following the commission report in October, Kennedy complied with its recommendation to provide for continual governmental action on behalf of women by creating the Interdepartmental Committee on the Status of Women and the Citizen's Advisory Council. These committees ensured ongoing leadership.

The Kennedy administration thus took the crucial first steps in improving the economic well-being of women. Through its Commission on the Status of Women, it, according to Cynthia Harrison, became the "starting point for governmental discussion of women's status that continued for at least two decades." By publicizing discrimination and injustice, that commission contributed to the establishment of commissions on the state level. It also unwittingly spurred the women's rights movement, which went beyond the administration's limited goals and its view of women's primary role as mother and homemaker. Kennedy, in fact, wondered how women could meet their responsibilities to their children and also make a contribution to society. He assumed that most women worked to support their families. The commission furthermore argued that women workers had "special" attributes which might permit "justified" discrimination. All of these assumptions would be called into question, as would traditional roles for women. In May 1963 Friedan, in her bestseller, called the American home a "comfortable concentration camp," an assessment that most likely troubled Kennedy, Peterson, and the commission members.

THE SPACE PROGRAM

Kennedy's quest to place a man on the moon by 1970 became a much more visible symbol of the New Frontier. It also remains a lasting legacy that can best be understood in the context of the Cold War. The anticipated cost of some $30 billion to $40 billion achieved congressional support because Kennedy so successfully tied it to Cold War considerations.

Interest in space came as a consequence of the Soviet launching of *Sputnik* into orbit in 1957, sending shock tremors nationwide that the Soviets were winning the war in space. In the Senate Lyndon Baines Johnson insisted that the "control of space means the control of the world. From space, the masters of infinity would have the power to control the earth's weather, to cause drought and flood, to change the tides and raise the levels of the sea, to divert the gulf stream and change temperate climates to frigid." Johnson and others challenged the nation to overtake Soviet domination of space. The frenetic activity that followed included the creation of the National Aeronautics and Space Administration (NASA); the Special Committee on Space and Aeronautics in the Senate, chaired by Johnson; a science adviser to the president; the implementation of the space program by NASA; and a nine-member Space Council, involving the president, the secretaries of state and defense, and the director of NASA, to establish a comprehensive policy and select specific programs.

The Eisenhower administration never shared the concerns and enthusiasm of those committed to an energetic space program. Ike denied that the United States was competing with the Russians and played down the military and technological significance of *Sputnik*. Although he unenthusiastically backed Project Mercury's objective of sending an American into space, he balked at a projected manned lunar landing by 1970. At a December 1960 White House meeting he asked why such an extravagant commitment should be made. When someone compared the venture to Columbus's voyage to America, Ike reportedly responded that he was "not about to hock [the] jewels" in order to land on the moon.

John Kennedy sought to capitalize on Eisenhower's sluggish response, despite expressing no interest in or knowledge of space issues prior to 1960. On more than thirty occasions, however, he told campaign audiences that our failure to be number one in space had cost Americans dearly. He argued that Third World nations now viewed the Soviet Union as equal if not superior to the United States. Soviet space successes would reach even higher levels as the result of Yuri Gagarin's round-the-earth flight on 12 April 1961. The Soviet became the first human in space, an accomplishment Khrushchev eagerly exploited as another Communist triumph over a decaying capitalist system.

In an important White House meeting two days after Gagarin's flight, Kennedy impatiently questioned the experts about how the United States might overcome the Soviet advantage: "Is there any place where we can catch them? What can we do? Can we go around the moon before them? Can we leapfrog?" The disastrous consequences of the Bay of Pigs operation on 17 and 18 April brought on even greater concern about the erosion of America's prestige as well as his own. Consequently, Kennedy felt even more pressure to respond.

Then on 5 May, after several postponements, Alan Shepard soared into suborbital space before a national TV audience in Project Mercury's initial venture, making him a hero to an American public anxiously awaiting some good news. Few people knew that Shepard's flight had nearly been canceled because of a fear of failure in the face of considerable hype. Had Shepard met with disaster, the project would have been in jeopardy. As it turned out, Shepard's achievement pumped new blood into a program that Kennedy had tentatively decided to move forward.

Kennedy had laid the groundwork for such action by asking Vice President Johnson to convene the Space Council to determine whether the

United States had the capability of beating the Soviets in a manned lunar enterprise and what it would cost the taxpayer. Kennedy also talked with hundreds of people about the feasibility of the project. Nine days later Johnson, after pressing NASA, submitted recommendations to include the manned lunar landing as the major objective of the space program. Kennedy's decision became public in a 25 May speech before Congress: "This nation should commit itself to achieving the goal, before this decade is out, of landing a man on the moon and returning him safely to earth. No single project . . . will be more exciting, or more impressive to mankind, or more important for the long-range exploration of space; and none will be so expensive to accomplish."

Nothing troubled the president more than the attendant financial obligation. The anticipated outlay over a ten-year period aroused his concern about deficits. Moreover, economists had informed him that the nature of the expenditure would only minimally promote economic growth. He knew the immense challenge of developing powerful booster rockets capable of sending a manned capsule into space. The United States seemed years behind the Soviets in rocket thrust development, thanks ironically to American technology, which so reduced the weight of the U.S. missiles that rockets as powerful as the Soviets' had previously not been needed. Just as troubling, scientists remained unconvinced that a manned lunar venture promised as much scientific gain as other space endeavors. Even James Webb, the director of NASA, soon expressed doubts about making the lunar landing the top priority, causing Kennedy to reply that the government was spending "fantastic" amounts on the space race, and if beating the Soviets to the moon were not the objective, then "we shouldn't be spending this kind of money because I'm not that interested in space."[7]

Obviously, there would have been no race to the moon without the Cold War; the space program became as much a part of that conflict as Cuba, Berlin, and Laos. With typical hyperbole Johnson stated that he did not "believe that this generation of Americans is willing to resign itself to going to bed each night by the light of a Communist moon." Others also feared—and exploited—the military implications of Soviet dominance of space. Kennedy saw a lunar commitment as a way to restore U.S. prestige, particularly with Third World nations, the new battleground of the Cold War. A moon launch would lessen the frustrations of Cuba, Southeast Asia, and Berlin. Kennedy's concerns touched on personal, foreign, and domestic considerations. Furthermore, it fit his New Frontier theme, preaching dedication and sacrifice. According to Robert Kennedy, it reflected the president's striving for excellence and admiration of courage. Additionally, a space race would unify Americans, creating a pride heretofore lacking. In a 12 September 1962 address in Houston, Kennedy rhetorically asked, "But why, some say, the moon? Why choose this as our goal? . . . Why does Rice play Texas?" Kennedy saw the race to the moon as a fitting challenge, one that America could win.

Kennedy had grasped that the United States had the science and technology to overcome Soviet advantages. He skillfully cast the United States as an underdog while accomplishments slowly unfolded. In February 1962 John Glenn flew around the earth in his Mercury capsule *Friendship,* equaling Gagarin's feat and making Glenn another hero of his times. He had been helped by a space budget that had jumped to $1.8 billion for 1962. NASA's budget doubled one year later. In January 1963 Kennedy also announced a successful unmanned Mariner flight past Venus and, one day before his assassination, referred to the completion of the "largest booster in the world," the Saturn C-1 rocket, soon to carry the largest payload ever to be sent into space.

By 1963, however, the space program faced criticism inside and outside of Congress because of escalating costs, which ultimately exceeded $30 billion by 1969. Housing and education programs, liberals argued, deserved more funding, and the intensification of racial discontent further heightened the need to refocus on domestic problems as priorities. Sociologist Amitai Etzioni called the Apollo program a "moondoggle." Conservative Republicans clamored for shifting funds into military projects such as the Titan-3 missile and space stations. The House Space Committee even recommended a reduction in space appropriations.

The truth is that the race to the moon seemed less pressing by 1963. Journalists repeatedly printed stories indicating that the Soviets were disengaging from the attempt. According to one contemporary authority, the USSR was focusing on space stations and unmanned explorations, reinforcing Khrushchev's 1961 claim at Vienna that he had no compulsion to go to the moon. The United States, he said, was rich; it should go first. Furthermore, the Cuban missile crisis of October 1962 had shown Americans the frightening aspects of technology in a thermonuclear era, leading to improved relations between the two superpowers. Kennedy talked even more openly now about space cooperation with the Soviets, including a joint moon launch, which few experts took seriously, given the existing mutual suspicions. Still, this contributed to the congressional opposition toward the space program in 1963.

Kennedy remained solidly behind the Apollo project to the end. His comments at an April 1963 press conference expressed his beliefs: "I have seen nothing . . . that has changed my mind about the desirability of our continuing this program." Johnson extended the commitment, even managing to increase the space budget to over $5.2 billion in 1964 before facing the strains of Vietnam, mounting social tensions at home, inflation, and Apollo cutbacks. Finally on 20 July 1969 four American astronauts landed their module on the moon. Advocates everywhere shared in the glory of that accomplishment, and many remembered Kennedy on that special day. But what did it all mean to those who lived in 1969? Did it represent the triumph of technology, with all of its psychological and material benefits and potential dangers? Was it instead a wasteful, misguided effort, given the enormous social ills afflicting the American society of the 1960s? Or was it a "delayed consequence of the Cold War, beginning with President Kennedy's resolve to outrace the Russians"? Americans at the time were not altogether sure. Regardless, the Apollo program will always be inexorably linked to Kennedy.

THE PEACE CORPS

Even more than the space program, the Peace Corps represented Kennedy's "most affirmative and enduring legacy," as Gerard T. Rice, the corps' leading scholar puts it. Elizabeth Cobbs Hoffman, another Peace Corps historian, likewise argues that the Peace Corps represented Kennedy's chief instrument to convey America's sense of "promise" to the world. It enabled more than one hundred thousand Americans to serve in Third World countries over a twenty-five year period. The prevailing popular image remains a romantic one of "idealistic, patriotic, freedom-loving" young Americans, enduring in mud huts with the "patience of Job, the forbearance of a saint, and the digestive system of an ostrich." In the process they contributed much to the improvement of the American image abroad and provided useful skills to emerging nations as well as eventually educating Americans about Third World cultures.

The idea of the Peace Corps predated the Kennedy presidency. During the 1930s the Civilian Conservation Corps and the National Youth

Administration were the Roosevelt administration's domestic equivalents. The idealism of that era was not lost to those in the 1950s who envisioned that government could create comparable programs in the Third World. By the late 1950s Senator Hubert Humphrey called for a Peace Corps, the first use of that specific name. In the House of Representatives Henry Reuss (D-Wis.) proposed the idea in 1957. Three years later the House provided ten thousand dollars for a study of a Point Four Youth Corps. Ike later labeled such a commitment a "juvenile experiment."

Kennedy remained silent on the topic until late in the 1960 campaign. At 2 A.M., in an appearance at Ann Arbor, Michigan, immediately following his debate with Nixon on 14 October, he met with ten thousand excited University of Michigan students—including Tom Hayden, the future founder of the Students for a Democratic Society. He asked how many would be prepared to give years of their lives working in Asia, Africa, and Latin America. The overwhelming response to this and other related questions reaffirmed for Kennedy an emerging idealism among college youth, described by the *Harvard Crimson:* "This is the first generation of students which is not going to school for purely economic reasons."

Not until the last week of the campaign, however, did Kennedy propose a Peace Corps in a speech at the San Francisco Cow Palace. He spoke eloquently of talented young men and women, well trained in the languages, skills, and customs of the host country, who would serve a three-year tour as an alternative to military service. By helping impoverished nations help themselves, Kennedy asserted, volunteers could erase the image of the "Ugly American" and overcome the efforts of Khrushchev's "missionaries." Kennedy clearly viewed the idea of the Peace Corps as more than altruistic; he saw the corps as another tool in the Cold War. He subsequently spoke of halting communist expansion by helping to develop the resources of the Third World. The Peace Corps also became a symbol of the nation's moral impulse and of Kennedy's own call for sacrifice and drive for excellence. According to one Gallup survey, 71 percent favored the idea, while only 18 percent opposed it. Clearly, it also served to improve his election chances.

The Peace Corps' phenomenal positive image, however, came about only as a result of some fortuitous circumstances. Most importantly, Kennedy made his brother-in-law Sargent Shriver the director. The perfect choice, Shriver was an idealist with a world of experience in business, education, and international travel. Handsome, tireless, vibrant, and caring, he became the prototypical New Frontiersman. His charisma helped to attract a talented supporting cast, including Harris Wofford, Kennedy's former civil rights adviser; twenty-six-year-old Bill Moyers, Johnson's key aide; and William Haddad, a former prize-winning journalist for the *New York Post*. The staff soon reflected the personality of Shriver in its hard-driving idealistic ways.

The impetus for the Peace Corps came from a task force headed by Shriver, which proposed a large and independent agency to begin activities almost immediately. Significantly, the military service exemption was removed for political reasons. To avoid probable congressional delay, Shriver recommended that Kennedy issue an executive order to give the organization life through the first year. From the outset Sorensen and other White House staffers reacted negatively to this approach. They pondered the potential dangers of sending youthful Americans abroad as part of a hastily conceived program. They favored a smaller, lower cost, less ambitious operation tied to the overall federal assistance program.

Though Kennedy agreed to issue an executive order, he too felt that the Peace Corps should come under the newly proposed Agency for International Development (AID), along with Food for Peace and other related agencies. This made administrative and political sense, particularly since it would facilitate congressional approval. Shriver argued that under this arrangement the Peace Corps would lose its "distinctive identity and appeal." Kennedy remained unpersuaded, at least until his vice president reinforced Shriver's concerns. Moyers had taken the matter to Johnson, who immediately responded, arguing that under AID the Peace Corps would become "just another box in an organizational chart, reporting to a third assistant director of personnel for the State Department." According to one contemporary, Johnson soon "collared Kennedy . . . and in the course of the conversation badgered him so much that Kennedy finally said all right." The action proved consequential: the Peace Corps could now freely develop without the burden of bureaucratic restrictions.

Perhaps initially the Peace Corps became more independent than it wished to be, as White House staffers and the president reacted coolly toward it following the organizational fight. Almost until the end, the White House refused to fight for the bill to extend the corps' existence after 1961. Shriver, told by Kennedy that he was on his own after failing to accept White House advice, worked the congressional offices and corridors with such passion that he won the admiration of countless congressmen. Many in the affirmative majority probably voted more for Shriver than for the program. Shriver also soon won the approval of Kennedy, who quipped: "I don't think it is altogether fair to say that I handed Sarge a lemon from which he made lemonade, but I do think he was handed one of the most sensitive and difficult assignments which any administration in Washington has been given in this century." Kennedy eventually took great pride in the Peace Corps and often asked visitors how the "kids" were doing. He did whatever the organization asked him to do, meeting with volunteers, participating in ceremonies, and ensuring that the CIA stayed out of its activities. Yet he generally left the Peace Corps alone, knowing that it was in good hands.

The Peace Corps in the Kennedy years sent volunteers to forty-four countries requesting Americans. The thousands who served underwent intense training on college campuses before qualifying for foreign service. In fact, from 1961 to 1963, 22 percent of all trainees failed to make it through the program. The objectives were threefold: to provide a needed skill to an interested country; to increase the understanding of Americans by other people; and to increase American understanding of non-Americans. For the most part the corps generally met these goals despite the inevitable problems of too many volunteers lacking necessary skills, finding themselves with no definite jobs, or having too little to do. Contrary to myth, few lived in mud huts; most taught English in schools. Although Shriver and other Peace Corps administrators painted a romantic picture, the fact is that volunteer life sometimes involved frustration and failure as much as success. In rarer instances volunteers even committed public and private indiscretions that necessitated their recall.

Yet stories abound of individual achievement and sacrifice. One young volunteer in Panama stayed away from the Peace Corps office in Panama City for ten months while working alone with Caribbean coastal Indians. Every couple of weeks he navigated up the river to deliver pig meat, fish, and rice to local communities. Paul Tsongas, a future Democratic senator from Massachusetts, lived with ten students in an Ethiopian village where he not only taught mathematics and science but also constructed timber footbridges over muddy streams and ditches. One popular volunteer in the Liberian bush became so culturally immersed that the local tribe adopted him as a son. A black corpsman in Tanzania, hailed as "Negro Bwana," enraptured his community to the extent that villagers offered him a wife and a small farm to entice him to stay. In so many different settings and ways barriers broke down, encouraging Third World peoples to cast aside their suspicions and to express genuine sorrow when volunteers left their communities. For this reason, Peace Corps volunteers have been called Kennedy's "Real Best and Brightest."

The Peace Corps served as an effective instrument in improving Third World relations. It transcended the Bay of Pigs, the missile buildup, and the other negative aspects of the Kennedy foreign policy and furthered the impression that Kennedy understood and empathized with the national aspirations and problems of Third World peoples. Yet its greatest success came as a result of its refusal to push the merits of U.S. foreign policy upon host nations. By ignoring ideology and responding to needs and problems, it won over many Third World people, including President Kwame Nkrumah of communist-leaning Ghana, who continually requested more Peace Corps volunteers. Paradoxically, it thus became an important element of U.S. foreign policy. The American people realized its significance in a 1963 Harris Poll when they rated it the third most popular activity of the Kennedy administration, after "national security" and "Berlin."

Recent studies further document its successes, even though the Peace Corps did little to achieve national economic growth in host countries. Its person-to-person approach elevated the lives of many impoverished people. No agency showed others the idealistic side of America more clearly. Moreover, the volunteers' overseas experiences would serve them well, as many former members went into the Foreign Service and other governmental agencies, bringing an understanding of Third World cultures heretofore lacking. Other former volunteers carried that idealism and knowledge into the schools as teachers or graduate students. Many others soon found themselves involved in the anti-Vietnam and civil rights protest movements. Even before the return of those volunteers, Kennedy's Peace Corps idea had inspired young Americans to seek a better world at home too.

CIVIL RIGHTS

No domestic issue occupied Kennedy's presidency more over a longer duration than civil rights. And no domestic matter of that time has invited as much attention among scholars. Disagreement has existed over the purity of Kennedy's commitment. Even though virtually every scholar has portrayed Kennedy as initially cautious and concerned about the political ramifications of moving against a hostile Congress, questions have arisen about whether he genuinely had the interests of African Americans at heart or whether he saw black activism as a hindrance to his own political fortunes and foreign policy objectives. More important, differences have emerged over the extent of Kennedy's accomplishments in the area of civil rights.

As a congressman and senator from Massachusetts—a state that lacked a sizable black population—Kennedy had not been particularly sensitive to the problems of African Americans, though he had supported civil rights legislation in the 1950s. His unexpected popularity with southern delegates during his unsuccessful drive for the vice presidential nomination in 1956 seemed to bode ill, even though his remark—"I'm going to sing Dixie for the rest of my life"—remained private. More disturbingly, Kennedy voted for the pro-South jury trial amendment to the Civil Rights Act of 1957. It is fair to say that Kennedy's political ambitions had made him sensitive both to Southern and African American feelings. He sought to win over black voters by proposing to advance civil rights appreciably. At the same time, he appeased the South by selecting a Texan, Lyndon Johnson, as his running mate and by criticizing Eisenhower for using federal troops to enforce school desegregation in Little Rock in 1957.

Beginning on 1 February 1960, the civil rights movement generated new intensity when four black freshmen at North Carolina Agricultural and Technical State University sat at the lunch counter of the Woolworth store in downtown Greensboro to protest a "whites only" policy. They inspired similar sit-in demonstrations across the South, awakening a generation of young activists, black and white, numbering in the tens of thousands. The names of civil rights leaders, such as Martin Luther King Jr., appeared with greater frequency in the press, as did civil rights organizations such as the Congress of Racial Equality (CORE), the Southern Christian Leadership Conference (SCLC), and, above all in 1960, the Student Nonviolent Coordinating Committee (SNCC).

Young activists found inspiration in Kennedy's presidential campaign. His speeches promised to use the "full moral force and political power of the Presidency to obtain for all Americans . . . equal access to the voting booth, the school room, to jobs, to housing and to public facilities, including lunch counters." Kennedy recognized that racism weakened the United States because of its wastefulness and divisiveness. It also debilitated the country internationally as the United States sought to improve relations with African nations and to capitalize on Soviet human rights violations.

At the risk of losing Southern backing, he also identified himself more fully with black America by calling Coretta Scott King, wife of the civil rights leader, on 20 October to express his concern about the arrest of her husband in Georgia, a call Republican nominee Richard Nixon refused to make. Finally, even though Kennedy's inauguration address failed to address domestic issues such as civil rights, it spoke of freedom, commitment, and sacrifice. By their actions student civil rights activists naturally felt that they were answering Kennedy's call to do something for their country. To them Kennedy's New Frontier embodied change and hope.

One day after Kennedy's inauguration, African American James Meredith applied for admission to the University of Mississippi, arguably the most racist of the southern segregated universities. Soon thereafter, however, black leaders became disappointed when the president suggested that there would be no civil rights legislation in 1961. His miniscule election victory, a stronger conservative coalition in Congress, and unfavorable public opinion became compelling considerations. He also believed that if he pushed civil rights, then reforms such as medicare, minimum wage increases, and federal aid to education would probably fail, hurting blacks in the process.

President Kennedy at first sought to divert civil rights activities to the Department of Justice, thereby lessening the emotional impact of the racial controversy by emphasizing the legal dimension over the moral. His brother Robert, who commented that he did not stay "awake nights worrying about civil rights" before becoming attorney general, consequently had free rein to enforce the law vigorously against civil rights violations. He delegated civil rights matters to an extremely competent, youthful staff of Ivy League law graduates after outlining the enforcement philosophy in his first public speech, delivered at the University of Georgia on 6 May 1961. He suggested that the administration would seek strict compliance with civil rights statutes and court orders through amicable negotiation. If voluntary compliance failed, then the administration would undertake legal action. He tempered his remarks by emphasizing that racial discrimination remained a national problem. He stressed the need to avoid violence and incidents such as the one at Little Rock Central High in 1957.

Yet next to Eisenhower, President Kennedy seemed a breath of fresh air to many blacks. Through executive action he significantly improved the lot of some black Americans, which had a symbolic impact. Noticing an all white Coast Guard unit at the inauguration parade, he pressured the academy to recruit blacks. By executive order, he also created the President's Committee on Equal Employment Opportunity (PCEEO), chaired by the vice president, to ensure that all Americans would have equal employment within government and "with those who do business with government." The PCEEO had unprecedented powers to institute investigations and to terminate contracts where discrimination existed. And no other president had provided blacks with as many federal appointments. "Kennedy was so hot on the department heads, the cabinet officers, and agency heads that everyone was scrambling around trying to find himself a Negro in order to keep the President off his neck," wrote Roy Wilkins, head of the National Association for the Advancement of Colored People (NAACP). The Civil Service Commission made a major effort to recruit blacks at college campuses. Kennedy also appointed some forty blacks to top administration posts, including Robert C. Weaver as administrator of the Housing and Home Finance Agency, slated for cabinet status; Andrew Hatcher, associate White House press secretary; and Carl Rowan, deputy assistant secretary of state for public affairs.[8] Additionally, Kennedy selected five black federal judges, including Thurgood Marshall, for the second circuit court of appeals in New York; Marshall was an important symbol to black America, given his role in *Brown v. Board of Education of Topeka*.

Other symbolic gestures abounded. Kennedy invited more blacks to the White House than any previous president had. Not only did they attend meetings and social functions, which were well publicized in the black press, but they also became the houseguests of Robert Kennedy and other New Frontiersmen. Moreover, the attorney general resigned, with attendant press coverage, from the exclusive Metropolitan Club after a six-month attempt to persuade its board of directors to admit blacks. Most significantly, the president withdrew his membership from the Cosmos Club following its rebuff of Carl Rowan. On the school desegregation front, Robert Kennedy threatened to seek contempt of court sentences against Louisiana officials if they continued to deny state funds to the recently desegregated schools of New Orleans. By September 1961 Atlanta and Memphis followed New Orleans in successful school desegregation efforts.

On another front, the Justice Department brought suits to end illegal violations of black voting rights in the South. In the Eisenhower period, the department had introduced only six suits in all and none in Mississippi, where only 6 percent of voting-age blacks were registered. The enormous effort required to win discouraged such actions. Yet Kennedy's

Justice Department instituted fifty-seven voting-rights suits, thirty of them in Mississippi, including one in Senator James Eastland's Sunflower County, an indication that the administration did not completely acquiesce to southern political power.

But neither the White House nor the NAACP controlled the timetable of the civil rights movement in 1961. It marched to the beat of more aggressive black organizations such as SNCC, CORE, and SCLC, all of whom felt the administration needed some nudging. James Farmer's rejuvenated CORE intended to force federal compliance with a 1960 Supreme Court decision, *Boynton v. Virginia,* which extended the court's prohibition of segregation on interstate buses to terminal facilities. Farmer sought to provoke southern authorities into arresting the Freedom Riders, thereby compelling the Justice Department to enforce the law of the land.

On 4 May seven blacks and six whites left Washington, D.C., on a Greyhound and a Trailways bus. They traveled south, where they challenged whites- and coloreds-only accommodations at terminal restaurants and restrooms. Violence first occurred at Rock Hill, South Carolina, where a black and a white Freedom Rider entered the whites-only Greyhound waiting room. Twenty thugs, wearing ducktail haircuts and leather jackets, mauled them before the police intervened. In the weeks ahead the national press soon reported other incidents, including bus burnings and beatings, most of them occurring in Alabama. Typically, the police came to the scene after the beatings, suggesting that local law enforcement deliberately delayed. The violence reached such threatening proportions in Montgomery, Alabama, that Attorney General Kennedy sent John Seigenthaler, an administrative assistant and Nashville native, there. While Seigenthaler helped victims into his car, he was knocked unconscious. A shocked and angry Robert Kennedy—"he looked like he'd just been poleaxed himself"—telephoned Seigenthaler at the hospital. Kennedy's characteristic use of humor to show affection soon followed, as he thanked his assistant for helping with the black vote.

In many ways the Freedom Rides represented a frustrating experience for the Kennedys. The rides revealed, first of all, the Kennedys' underestimation of the depth of the problem. Civil rights was not merely a political matter that could easily be orchestrated from the White House by pulling the right strings with business, political, educational, and judicial leaders. The president, preoccupied with Khrushchev and the Berlin crisis, showed a profound ignorance when he angrily asked Harris Wofford, his civil rights adviser, to tell the Freedom Riders to "call it off." Kennedy saw that activity as an embarrassment because communist propaganda would seek to exploit apparent American human rights violations. This would have a particular affect on Third World countries, which the administration sought to keep out of the Soviet camp.

The attorney general reacted more emotionally. On the one hand, according to Deputy Attorney General for Civil Rights Burke Marshall, Kennedy's compassion for the underdog might have made him a Freedom Rider as a private citizen. But as his brother's agent, it angered him that the rides continued. All of this, he thought, weakened the U.S. image abroad, which led him to question the riders' patriotism. Yet he reacted even more strongly against the violation of the activists' constitutional rights and the attendant violence. He also gradually became more aware of the racial militancy of the South, for which negotiations offered no easy solutions. "Despite the enlightened Southerners among us," Robert Kennedy later admitted, "we lacked a sense of Southern history."

The attorney general became the administration's point man during the Freedom Ride crisis. He sought to protect the activists rather than to engage in a civil rights crusade that would turn the Democratic South against the administration as well as exacerbate the conflict. He knew that 63 percent of the American people opposed the Freedom Rides. Former President Harry Truman helped little by railing publicly against meddling northern "busybodies." Yet Kennedy could not permit Freedom Riders to remain at the mercy of southern police authority, nor could he be indifferent to defending their constitutional rights, no matter how much he might have disagreed with their methods.

Robert Kennedy's efforts at crisis management became more severely tested after he failed to win the cooperation of southern governors. Nor could he rely on the support of FBI Director J. Edgar Hoover, who insisted that the FBI was not a protection agency. More to the point, Hoover deplored the civil rights movement and considered the Freedom Riders law breakers. His agents in the South, native southerners sensitive to the biases of local communities, did nothing more than take notes as they witnessed southern brutality. Some worked with southern law enforcement officials in ways that hurt civil rights activists.

The attorney general consequently employed federal marshals—not troops—to protect the Freedom Riders, after obtaining an injunction against those interfering with interstate travel. That obligation to protect the Freedom Riders had finally overcome his sensitivity to a federal system that placed law enforcement in the hands of local authorities. He deployed marshals in Montgomery, Alabama, and elsewhere to protect activists. He also pushed for a ruling from the Interstate Commerce Commission, decreeing that all seating on interstate buses would be without reference to race, color, or creed and that all terminals would be integrated. By fall 1961 this had been largely implemented. Overall, the Kennedy administration had handled the Freedom Ride crisis reasonably well. Much of the credit belongs to Robert Kennedy who kept his brother out of the crisis. He had preserved the constitutional rights of interstate travelers in a way that satisfied moderates both North and South. However, this approach failed to mollify many northern liberals, who criticized him for not embracing the moral cause of the Freedom Riders. At the same time southern extremists accused him of aiding and abetting a communist instigated movement. Still, such opposition hurt the administration very little in 1961.

By the end of the summer the civil rights movement had entered a different phase, now centering on black voter registration in the South. Kennedy's Justice Department strongly encouraged this approach. That sort of commitment seemed a suitable substitute for civil disobedience, which inflamed southern emotions. One black scholar called it Kennedy's effort to "get the niggers off the street." A series of meetings between the Justice Department and black civil rights groups in the summer of 1961 led to the formation of the Voter Education Project, financed by private foundations, to embark on an $870,000 registration campaign from April 1962 to October 1965. SNCC, buoyed by its recent successes, played the key role, attracting hundreds of students to the project. Ironically, this new venture created even more problems for the Kennedy administration.

Difficulties began when Robert Kennedy and Burke Marshall left SNCC officials with the clear impression that the department would protect those engaged in voter registration. Kennedy, arguing that the greatest registration potential existed in southern cities, probably did not anticipate that SNCC workers would concentrate on the most remote, rural counties, deep in the black belt of Mississippi and southwest Georgia where no blacks were registered. In fact, places such as McComb, Mississippi, soon experienced baptisms of fire. Aggressive SNCC workers assisted blacks in registering only to see them lose their tenancy and welfare assistance. SNCC volunteers also faced assaults from private citizens and good old boy sheriffs. From 1961 to 1963 SNCC recorded some sixty-two incidents of racial violence in Mississippi alone. One civil rights activist complained, "To have the FBI looking out of the courthouse windows while you were being chased down the street by brick throwers deeply offended the sensibilities. So people wept and cursed Robert Kennedy and Burke Marshall more than the FBI, whom they never had any confidence in to begin with."

SNCC workers felt especially betrayed after their frantic calls and letters to the Justice Department brought only polite and sympathetic replies. The department, Justice officials explained, was powerless to act because the federal system prohibited the national government from interfering with local enforcement. Only if local authorities showed themselves wholly incapable of upholding law and order could Washington intervene. This doctrine clearly had the backing of most in Justice, including the attorney general, who later somewhat callously asserted that "Mississippi is going to work itself out. . . . Maybe it's going to take a decade and maybe a lot of people are going to be killed in the meantime. . . . But in the long run I think it's for the health of the country and the stability of the system." The Justice Department condemned the violence and sought to negotiate with southern officials to end it, but did little else.

Not surprisingly, civil rights attorneys questioned the assumptions of the administration's federalist approach. They argued that by using U.S. criminal codes, the Justice Department could have instituted legal action against civil rights violations and police brutality. They also challenged the department's refusal to employ marshals or to seek injunctions to protect SNCC workers because of the alleged lack of statutory authority or interstate activity. In *Kennedy Justice*, Victor Navasky noted the curious inconsistency between Robert Kennedy's overcautious approach to civil rights and his obsessive war against organized crime, where he often overreached his authority. To Navasky, federalism "was an enlightened apology for the existing order," a conclusion that several later scholars understandably share.

Undoubtedly, federalism partly served as a cover for the administration's other reservations about interfering with southern justice. Those included Justice's lack of staff resources, given the unavailability of the FBI in civil rights matters and the Civil Rights Division's heavy involvement in voting-rights suits. The point is that there were too many McCombs. Furthermore, Robert Kennedy remained personally apprehensive about using force in the South. Thus it is no wonder that idealistic and defenseless SNCC and CORE workers came to view the Kennedy administration as the enemy in 1962. As white violence continued, they also called into question King's nonviolent and integrationist approaches. Partly from the crucible of the voter registration movement, then, emerged the driving force of Black Power as an eventual major component of SNCC and CORE. As a result of the shift, the administration's attitude toward those organizations became more negative. In 1962 James Farmer of CORE, when meeting with the Kennedy brothers, detected a "little coldness and aloofness and perhaps suspicion even."

The administration also found itself at odds in 1962 with those who expected it to end discrimination in housing, which Kennedy in the 1960 campaign had expounded could be accomplished with a "stroke of the presidential pen." By inundating him with pens and instituting an "ink for Jack" drive, critics now prodded him to issue an executive order. Politics constituted the major reason for the hesitancy. The administration believed that it would jeopardize congressional approval of the Department of Urban Affairs bill and the planned appointment of Robert Weaver as the first black cabinet member. Kennedy's initial instincts were to issue the order anyway, but advisers talked him out of it at a November 1961 meeting. Ironically, Kennedy failed to obtain the urban affairs bill.

The proposed housing order then became enmeshed in the politics of the congressional election of 1962. According to Robert Kennedy, even several northern liberal congressmen wanted no order until after the November election because it might hurt them at home. The announcement of the order belatedly came on Thanksgiving Eve 1962, sandwiched between two significant foreign policy statements; the president hardly could have lessened the impact of its publicity. Moreover, the administration restricted Executive Order 11063 to housing facilities owned or operated by the federal government and to those obtaining federal loans, grants, or loan guarantees. The law was not retroactive nor did it apply to private bank loans covered by the Federal Deposit Insurance Corporation (FDIC). The administration hesitated to go further because it doubted that it had the authority through executive action to impose restrictions on the potentially recalcitrant FDIC. As Marshall soon admitted, the housing order "has not been very meaningful."

The President's Commission on Equal Employment Opportunity also proved disappointing, especially the Plans for Progress project. Herbert Hill of the NAACP called Plans for Progress "one of the great phonies of the Kennedy administration's civil rights programs." It had sought to negotiate agreements with private corporations to hire more blacks, and many companies had willingly agreed to participate. All of this had occurred in the midst of considerable fanfare, but in the process the PCEEO had exaggerated its successes and misrepresented the statistics. A 100 percent increase in black employment meant little, the administration soon acknowledged, if the number of blacks in a major company jumped from one to two. Aside from the Plans for Progress fiasco, the PCEEO also failed to raise black employment substantially in federal agencies or in corporations doing business with the federal government. One study revealed that in Birmingham, Alabama, black employment in federal agencies amounted to .001 percent of the total work force.

The Kennedys privately blamed the PCEEO's chairman, Lyndon Johnson, for the shortcomings. According to Robert Kennedy, who came to dislike Johnson more and more, the president "almost had a fit" when he saw the uncomplimentary statistics. In blaming the vice president, President Kennedy supposedly said, "That man can't run this committee. Can you think of anything more deplorable than him trying to run the United States?" Yet he remained reluctant to make changes so as not to offend Johnson. Robert did not share such sensitivity. On one occasion, he and Marshall attended a PCEEO meeting where Kennedy expressed dissatisfaction with the lack of significant progress. When the vice president began to defend the committee, Kennedy and Marshall walked out. They had reason to be disappointed. Despite some twenty-five thousand all-white companies under federal contract, the PCEEO never once used its authority to terminate a work agreement. Yet Johnson was only reflecting the administration's cautious style and approach. Nonetheless, the PCEEO experience, with all of the attending criticism, probably contributed to the president's eventual decision to play down executive action.

In 1962, however, a limited legislative approach also proved frustrating and failed to achieve any real progress. Despite congressional approval of the poll tax amendment (ratified in 1964), the administration failed to obtain a literacy test bill enabling blacks with a sixth-grade education to vote. Furthermore, the president found himself in the political position of having to appoint segregationist judges in the South. Five of the six appointments in the southern Fifth Circuit were segregationists, including the notorious William Harold Cox of Mississippi. Cox had the enthusiastic endorsement of his former college roommate, Mississippi Senator James Eastland, chairman of the Senate Judiciary Committee. Without selecting

Cox, Kennedy probably would not have had the Judiciary Committee's approval of Thurgood Marshall's judicial appointment or its support on other appointments or issues. Besides, Cox had obtained the American Bar Association's rating of Extremely Well Qualified and had promised the attorney general that holding up the Constitution "would never be a problem." Nevertheless, Roy Wilkens, executive secretary of the NAACP, prophetically warned that "for 986,000 Negro Mississippians, Judge Cox will be another strand in their barbed wire fence, another cross on their weary shoulders and another rock in the road up which their young people must struggle." Within weeks after Cox's appointment, he referred to Negro litigants as "niggers" and unlawfully obstructed black voter registration drives and other civil rights activities in Mississippi.

Historian Carl Brauer provides the most sympathetic assessment of the administration's judicial difficulties. Besides having to deal with powerful southern senators who favored their own judicial candidates, the Kennedy administration, he contended, had to accept the fact that civil rights sympathizers in the Deep South were ostracized. Consequently, their judicial or legal careers were not prominent enough to qualify them for federal judicial appointment, nor did they have the necessary political connections. Still, the southern judges appointed under Eisenhower had at least as good a record on civil rights, despite Kennedy's pledge to do more for black America.

No wonder the limitations of Kennedy's civil rights actions seemed much more pronounced to activists in 1962. King accused him of "aggressively driving toward the limited goal of token integration," and another black activist claimed that "we've gotten the best snow job in history. We lost two years because we admired him." The administration faced the same strictures from the white South, epitomized in the desegregation crisis at the University of Mississippi in September, which thrust the civil rights conflict again to the forefront. Once more the administration found itself in crisis management.

The issue arose over James H. Meredith's desire to enroll at the University of Mississippi in the fall of 1962. A twenty-eight-year-old grandson of a slave, the quiet, slim, and unflappable Meredith asked for the assistance of the NAACP after the university failed to admit him. The NAACP obtained a circuit court order commanding the university to enroll Meredith. Because of the school's continued resistance, the court gave the Justice Department permission to seek compliance. For political, legal, and moral reasons the department had no alternative but to force the desegregation of the Oxford, Mississippi, campus. It sought to do so without the employment of federal troops, whose presence would symbolize Reconstruction.

The initial conflict pitted Robert Kennedy against Mississippi Governor Ross Barnett. Following Barnett's delaying tactics, Kennedy sanctioned the deployment of five hundred marshals on campus to protect Meredith as he registered for classes. That invited a backlash that went deeper than the enrollment of a black student. It summoned the nostalgic, bitter emotions of the "lost cause," in which Mississippians sought once again to grasp a fallen standard previously held by Jefferson Davis and his Confederate legions.

As a result, on Sunday, 30 September, a large number of angry students and armed outsiders approached the administration building where the marshals were positioned to protect Meredith. To combat the rock- and bottle-throwing mob, the marshals employed tear gas. Later that day an even angrier crowd, led by armed good old boys, responded with gunfire, killing two, including a French reporter, and wounding twenty-eight. Not knowing that violence had erupted, President Kennedy addressed a national television audience, speaking loftily of the past courage, patriotism, and contributions of Mississippians. He then reminded viewers that "Americans are free, in short, to disagree with the law but not to disobey it." That the latter occurred left no alternative to federal intervention. He appealed to Mississippians to uphold the "tradition of honor and courage won on the field of battle and on the gridiron as well as the university campus."

Kennedy's conciliatory remarks probably had no impact on University of Mississippi students, nor did he change the avowed segregationists, who found more reason to detest him. Yet his efforts to retain moderate support from the business, academic, and professional communities proved more successful. Business in particular took to heart Kennedy's appeals that compliance, rather than rebellion, best served the state's economic interests.

That moderation became more severely tested later that Sunday, following the threatened marshals' request to draw their pistols. However, the president, Robert Kennedy, and others who stayed at the White House command post throughout the night remained cool and under control. The attorney general relayed President Kennedy's order that the marshals must not fire their weapons unless Meredith's life was endangered. As the situation worsened the president had no alternative but to employ federal troops. He had wisely federalized the Mississippi National Guard and ordered United States Army units to nearby Memphis. They were soon brought on campus to enable Meredith to register. Almost miraculously, neither Meredith nor the marshals suffered any fatalities. Meredith graduated the next year, and other blacks then matriculated at the University of Mississippi without incident.

For the Kennedys the University of Mississippi fight represented yet another successful example of crisis management—one that had the approval of the American majority. More importantly, it left an enduring intellectual impact on Kennedy, causing him to recast traditional beliefs about Reconstruction following the Civil War—and hence race relations during the 1960s. The way in which Mississippians reacted emotionally and distorted the marshals' actions appalled Kennedy, making him wonder if such distortions might have existed nearly a hundred years earlier. Robert Kennedy recalled that his brother "would never believe a book on Reconstruction again," at least not one that dwelled on the "terrible tales of the northern scalawag troops." The attorney general helped expose him to the new interpretations of Reconstruction history by inviting the distinguished professor David Donald to a White House seminar. Donald more charitably interpreted the motivations of Radical Republicans, such as Charles Sumner and Speaker of the House Thaddeus Stevens, and more critically assessed southern reaction to Reconstruction—an analysis that challenged Kennedy's earlier views in his 1956 *Profiles in Courage*. The crisis at Ole Miss, more than Donald, however, had influenced the president to consider a fresh historical perspective, one that still competed with his political pragmatism as 1963 unfolded.

That new year marked the centennial celebration of Lincoln's Emancipation Proclamation. On 12 February, Lincoln's birthday, Kennedy sponsored a White House reception for eight hundred African American leaders and their spouses. This unprecedented reception symbolized how far the White House had come in reaching out to the black establishment. Yet there were several conspicuous absences, including longtime activist A. Philip Randolph, who thought the Kennedys had not done enough for blacks, and Martin Luther King Jr., vacationing on the Caribbean island of Jamaica and planning his campaign to combat Jim Crow in Birmingham, Alabama.

Birmingham, the Johannesburg of the South, was arguably the most segregated urban center in Dixie. Blacks faced Whites Only signs at restaurants, restrooms, and water fountains and held the most menial jobs. Challenged by competing civil rights organizations, pressured by his own followers, and frustrated by the seeming ambivalence of the Kennedy administration, King decided to act in early April. Aided by substantial local black support, King engineered a protest campaign that included sit-ins at downtown stores, street marches, and pray-ins. On Good Friday, 12 April, King was incarcerated for violating an injunction against demonstrations. His "Letter from the Birmingham Jail," an eloquent justification for civil disobedience and nonviolent protest, soon followed. King sought "to create a situation so crisis-packed that it will inevitably open the door to negotiation." Otherwise black frustration and injustice would lead to street violence and black nationalist ideologies, which King wished to avoid.

The Birmingham crisis escalated after King's release a week later. For the first time he mobilized more than one thousand children in street marches on 2 May, and most of them were arrested. As demonstrators filled the jails, other protesters also fell victim to "Bull" Connor, the enraged police commissioner, who used police dogs, high-pressure fire hoses, and nightsticks to punish them. Vivid images of lunging police dogs and blacks tumbling before powerful jets of water dominated the evening television news, causing the president to remark that the pictures made him "sick." Connor soon became a symbol of racial oppression, and King reemerged as the most prominent force in the movement.

The Kennedy administration played a key role in that crisis. Once again the president had telephoned Coretta Scott King, and he and Robert had helped to ease her husband's confinement. On 4 May the attorney general sent Marshall and an assistant to Birmingham to mediate between the two sides. Andrew Young of SCLC later testified that the "Justice Department did a tremendous behind-the-scenes job of pulling the Birmingham community together." Kennedy meanwhile used the occasion of a press conference to goad Birmingham business leaders to meet "the justifiable needs of the Negro community," which resulted in a satisfactory agreement for both Kennedy and King. The white leadership pledged to desegregate public facilities such as lunch counters within ninety days, to promote blacks from menial positions, and to hire other blacks within sixty days. Birmingham had elevated the intensity of the movement to a much higher level, inspiring more blacks to move into the streets and spawning demonstrations in several other southern communities. It also caused "blacks en masse [to forsake] gradualism for immediacy."

After Birmingham the Kennedy administration found itself further entangled in the movement. For Robert Kennedy especially, it remained a learning experience. His exploratory breakfast session on 23 May with the brilliant black writer James Baldwin led to a meeting that Kennedy had arranged at the family apartment in New York City. Baldwin and thirteen other black personalities, including Kenneth Clark, a well-known psychologist; famous entertainers Harry Belafonte and Lena Horne; Lorraine Hansberry, an accomplished playwright; and Jerome Smith, a CORE field worker victimized by Mississippi justice, participated.

Kennedy began the meeting by asking them to get involved in the civil rights movement and then proceeded to outline the administration's accomplishments. Smith, who stammered when upset, set the tone by professing to be nauseated from having to share the same room with the attorney general, volunteering that "I've seen what government can do to crush the spirit and lives of people in the South." He vividly recalled waiting vainly in a Mississippi jail for the FBI or the Justice Department to respond. He expressed shame for his country and an unwillingness to defend it militarily. All of this shocked Kennedy, who took it personally and turned his back on Smith. "That was a mistake," Baldwin later said, "because when he turned his back toward us . . . Lorraine Hansberry said, 'You've got a great many very accomplished people in the room, Mr. Attorney General. But the only man you should be listening to is that man over there.'" For three excruciating hours, then, Kennedy heard what it meant to be black in a racist society. He also heard their denunciations of the FBI and the administration in general. He at first defended himself but ended up silent and tense.

Clark left the meeting convinced "that this man was an extraordinarily insensitive person, extraordinarily loyal to his brother. . . . I did not leave there feeling that he was a racist, by any means [but he did] not have empathy." Kennedy returned to Justice angry and hurt, yet soon afterward he tried to comprehend more deeply what had happened. He pondered that if he had had Smith's experience, he too might not want to fight for his country. One of Kennedy's "greatest gifts," according to biographer Evan Thomas, "was his capacity to see from the other side."[9] Kennedy eventually reestablished ties with those who attended that meeting. The Baldwin group had alerted him to the intensity of the blacks' frustration and to the need for government to do more. The New York encounter became a defining moment in Robert Kennedy's odyssey, as did the beating of his aide John Seigenthaler in Alabama in 1961, which personalized a developing anger toward segregationists, and the Ole Miss crisis the following fall. As a consequence, in the summer of 1963 no one in the administration felt more strongly about pushing for civil rights legislation.

The desegregation crisis at the University of Alabama came first, however. The Kennedys had heard that spring from the university president that two blacks sought entry for the summer term. The cocky and pugnacious George Wallace, elected governor on a segregationist platform in 1962, opposed their admission and, of course, had considerable support from the Ku Klux Klan, whose national headquarters virtually bordered the university's main campus in Tuscaloosa.[10] Yet the situation in Alabama seemed less ominous than it had at Ole Miss. The university president, its faculty, and its trustees disagreed with Wallace, as did many state officials. Moreover, most newspapers and business establishments turned against the governor. To activate corporate disapproval, "we wrote down . . . the names of every company with . . . more than 100 employees," Robert Kennedy recalled. "All those names were distributed at a Cabinet meeting. . . . Then, we got in touch with the heads of all the other departments and agencies in the government." They made calls to company executives with whom they had associations. Corporate interests understood that any repeat of the crisis at the University of Mississippi would be detrimental to business. Wallace received fifteen to twenty calls a day from concerned businessmen.

By registration day on 11 June, Wallace clearly wanted a way to save face. He planned to stand in the "school house" door before yielding to overwhelming federal force. The Kennedy administration wisely took him seriously; federal troops sat in helicopters at nearby Fort Benning, Georgia. On campus Assistant Attorney General Nicholas Katzenbach went face to face with Wallace, who positioned himself behind a lectern in front of the registration building. After delivering a prepared statement, Wallace refused to step aside. Katzenbach and a small number of marshals returned to their cars, where Vivian Malone and James Hood, the two black students, sat. As planned, the marshals escorted them to the dormitories. President Kennedy thereupon federalized the Alabama National Guard, signaling Wallace that he intended to enforce the court order militarily if necessary. In the afternoon the students registered without opposition, and Alabama became the last southern state to begin the integration of its universities.

That evening President Kennedy delivered a moving address on civil rights, which some considered his best effort. The day before he had given an equally inspiring speech at American University, expressing his desire for "genuine" peace and calling for the reexamination of American attitudes toward the Cold War and the Soviet Union. In a speech devoted almost entirely to foreign policy, he also asked Americans to examine their attitudes toward freedom at home. "In too many of our cities today," Kennedy argued, "the peace is not secure because freedom is incomplete." Consequently, "it is the responsibility of the . . . government to provide and protect that freedom for all of our citizens by all means within [its] authority." That commentary is just one of many indications that Kennedy viewed foreign and domestic matters as inseparable.

Kennedy requested airtime for 11 June to be used only in the event that desegregation at the University of Alabama failed to go well, but his brother persuaded him to speak anyway. As it turned out, Ted Sorensen barely managed to complete the speech in time. Kennedy had constructed his own outline while waiting for the draft, and that effort comprised the concluding portion of the address.

Kennedy became the first president to focus on the moral dimension of civil rights. No longer was government responding solely to restore order, protect lives, or enforce court orders; it was doing so, Kennedy asserted, because it was the right thing to do. "We are confronted primarily with a moral issue," he eloquently continued. "It is as old as the scriptures, and is as clear as the American Constitution. The heart of the question is whether all Americans are to be afforded equal rights and equal opportunities, whether we are going to treat our fellow Americans as we want to be treated. If an American, because his skin is dark, cannot eat lunch in a restaurant open to the public, if he cannot send his children to the best school available, if he cannot vote for the public officials who represent him, if, in short, he cannot enjoy the full and free life which all of us want, then who among us would be content to have the color of his skin changed and stand in his place? Who among us would then be content with the counsels of patience and delay?" Kennedy asked individual Americans to examine their own consciences on this issue. His message moved an overjoyed King who labeled it "eloquent" and "profound." Calling it the "message I had been waiting to hear," Roy Wilkens "fell asleep that night feeling new confidence."

To address the discrimination problem, Kennedy urged private enterprise and municipal leaders to employ blacks and desegregate public facilities. He pointed out that communities suffering from racial disturbances attract less capital and business. After having spent weeks encouraging business leaders and mayors to respond, he realized, however, that some were unwilling to act alone. Therefore, in the 11 June address, he announced a comprehensive civil rights bill to be submitted to Congress in seven days. It represented an admission that the administration needed to go beyond executive action.

The metamorphosis had begun in late 1962, a time of frustration for the administration over growing southern violence, the slowness of civil rights advances, and criticism from virtually all civil rights groups. Even some Republicans flayed the administration for its failure to push civil rights legislation. Kennedy recognized the discontent and perceived a need for action. He proposed a modest bill in February 1963 to improve black voting rights and to assist school desegregation financially.

Yet it took Birmingham to move the civil rights movement to center stage in dramatic fashion—thanks to the leadership of King and other activists and the shocking reaction of Connor, whom Kennedy quipped did as much for civil rights as anyone. As more Americans became appalled by injustice to blacks and as their concern about increasing violence grew, Kennedy felt the need to cool tensions in the South. Otherwise, further demonstrations could lead to more violence, possibly necessitating federal military intervention. Furthermore, if his administration failed to address the moral imperatives of racism, it might lose not only the black community but also the opportunity to respond forcefully to wrongs that Kennedy knew existed.

Kennedy's focus on the moral dimension was not wholly political. The Ole Miss crisis had intellectually altered his view of southern Reconstruction. Given also his own experience with bigotry in the 1960 campaign, he could speak movingly on 11 June 1963 that "no one has been barred on account of his race from fighting or dying for America—there was no 'white' or 'colored' signs on the foxholes or graveyards of battle." That paralleled his statement on religious intolerance in the 1960 West Virginia primary: "Nobody asked me if I was a Catholic when I joined the

United States Navy. Nobody asked my brother [Joe] if he was a Catholic or Protestant before he climbed into an American bomber plane to fly his last mission."

Kennedy strove to shift the activity from street demonstrations to the White House, recognizing that great leaders must seize the moment to take charge. Considering himself an activist president, he placed himself in the tradition of Lincoln, one hundred years after the Emancipation Proclamation. And as Lincoln had drafted the proclamation partly to keep England out of the American Civil War, so too did Kennedy respond in part because racial injustice at home resonated poorly with Third World countries whose support he sought in the battle against communism. In his 11 June speech he referred to the "worldwide struggle to promote and protect the rights of all who wish to be free." Politically, Kennedy's new commitment involved risks because of the likely alienation of southern Democrats and the difficulties of passing civil rights legislation.

"This is a very serious fight," Kennedy acknowledged to King in June. "We're in this up to the neck. The worst trouble of all would be to lose the fight in Congress. . . . A good many programs I care about would go down the drain . . . so we are putting a lot on the line. What is important is that we preserve confidence in the good faith of each other." All of this explains why the president faced so much hesitation from his staff. Vice President Johnson recommended delay until the approval of the tax cut and until the president had laid a better foundation for its passage, including winning over Everett Dirksen (R-Ill.), the Senate minority leader, and other Republicans. He also wished for a joint declaration of support from the three former presidents—Hoover, Truman, and Eisenhower. By speaking in southern states on the incongruity of serving in Vietnam while not being able to buy a cup of coffee in a Mississippi lunchroom, Johnson argued that civil rights be made more of a moral issue. His advice caused Kennedy to focus more on the moral aspects and to lobby Congress more intently. Yet only the attorney general pushed strongly for a civil rights bill in June; he had immense influence in large part because his instincts mirrored the president's.

Robert Kennedy also shaped the writing of the bill. Its key feature, the public accommodations provision, would guarantee citizens equal access to hotels, restaurants, places of amusement, and retail establishments, effectively removing most of the reasons for the recent protest. The bill also further challenged the denial of black voting rights. It gave greater authority to the attorney general in matters of school desegregation and provided for technical and financial assistance to schools undergoing desegregation. It also recognized the need to improve economic opportunities for blacks by expanding various development and training programs and by ending racial discrimination in the workplace. It fell short of what civil rights leaders wanted by failing to provide for a Title III provision that would have authorized the attorney general to institute suits on a variety of civil rights infractions, including school segregation. Nor did the bill include a strong Fair Employment Practice Commission (FEPC) provision with statutory authority to end discrimination on the part of employers and labor unions. Kennedy would only endorse the idea, which was incorporated into a separate nonadministration proposal.

For the remainder of Kennedy's life, debate swirled around the nature of the bill. The problem became more acute after the liberal-dominated House Judiciary Subcommittee loaded it down with FEPC, Title III, a broader public accommodation provision, and other clauses. In the process subcommittee liberals alienated the Republican congressional leadership that initially had expressed a willingness to work with the administration. Robert Kennedy angrily referred to such liberals as obstructionist "sons of bitches," accusing them of "being in love with death."

Domestically, nothing occupied the administration more that summer and fall than civil rights. The president staged several White House meetings involving White House, congressional, and civil rights leaders to work out an acceptable compromise. He consulted Eisenhower, who thought an omnibus bill a mistake but expressed a willingness to cooperate. All of this resulted in an informal agreement to work closely with the Republican leadership to modify the bill in the House Judiciary Committee. House Minority Leader Charles Halleck and William M. McCulloch (Ohio), ranking Republican on the Judiciary Committee, who Kennedy believed could deliver sixty house colleagues, became the key people. They both sought a reasonable bill.

White House tapes of those meetings reveal the president's developing relationship with Halleck and McCulloch over civil rights. The Kennedys, however, never did understand why some Republicans cooperated so willingly. President Kennedy conceded that conscience motivated McCulloch but "trying to touch Charlie is like trying to pick up a greased pig." Yet Halleck's biographer echoed Halleck's assertion that civil rights was "not a political question but a matter of what's right." At any rate, Halleck's surprising support soon invited strong criticism from the Republican rank and file. Meanwhile, the president had calculated that forty-four senators favored the administration's bill and forty opposed, not nearly enough for cloture. He consequently focused on twenty-five swing votes, most of them Midwest Republicans, figuring that probably only Senate Minority Leader Dirksen's support could win them over. Kennedy had a close relationship with Dirksen, whom he wooed through patronage and by not strongly opposing his reelection in 1962. More than likely, he would have come over had Kennedy lived; but just as likely, this would have come at the expense of FEPC, Title III, or perhaps a broad accommodation section.

In the House, as it turned out, Halleck directed the bipartisan measure out of the Judiciary Committee in October. At this stage the legislative proposal remained stronger than the administration's original effort since it provided for a watered-down Title III and a permanent Civil Rights Commission. It figured to clear the House Rules Committee, despite the delaying tactics of Chairman Howard Smith. Kennedy expected the House to pass it in early 1964. The Senate vote on cloture would supposedly occur sometime that spring. After Kennedy's assassination the Johnson administration succeeded in getting the bill through the Senate on 10 June 1964. It seems clear that Kennedy's efforts, not his death, had contributed most to its passage. Had he lived, there would have been a law, even though different content and time frames would have resulted.

In Kennedy's last months the administration had also become entangled in two related civil rights issues involving Martin Luther King Jr. and the March on Washington. In both instances the administration sought to impose more control over the civil rights movement. At the same time, the Kennedys remained somewhat suspicious of King, having received reports from FBI Director Hoover that King had been consorting with known Communists. Hoover, believing that Communists had first infiltrated the civil rights movement in the mid-1950s and hoping to use that concern to break the movement, charged that Stanley Levison, a New York lawyer and longtime King adviser and speechwriter, was a key figure in the Soviet intelligence apparatus in the United States. Without obtaining conclusive evidence from the bureau, the attorney general authorized the wiretapping of Levison's office telephone and eventually King's office and home phones after King refused to break completely with his friend and adviser. Hoover also proceeded to bug King indiscriminately.

In June 1963 the president spoke to King in the White House Rose Garden about the danger of associating with Levison. Kennedy warned that the FBI had King's associates under electronic surveillance, causing King to conclude that Kennedy's stroll in the garden must have reflected the president's own fears of Hoover. While extensive wiretapping failed to reveal evidence of Communist links to any civil rights activist, the taps inexcusably continued until 1965.

This episode reveals more than the Kennedys' desire to protect themselves, civil rights legislation, and King; it shows their continued belief in an internal Communist menace. Robert Kennedy thought Levison was an important Communist who had a dangerous influence on King, and he was particularly troubled that King laughed about such allegations. Even though David Garrow's study on the FBI confirms Levison's early Communist affiliations, Garrow reveals that Levison broke with the movement in 1955 and that the bureau had no firsthand evidence that he had resumed those ties during the Kennedy era. Yet Hoover continued to probe indiscreetly into King's private life, a practice he first had begun against others during the 1930s. Meanwhile, Robert Kennedy continued to advise the president that King remained a potential problem.

The black leader's planned march on Washington in the summer of 1963 posed additional vexations. President Kennedy initially seemed as unenthusiastic about this effort as Franklin Roosevelt had been about a similar planned march in 1941. The administration had two concerns: the march would be directed against the government for not moving faster on civil rights, and it would jeopardize the civil rights bill. "We want success in Congress," the president said to civil rights leaders on 22 June, "not just a big show at the Capitol. Some of these people are looking for an excuse to be against us. I don't want to give any of them a chance to say, 'Yes, I'm for the bill, but I'm damned if I'll vote for it at the point of a gun.'" King argued that he had "never engaged in any direct action movement which did not seem ill timed. Some people thought Birmingham ill timed." "Including the Attorney General," Kennedy responded.

Despite the advice of several congressmen, Kennedy wisely endorsed the march after ensuring that it would serve the administration's purpose. In several ways he contributed to its colossal success. He worked closely with Walter Reuther, the autoworkers' union leader, to involve the labor movement, churches, and other groups, making it interracial. The attorney general put one staffer on the project full time for four weeks to guarantee that toilets, food, drinks, and other essentials would be provided. The administration had also induced the movement's leaders to shift the program from the Capitol to the Lincoln Memorial. Even the speeches came under indirect scrutiny by the administration, as march organizers forced John Lewis, chairman of SNCC, to tone down his denunciation of the administration's civil rights bill. It is little wonder that critics charged Kennedy with co-opting the movement and that black militant Malcolm X called it "The Farce on Washington."

Yet a quarter of a million people came to Washington on 28 August in an upbeat, orderly procession of interracial solidarity. They were moved by the music of Joan Baez ("We Shall Overcome"); Peter, Paul and Mary; Bob Dylan; and Mahalia Jackson and by the addresses of so many others. Perhaps King's greatest speech stirred them most. Standing before the Lincoln Memorial, as a bright sun glistened on the reflecting pool and upon thousands of people around it, he expressed that immortal ideal of equality for all. Afterward King and the other march leaders visited the White House for a meeting and refreshments. Kennedy greeted them by saying, "I have a dream." Never before had the civil rights movement evoked such a positive image of goodwill, strengthening popular support for civil rights legislation.

The year's civil rights successes had culminated in the March on Washington. In his remaining days Kennedy had reason to take pride in those recent advances, including the desegregation of the University of Alabama, the Birmingham agreement, the Kennedys' sustained dialogue with private industry and local governments to end discriminatory practices, and the most comprehensive civil rights bill in American history, a clear indication that the president had come full circle regarding his campaign promises. These, along with the earlier gains, had grudgingly mollified many civil rights leaders. Even King probably would have endorsed Kennedy in 1964. Of course, SNCC, CORE, and the Black Muslims remained another matter. John Lewis of CORE spoke for many when he called Kennedy's civil rights bill "too little, too late." Years later black historian Vincent Harding more thoughtfully expressed the movement's differences with the Kennedys when he categorized them as liberals who sought reform by working with the southern power structure. Even though the Kennedys sought to avoid a "tearing of the [societal] fabric," such tearing, Harding contended, "was absolutely necessary for something real to take place."

Harris Wofford compared Kennedy to Abraham Lincoln, who, unlike the abolitionists, saw black rights in the broader context of other conflicting goals and problems. Lincoln too had come under fire for temporizing and limiting the scope of his Emancipation Proclamation. As agents of change both Kennedy and Lincoln stood well behind advancing social forces, but their restraining actions made those changes more acceptable. In Kennedy's case, he tried to nudge civil rights forward without severing ties with the white South. In Kennedy's lifetime, no American president—including Franklin Roosevelt and Harry Truman—could have served the black cause better.

As a result, Kennedy's support in Dixie eroded substantially. In a September Gallup poll, although 89 percent of blacks approved of his presidency, 70 percent of southern whites thought that he was pushing integration too fast, compared to 50 percent of all Americans who agreed. His approval rating in the South dropped from 60 percent in March to 44 percent in September. A realignment was emerging that would eventually make the Democratic South a bastion of Republicanism. Kennedy anticipated its implications, knowing that increased black votes in Dixie would not make up for southern white disaffections to the GOP. He remained hopeful that increased northern support would compensate for the loss, particularly if the Republicans nominated archconservative Barry Goldwater in 1964. In his last days Kennedy viewed the future with confidence, bolstered by a 62 percent overall approval rating in September and encouraged by a belief that racial progress seemed inevitable.

CONCLUSION

John Kennedy served less time than any other elected president in the twentieth century, with the exception of Warren G. Harding. As already indicated, that fact alone affected his presidency. Many of his programs were still pending at the time of his unexpected death, some of which would surely have passed had he lived. He also faced the constraints of an antiwelfare coalition in Congress that had plagued Democratic presidents since 1938. The highly rated Truman proved no more effective in combating it despite having a much greater election mandate than Kennedy. Moreover, an antiliberal backlash that reached its peak in the Reagan era has further undercut Kennedy's domestic goals and accomplishments. Consequently, to reach a judicious evaluation of Kennedy's domestic presidency, ideology must be taken out of the equation.

Two key questions can be asked about Kennedy's domestic performance. To what extent did he achieve the goals he had set in the 1960 campaign and in various messages to Congress and the American people? And did he leave the country in better shape as a result of that abbreviated tenure?

In 1960 candidate Kennedy had criticized the Eisenhower administration for ignoring urban deterioration, an emerging civil rights movement, a stagnating economy in which the growth rate had fallen to a modest 2.5 percent, and a balance of payments deficit that had drained the gold reserves. Poverty afflicted the elderly, blacks, Hispanics, and rural Americans. Also, agriculture, despite huge subsidies to major commercial farmers, and public education both suffered vexatious reversals. In the face of Soviet scientific advances, particularly in space, the American spirit also seemed to be flagging.

Kennedy promised Americans a dynamic presidency—one that would formulate and fight for legislation and provide moral and political leadership. In the tradition of his Democratic predecessors, he pledged to alleviate economic stagnation, rising unemployment, wide scale poverty, and urban squalor. He proposed expanded coverage and increases in Social Security benefits and the minimum wage, a housing program under a new Housing and Urban Affairs Department, urban renewal, tax incentives, federal aid to education, and health care for the aged. He also pledged to end racial discrimination, combat the farm problem, and preserve America's national resources. All of this, he acknowledged, would not be finished in the "first thousand days" nor "in the life of this administration."

Kennedy fell far short of his ambitious domestic objectives; he failed to implement his key programs for civil rights, medical assistance for the aged, education, and poverty. Most disconcerting was Kennedy's initial wavering leadership in advancing civil rights. Largely in response to intense pressure from black activists, however, he did morally commit the presidency to the movement by 1963—resulting in the Civil Rights Act of 1964. In the end, no president before him had more fully embraced the black cause.

Moreover, Kennedy's policies, culminating in the tax cut of 1964, ended economic stagnation and reduced unemployment and the balance of payments deficit, making the 1960s a good time to live for most Americans. Kennedy also provided job training programs, updated traditional New Deal commitments such as Social Security and the minimum wage, and reduced job discrimination against women. Despite failing to obtain comprehensive agricultural legislation, he eased farm problems and extended rural assistance. He responded to the needs of juvenile delinquency and mental retardation, implemented the first significant housing program since 1949, and began urban renewal. He also accomplished some limited educational objectives, thus paving the way for Johnson's sweeping reforms of 1965. Through such initiatives as the space program and the Peace Corps, and through inspiring rhetoric, the national spirit was changing too. Even though several major domestic objectives remained unfulfilled, Kennedy left the country better off than he found it in 1961. Partly because of Kennedy's efforts, the national mood seemed more receptive to change by 1963. Arguably, these last two points represent Kennedy's greatest domestic legacy.

Of the nine presidents who served less than one full term, Kennedy alone was ranked above average in the 1982 Murray-Blessing presidential evaluation poll of some thousand scholars, a ranking that I believe he deserves. Even though Kennedy ranked eleventh in domestic policy, he slipped to eighteenth overall in the 1996 *Chicago Sun-Times* survey of fifty-eight presidential scholars, several of whom have written books on Kennedy. Four years later, in the same sponsored survey, he slipped one more position both in the overall and domestic rankings.[11] Only time will tell whether his abbreviated domestic record will continue to contribute to his declining positive image.

NOTES

I wish to thank the University Press of Kansas for permission to use material from my 1991 work, *The Presidency of John F. Kennedy*. Unless otherwise noted, the sources for all quotations can be found in that book or in the *Public Papers of the Presidents of the United States: John F. Kennedy*.

1. The recent public opinion polls include the Marist poll of 1993 in which 21 percent listed Kennedy as their favorite executive followed by Lincoln at 20 percent; a 1996 *New York Times*/CBS poll overwhelmingly ranked Kennedy number one on the question, "Who would you choose to run the country?" In a February 2001 Gallup poll Kennedy fell to second place (15 percent to Ronald Reagan's 18 percent) in response to the question, "Who do your regard as the greatest United

States President?" For cover stories, *Time,* 17 November 1997, for example, featured Seymour Hersh's *Dark Side of Camelot,* and *Newsweek,* 14 August 2000, Evan Thomas's *Robert Kennedy: His Life.* No recent Kennedy tragedy commanded more attention than John F. Kennedy Jr.'s, death in July 1999; he appeared on the cover of virtually every news magazine.

2. See, for example, the University of Illinois at Chicago/*Chicago Sun Times* Survey on the American Presidency published in the *Chicago Sun Times* on 1 October 2000.

3. The bibliographical data for books and historians mentioned in the text can be found in the selected readings.

4. For Kennedy's trade policy, see Thomas W. Zeiler, "Meeting the European Challenge: The Common Market and Trade Policy," in *Kennedy: The New Frontier Revisited,* ed. Mark J. White (London: Macmillan Press, 1998), 132–54.

5. See Thomas G. Smith, "John F. Kennedy, Stewart Udall, and New Frontier Conservation," *Pacific Historical Review,* 64 (August 1995), 329–62 and Thomas Clarkin, *Federal Indian Policy in the Kennedy and Johnson Administrations, 1961–1969* (Albuquerque: University of New Mexico Press, 2001).

6. Most of Galbraith's perceptive memoranda can be found in John Kenneth Galbraith, *Letters to Kennedy* (Cambridge, Mass.: Harvard University Press, 1998).

7. White House Tape Recording #63, John Fitzgerald Kennedy Library, Boston, Massachusetts.

8. For an account of two African Americans, Andrew Hatcher and Frank Reeves, who served on Kennedy's White House staff, see James N. Giglio, "The Tide Turns: Kennedy," *American Visions* (February/March 1995), 40–41.

9. Evan Thomas, *Robert Kennedy: His Life* (New York: Simon and Schuster, 2000), 245.

10. For the most recent account on Wallace and the University of Alabama crisis, see Dan T. Carter, *The Politics of Rage: George Wallace, the Origins of New Conservatism, and the Transformation of American Politics* (New York: Simon and Schuster, 1995), 133–55.

11. *Chicago Sun Times,* 18 November 1996; *Chicago Sun Times,* 1 October 2000.

Documents

1

KENNEDY INAUGURAL ADDRESS
20 JANUARY 1961

We observe today not a victory of party but a celebration of freedom—symbolizing an end as well as a beginning—signifying renewal as well as change. For I have sworn before you and Almighty God the same solemn oath our forebears prescribed nearly a century and three quarters ago.

The world is very different now. For man holds in his mortal hands the power to abolish all forms of human poverty and all forms of human life. And yet the same revolutionary beliefs for which our forebears fought are still at issue around the globe—the belief that the rights of man come not from the generosity of the state but from the hand of God.

We dare not forget today that we are the heirs of that first revolution. Let the word go forth from this time and place, to friend and foe alike, that the torch has been passed to a new generation of Americans—born in this century, tempered by war, disciplined by a hard and bitter peace, proud of our ancient heritage—and unwilling to witness or permit the slow undoing of those human rights to which this nation has always been committed, and to which we are committed today at home and around the world.

Source: John F. Kennedy, *Public Papers of the Presidents of the United States: John F. Kennedy, 1961,* vol. 1. (Washington, D.C.: GPO, 1961), 1–3.

Let every nation know, whether it wishes us well or ill, that we shall pay any price, bear any burden, meet any hardship, support any friend, oppose any foe to assure the survival and the success of liberty.

This much we pledge—and more.

To those old allies whose cultural and spiritual origins we share, we pledge the loyalty of faithful friends. United, there is little we cannot do in a host of cooperative ventures. Divided, there is little we can do—for we dare not meet a powerful challenge at odds and split asunder.

To those new states whom we welcome to the ranks of the free, we pledge our word that one form of colonial control shall not have passed away merely to be replaced by a far more iron tyranny. We shall not always expect to find them supporting our view. But we shall always hope to find them strongly supporting their own freedom—and to remember that, in the past, those who foolishly sought power by riding the back of the tiger ended up inside.

To those peoples in the huts and villages of half the globe struggling to break the bonds of mass misery, we pledge our best efforts to help them help themselves, for whatever period is required—not because the communists may be doing it, not because we seek their votes, but because it is right. If a free society cannot help the many who are poor, it cannot save the few who are rich.

To our sister republics South of our border, we offer a special pledge—to convert our good words into good deeds—in a new alliance for progress—to assist free men and free governments in casting off the chains of poverty. But this peaceful revolution of hope cannot become the prey of hostile powers. Let all our neighbors know that we shall join with them to oppose aggression or subversion anywhere in the Americas. And let every other power know that this Hemisphere intends to remain the master of its own house.

To that world assembly of sovereign states, the United Nations, our last best hope in an age where the instruments of war have far outpaced the instruments of peace, we renew our pledge of support—to prevent it from becoming merely a forum for invective—to strengthen its shield of the new and the weak—and to enlarge the area in which its writ may run.

Finally, to those nations who would make themselves our adversary, we offer not a pledge but a request: that both sides begin anew the quest for peace, before the dark powers of destruction unleashed by science engulf all humanity in planned or accidental self-destruction.

We dare not tempt them with weakness. For only when our arms are sufficient beyond doubt can we be certain beyond doubt that they will never be employed.

But neither can two great and powerful groups of nations take comfort from our present course—both sides overburdened by the cost of modern weapons, both rightly alarmed by the steady spread of the deadly atom, yet both racing to alter that uncertain balance of terror that stays the hand of mankind's final war.

So let us begin anew—remembering on both sides that civility is not a sign of weakness, and sincerity is always subject to proof. Let us never negotiate out of fear. But let us never fear to negotiate.

Let both sides explore what problems unite us instead of belaboring those problems which divide us.

Let both sides, for the first time, formulate serious and precise proposals for the inspection and control of arms—and bring the absolute power to destroy other nations under the absolute control of all nations.

Let both sides seek to invoke the wonders of science instead of its terrors. Together let us explore the stars, conquer the deserts, eradicate disease, tap the ocean depths and encourage the arts and commerce.

Let both sides unite to heed in all corners of the earth the command of Isaiah—to "undo the heavy burdens . . . (and) let the oppressed go free."

And if a beach head of cooperation may push back the jungle of suspicion, let both sides join in creating a new endeavor, not a new balance of power, but a new world of law, where the strong are just and the weak secure and the peace preserved.

All this will not be finished in the first one hundred days. Nor will it be finished in the first one thousand days, nor in the life of this Administration, nor even perhaps in our lifetime on this planet. But let us begin.

In your hands, my fellow citizens, more than mine, will rest the final success or failure of our course. Since this country was founded, each generation of Americans has been summoned to give testimony to its national loyalty. The graves of young Americans who answered the call to service surround the globe.

Now the trumpet summons us again—not as a call to bear arms, though arms we need—not as a call to battle, though embattled we are—but a call to bear the burden of a long twilight struggle, year in and year out, "rejoicing in hope, patient in tribulation"—a struggle against the common enemies of man: tyranny, poverty, disease and war itself.

Can we forge against these enemies a grand and global alliance, North and South, East and West, that can assure a more fruitful life for all mankind? Will you join in that historic effort?

In the long history of the world, only a few generations have been granted the role of defending freedom in its hour of maximum danger. I do not shrink from this responsibility—I welcome it. I do not believe that any of us would exchange places with any other people or any other generation. The energy, the faith, the devotion which we bring to this endeavor will light our country and all who serve it—and the glow from that fire can truly light the world.

And so, my fellow Americans: ask not what your country can do for you—ask what you can do for your country.

My fellow citizens of the world: ask not what America will do for you, but what together we can do for the freedom of man.

Finally, whether you are citizens of America or citizens of the world, ask of us here the same high standards of strength and sacrifice which we ask of you. With a good conscience our only sure reward, with history the final judge of our deeds, let us go forth to lead the land we love, asking His blessing and His help, but knowing that here on earth God's work must truly be our own.

2

EXCERPT FROM COMMENCEMENT ADDRESS AT YALE UNIVERSITY 11 JUNE 1962

Let me begin by expressing my appreciation for the very deep honor that you have conferred upon me. As General de Gaulle occasionally acknowledges America to be the daughter of Europe, so I am pleased to come to Yale, the daughter of Harvard. It might be said now that I have the best of both worlds, a Harvard education and a Yale degree.

I am particularly glad to become a Yale man because as I think about my troubles, I find that a lot of them have come from other Yale men. Among businessmen, I have had a minor disagreement with Roger Blough, of the law school class of 1931, and I have had some complaints, too, from my friend Henry Ford, of the class of 1940. In journalism I seem to have a difference with John Hay Whitney, of the class of 1926—and sometimes I also displease Henry Luce of the class of 1920, not to mention also William F. Buckley, Jr., of the class of 1950. I even have some trouble with my Yale advisers. I get along with them, but I am not always sure how they get along with each other.

I have the warmest feelings for Chester Bowles of the class of 1924, and for Dean Acheson of the class of 1915, and my assistant, McGeorge

Source: John F. Kennedy, *Public Papers of the Presidents of the United States: John F. Kennedy, 1962*, vol. 2. (Washington, D.C.: GPO, 1962), 470–75.

Bundy, of the class of 1940. But I am not 100 percent sure that these three wise and experienced Yale men wholly agree with each other on every issue.

So this administration which aims at peaceful cooperation among all Americans has been the victim of a certain natural pugnacity developed in this city among Yale men. Now that I, too, am a Yale man, it is time for peace. Last week at West Point, in the historic tradition of that Academy, I availed myself of the powers of Commander in Chief to remit all sentences of offending cadets. In that same spirit and in the historic tradition of Yale, let me now offer to smoke the clay pipe of friendship with all of my brother Elis, and I hope that they may be friends not only with me but even with each other.

In any event, I am very glad to be here and as a new member of the club, I have been checking to see what earlier links existed between the institution of the Presidency and Yale. I found that a member of the class of 1878, William Howard Taft, served one term in the White House as preparation for becoming a member of this faculty. And a graduate of 1804, John C. Calhoun, regarded the Vice Presidency, quite naturally, as too lowly a status for a Yale alumnus—and became the only man in history to ever resign that office.

Calhoun in 1804 and Taft in 1878 graduated into a world very different from ours today. They and their contemporaries spent their entire careers stretching over 40 years in grappling with a few dramatic issues on which the Nation was sharply and emotionally divided, issues that occupied the attention of a generation at a time: the national bank, the disposal of the public lands, nullification or union, freedom or slavery, gold or silver. Today these old sweeping issues very largely have disappeared. The central domestic issues of our time are more subtle and less simple. They relate not to basic clashes of philosophy or ideology but to ways and means of reaching common goals—to research for sophisticated solutions to complex and obstinate issues. The world of Calhoun, the world of Taft had its own hard problems and notable challenges. But its problems are not our problems. Their age is not our age. As every past generation has had to disenthrall itself from an inheritance of truisms and stereotypes, so in our own time we must move on from the reassuring repetition of stale phrases to a new, difficult, but essential confrontation with reality.

For the great enemy of the truth is very often not the lie—deliberate, contrived, and dishonest—but the myth—persistent, persuasive, and unrealistic. Too often we hold fast to the cliches of our forebears. We subject all facts to a prefabricated set of interpretations. We enjoy the comfort of opinion without the discomfort of thought.

Mythology distracts us everywhere—in government as in business, in politics as in economics, in foreign affairs as in domestic affairs. But today I want to particularly consider the myth and reality in our national economy. In recent months many have come to feel, as I do, that the dialog between the parties—between business and government, between the government and the public—is clogged by illusion and platitude and fails to reflect the true realities of contemporary American society.

I speak of these matters here at Yale because of the self-evident truth that a great university is always enlisted against the spread of illusion and on the side of reality. No one has said it more clearly than your President Griswold: "Liberal learning is both a safeguard against false ideas of freedom and a source of true ones." Your role as university men, whatever your calling, will be to increase each new generation's grasp of its duties.

There are three great areas of our domestic affairs in which, today, there is a danger that illusion may prevent effective action. They are, first, the question of the size and the shape of government's responsibilities; second, the question of public fiscal policy; and third, the matter of confidence, business confidence or public confidence, or simply confidence in America. I want to talk about all three, and I want to talk about them carefully and dispassionately—and I emphasize that I am concerned here not with political debate but with finding ways to separate false problems from real ones.

If a contest in angry argument were forced upon it, no administration could shrink from response, and history does not suggest that American Presidents are totally without resources in an engagement forced upon them because of hostility in one sector of society. But in the wider national interest, we need not partisan wrangling but common concentration on common problems. I come here to this distinguished university to ask you to join in this great task.

Let us take first the question of the size and shape of government. The myth here is that government is big, and bad—and steadily getting bigger and worse. Obviously this myth has some excuse for existence. It is true that in recent history each new administration has spent much more money than its predecessor. Thus President Roosevelt outspent President Hoover, and with allowances for the special case of the Second World War,

President Truman outspent President Roosevelt. Just to prove that this was not a partisan matter, President Eisenhower then outspent President Truman by the handsome figure of $182 billion. It is even possible, some think, that this trend may continue.

But does it follow from this that big government is growing relatively bigger? It does not—for the fact is for the last 15 years, the Federal Government—and also the Federal debt—and also the Federal bureaucracy—have grown less rapidly than the economy as a whole. If we leave defense and space expenditures aside, the Federal Government since the Second World War has expanded less than any other major sector of our national life—less than industry, less than commerce, less than agriculture, less than higher education, and very much less than the noise about big government.

The truth about big government is the truth about any other great activity—it is complex. Certainly it is true that size brings dangers—but it is also true that size can bring benefits. Here at Yale which has contributed so much to our national progress in science and medicine, it may be proper for me to mention one great and little noticed expansion of government which has brought strength to our whole society—the new role of our Federal Government as the major patron of research in science and in medicine. Few people realize that in 1961, in support of all university research in science and medicine, three dollars out of every four came from the Federal Government. I need hardly point out that this has taken place without undue enlargement of Government control—that American scientists remain second to none in their independence and in their individualism.

I am not suggesting that Federal expenditures cannot bring some measure of control. The whole thrust of Federal expenditures in agriculture have been related by purpose and design to control, as a means of dealing with the problems created by our farmers and our growing productivity. Each sector, my point is, of activity must be approached on its own merits and in terms of specific national needs. Generalities in regard to Federal expenditures, therefore, can be misleading—each case, science, urban renewal, education, agriculture, natural resources, each case must be determined on its merits if we are to profit from our unrivaled ability to combine the strength of public and private purpose.

Next, let us turn to the problem of our fiscal policy. Here the myths are legion and the truth hard to find. But let me take as a prime example the problem of the Federal budget. We persist in measuring our Federal fiscal integrity today by the conventional or administrative budget—with results which would be regarded as absurd in any business firm—in any country of Europe—or in any careful assessment of the reality of our national finances. The administrative budget has sound administrative uses . But for wider purposes it is less helpful. It omits our special trust funds and the effect that they have on our economy; it neglects changes in assets or inventories. It cannot tell a loan from a straight expenditure—and worst of all it cannot distinguish between operating expenditures and long term investment.

This budget in relation to the great problems of Federal fiscal policy which are basic to our economy in 1962, is not simply irrelevant; it can be actively misleading. And yet there is a mythology that measures all of our national soundness or unsoundness on the single simple basis of this same annual administrative budget. If our Federal budget is to serve not the debate but the country, we must and will find ways of clarifying this area of discourse.

Still in the area of fiscal policy, let me say a word about deficits. The myth persists that Federal deficits create inflation and budget surpluses prevent it. Yet sizeable budget surpluses after the war did not prevent inflation, and persistent deficits for the last several years have not upset our basic price stability. Obviously deficits are sometimes dangerous—and so are surpluses. But honest assessment plainly requires a more sophisticated view than the old and automatic cliche that deficits automatically bring inflation.

There are myths also about our public debt. It is widely supposed that this debt is growing at a dangerously rapid rate. In fact, both the debt per person and the debt as a proportion of our gross national product have declined sharply since the Second World War. In absolute terms the national debt since the end of World War II has increased only 8 percent, while private debt was increasing 305 percent, and the debts of State and local governments— on whom people frequently suggest we should place additional burdens— the debts of State and local governments have increased 378 percent. Moreover, debts, public and private, are neither good or bad, in and of themselves. Borrowing can lead to over-extension and collapse—but it can also lead to expansion and strength. There is no single, simple slogan in this field that we can trust.

Finally, I come to the problem of confidence. Confidence is a matter of myth and also a matter of truth—and this time let me take the truth of the matter first.

It is true—and of high importance—that the prosperity of this country depends on the assurance that all major elements within it will live up to their responsibilities. If business were to neglect its obligations to the public, if labor were blind to all public responsibility, above all, if government were to abandon its obvious—and statutory-duty of watchful concern for our economic health—if any of these things should happen, then confidence might well be weakened and the danger of stagnation would increase. This is the true issue of confidence.

But there is also the false issue—and its simple form is the assertion that any and all unfavorable turns of the speculative wheel—however temporary and however plainly speculative in character—are the result, and I quote, "a lack of confidence in the national administration." This I must tell you, while comforting, is not wholly true. Worse, it obscures the reality—which is also simple. The solid ground of mutual confidence is the necessary partnership of government with all of the sectors of our society in the steady quest for economic progress.

Corporate plans are not based on a political confidence in party leaders but on an economic confidence in the Nation's ability to invest and produce and consume. Business had full confidence in the administrations in power in 1929, 1954, 1958, and 1960—but this was not enough to prevent recession when business lacked full confidence in the economy. What matters is the capacity of the Nation as a whole to deal with its economic problems and its opportunities.

The stereotypes I have been discussing distract our attention and divide our effort. These stereotypes do our Nation a disservice, not just because they are exhausted and irrelevant, but above all because they are misleading—because they stand in the way of the solution of hard and complicated facts. It is not new that past debates should obscure present realities. But the damage of such a false dialogue is greater today than ever before simply because today the safety of all the world—the very future of freedom—depends as never before upon the sensible and clearheaded management of the domestic affairs of the United States.

The real issues of our time are rarely as dramatic as the issues of Calhoun. The differences today are usually matters of degree. And we cannot understand and attack our contemporary problems in 1962 if we are bound by traditional labels and wornout slogans of an earlier era. But the unfortunate fact of the matter is that our rhetoric has not kept pace with the speed of social and economic change. Our political debates, our public discourse—on current domestic and economic issues—too often bear little or no relation to the actual problems the United States faces.

What is at stake in our economic decisions today is not some grand warfare of rival ideologies which will sweep the country with passion but the practical management of a modern economy. What we need is not labels and cliches but more basic discussion of the sophisticated and technical questions involved in keeping a great economic machinery moving ahead.

The national interest lies in high employment and steady expansion of output, in stable prices, and a strong dollar. The declaration of such an objective is easy; their attainment in an intricate and interdependent economy and world is a little more difficult. To attain them, we require not some automatic response but hard thought. Let me end by suggesting a few of the real questions on our national agenda.

First, how can our budget and tax policies supply adequate revenues and preserve our balance of payments position without slowing up our economic growth?

Two, how are we to set our interest rates and regulate the flow of money in ways which will stimulate the economy at home, without weakening the dollar abroad? Given the spectrum of our domestic and international responsibilities, what should be the mix between fiscal and monetary policy?

Let me give several examples from my experience of the complexity of these matters and how political labels and ideological approaches are irrelevant to the solution.

Last week, a distinguished graduate of this school, Senator Proxmire, of the class of 1938, who is ordinarily regarded as a liberal Democrat, suggested that we should follow in meeting our economic problems a stiff fiscal policy, with emphasis on budget balance and an easy monetary policy with low interest rates in order to keep our economy going. In the same week, the Bank for International Settlement in Basel, Switzerland, a conservative organization representing the central bankers of Europe suggested that the appropriate economic policy in the United States should be the very opposite; that we should follow a flexible budget policy, as in Europe, with deficits when the economy is down and a high monetary policy on interest rates, as in Europe, in order to control inflation and protect goals. Both may be right or wrong. It will depend on many different factors.

The point is that this is basically an administrative or executive problem in which political labels or cliches do not give us a solution.

A well-known business journal this morning, as I journeyed to New Haven, raised the prospects that a further budget deficit would bring inflation and encourage the flow of gold. We have had several budget deficits beginning with a $12.5 billion deficit in 1958, and it is true that in the fall of 1960 we had a gold dollar loss running at $5 billion annually. This would seem to prove the case that a deficit produces inflation and that we lose gold, yet there was no inflation following the deficit of 1958 nor has there been inflation since then.

Our wholesale price index since 1958 has remained completely level in spite of several deficits, because the loss of gold has been due to other reasons: price instability, relative interest rates, relative export-import balances, national security expenditures—all the rest.

Let me give you a third and final example. At the World Bank meeting in September, a number of American bankers attending predicted to their European colleagues that because of the fiscal 1962 budget deficit, there would be a strong inflationary pressure on the dollar and a loss of gold. Their predictions of inflation were shared by many in business and helped push the market up. The recent reality of noninflation helped bring it down. We have had no inflation because we have had other factors in our economy that have contributed to price stability.

I do not suggest that the Government is right and they are wrong. The fact of the matter is in the Federal Reserve Board and in the administration this fall, a similar view was held by many well-informed and disinterested men that inflation was the major problem that we would face in the winter of 1962. But it was not. What I do suggest is that these problems are endlessly complicated and yet they go to the future of this country and its ability to prove to the world what we believe it must prove.

I am suggesting that the problems of fiscal and monetary policies in the sixties as opposed to the kinds of problems we faced in the thirties demand subtle challenges for which technical answers, not political answers, must be provided. These are matters upon which government and business may and in many cases will disagree. They are certainly matters that government and business should be discussing in the most sober, dispassionate, and careful way if we are to maintain the kind of vigorous economy upon which our country depends.

How can we develop and sustain strong and stable world markets for basic commodities without unfairness to the consumer and without undue stimulus to the producer? How can we generate the buying power which can consume what we produce on our farms and in our factories? How can we take advantage of the miracles of automation with the great demand that it will put upon highly skilled labor and yet offer employment to the half million of unskilled school dropouts each year who enter the labor market, eight million of them in the 1960's?

How do we eradicate the barriers which separate substantial minorities of our citizens from access to education and employment on equal terms with the rest?

How, in sum, can we make our free economy work at full capacity—that is, provide adequate profits for enterprise, adequate wages for labor, adequate utilization of plant, and opportunity for all?

These are the problems that we should be talking about—that the political parties and the various groups in our country should be discussing. They cannot be solved by incantations from the forgotten past. But the example of Western Europe shows that they are capable of solution—that governments, and many of them are conservative governments, prepared to face technical problems without ideological preconceptions, can coordinate the elements of a national economy and bring about growth and prosperity—a decade of it. . . .

3

EXCERPT FROM ADDRESS AT RICE UNIVERSITY ON THE NATION'S SPACE EFFORT 12 SEPTEMBER 1962

We meet at a college noted for knowledge, in a city noted for progress, in a State noted for strength, and we stand in need of all three, for we meet in an hour of change and challenge, in a decade of hope and fear, in an age of both knowledge and ignorance. The greater our knowledge increases, the greater our ignorance unfolds. . . .

Those who came before us made certain that this country rode the first waves of the industrial revolutions, the first waves of modern invention, and the first wave of nuclear power, and this generation does not intend to founder in the backwash of the coming age of space. We mean to be a part of it—we mean to lead it. For the eyes of the world now look into space, to the moon and to the planets beyond, and we have vowed that we shall not see it governed by a hostile flag of conquest, but by a banner of freedom and peace. We have vowed that we shall not see space filled with weapons of mass destruction, but with instruments of knowledge and understanding.

Yet the vows of this nation can only be fulfilled if we in this Nation are first, and, therefore, we intend to be first. In short, our leadership in sci-

Source: John F. Kennedy, *Public Papers of the Presidents of the United States: John F. Kennedy, 1962*, vol. 2. (Washington, D.C.: GPO, 1962), 668–69.

ence and in industry, our hopes for peace and security, our obligations to ourselves as well as others, all require us to make this effort, to solve these mysteries, to solve them for the good of all men, and to become the world's leading space-faring nation.

We set sail on this new sea because there is new knowledge to be gained, and new rights to be won, and they must be won and used for the progress of all people. For space science, like nuclear science and all technology, has no conscience of its own. Whether it will become a force for good or ill depends on man, and only if the United States occupies a position of pre-eminence can we help decide whether this new ocean will be a sea of peace or a new terrifying theater of war. I do not say that we should or will go unprotected against the hostile misuse of space any more than we go unprotected against the hostile use of land or sea, but I do say that space can be explored and mastered without feeding the fires of war, without repeating the mistakes that man has made in extending his writ around this globe of ours.

There is no strife, no prejudice, no national conflict in outer space as yet. Its hazards are hostile to us all. Its conquest deserves the best of all mankind, and its opportunity for peaceful cooperation may never come again. But why, some say, the moon? Why choose this as our goal? And they may well ask why climb the highest mountain. Why, 35 years ago, fly the Atlantic? Why does Rice play Texas?

We choose to go to the moon. We choose to go to the moon in this decade and do the other things, not because they are easy, but because they are hard, because that goal will serve to organize and measure the best of our energies and skills, because that challenge is one that we are willing to accept, one we are unwilling to postpone, and one which we intend to win, and the others, too.

It is for these reasons that I regard the decision last year to shift our efforts in space from low to high gear as among the most important decisions that will be made during my incumbency in the Office of the Presidency. . . .

4

EXCERPT FROM REMARKS
AT MEETING WITH
THE HEADQUARTERS
OF THE PEACE CORPS
14 JUNE 1962

I wanted to come over here this morning to express my very great appreciation to you for all that you have done to make the Peace Corps such an important part of the life of America and, though I hate to use this word which we have inherited from other days, the image of America overseas.

I don't think it is altogether fair to say that I handed Sarge [Shriver] a lemon from which he made lemonade, but I do think that he was handed and you were handed one of the most sensitive and difficult assignments which any administrative group in Washington has been given, almost, in this century.

The concept of the Peace Corps was entirely new. It was subjected to a great deal of criticism at the beginning. If it had not been done with such great care and really, in a sense, loving and prideful care, it could have defeated a great purpose and could have set back the whole cause of public service internationally for a good many years. That it has turned out to be the success that it has been has been due to the tireless work of Sargent Shriver, and to all of you. You have brought to Government service a sense of morale and a sense of enthusiasm and, really, commitment which has been absent from too many governmental agencies for too many years.

Source: John F. Kennedy, *Public Papers of the Presidents of the United States: John F. Kennedy, 1962*, vol. 2. (Washington, D.C.: GPO, 1962), 482.

So that while the Peace Corpsmen overseas have rendered unusual service, those of you who have worked to make this a success here in Washington I think have set an example for government service which I hope will be infectious. Government service should be, in these days when so much depends upon the United States, the most prideful of all careers. To serve in the United States Government, to be a public employee, to be a bureaucrat in the critical sense—that should be the greatest source of satisfaction to any American.

I hope that when the times are written and when we have moved on to other work inevitably the sense of having worked for the Government during important days will be the greatest source of pride to all of us.

You remember, in the Second World War, Winston Churchill made one of his speeches—I think at Tripoli, when the 8th Army marched in there—and said, "they will say to you 'What did you do during the great war?' and you will be able to say 'I marched with the 8th Army!'" Well, they may ask you what you have done in the sixties for your country, and you will be able to say, "I served in the Peace Corps, I served in the United States Government," and I think that people will recognize that you have made your contribution. . . .

5

EXCERPT FROM RADIO AND TELEVISION REPORT TO THE AMERICAN PEOPLE ON CIVIL RIGHTS 11 JUNE 1963

This afternoon, following a series of threats and defiant statements, the presence of Alabama National Guardsmen was required on the University of Alabama to carry out the final and unequivocal order of the United States District Court of the Northern District of Alabama. That order called for the admission of two clearly qualified young Alabama residents who happened to have been born Negro. That they were admitted peacefully on the campus is due in good measure to the conduct of the students of the University of Alabama who met their responsibilities in a constructive way.

I hope that every American, regardless of where he lives, will stop and examine his conscience about this and other related incidents. This nation was founded on the principle that all men are created equal, and that the rights of every man are diminished when the rights of one man are threatened.

Today we are committed to a worldwide struggle to promote and protect the rights of all who wish to be free. And when Americans are sent to Viet-Nam or West Berlin, we do not ask for whites only. It ought to be pos-

Source: John F. Kennedy, *Public Papers of the Presidents of the United States: John F. Kennedy, 1963*, vol. 3. (Washington, D.C.: GPO, 1963), 468–70.

sible, therefore, for American students of any color to attend any public institution they select without having to be backed up by troops.

It ought to be possible for American consumers of any color to receive equal service in places of public accommodation, such as hotels and restaurants and theaters and retail stores, without being forced to resort to demonstrations in the street, and it ought to be possible for American citizens of any color to register and to vote in a free election without interference or fear of reprisal.

It ought to be possible, in short, for every American to enjoy the privileges of being American without regard to his race or his color. In short, every American ought to have the right to be treated as he would wish to be treated, as one would wish his children to be treated. But this is not the case.

The Negro baby born in America today, regardless of the section of the Nation in which he is born, has about one-half as much chance of completing a high school as a white baby born in the same place on the same day, one-third as much chance of completing college, one-third as much chance of becoming a professional man, twice as much chance of becoming unemployed, about one-seventh as much chance of earning $10,000 a year, a life expectancy which is 7 years shorter, and the prospects of earning only half as much.

This is not a sectional issue. Difficulties over segregation and discrimination exist in every city, in every State of the Union, producing in many cities a rising tide of discontent that threatens the public safety. Nor is this a partisan issue. In a time of domestic crisis men of good will and generosity should be able to unite regardless of party or politics. This is not even a legal or legislative issue alone. It is better to settle these matters in the courts than on the streets, and new laws are needed at every level, but law alone cannot make men see right.

We are confronted primarily with a moral issue. It is as old as the scriptures and is as clear as the American Constitution.

The heart of the question is whether all Americans are to be afforded equal rights and equal opportunities, whether we are going to treat our fellow Americans as we want to be treated. If an American, because his skin is dark, cannot eat lunch in a restaurant open to the public, if he cannot send his children to the best public school available, if he cannot vote for the public officials who represent him, if, in short, he cannot enjoy the full and free life which all of us want, then who among us would be content to have the color of his skin changed and stand in his place? Who among us would then be content with the counsels of patience and delay?

One hundred years of delay have passed since President Lincoln freed the slaves, yet their heirs, their grandsons, are not fully free. They are not yet freed from the bonds of injustice. They are not yet freed from social and economic oppression. And this Nation, for all its hopes and its boasts, will not be fully free until all its citizens—are free.

We preach freedom around the world, and we mean it, and we cherish our freedom here at home but are we to say to the world, and much more importantly to each other that this is a land of the free except for the Negroes; that we have no second-class citizens except Negroes; that we have no class or caste system, no ghettoes, no master race except with respect to Negroes? Now the time has come for this Nation to fulfill its promise. The events in Birmingham and elsewhere have so increased the cries for equality that no city or State or legislative body can prudently choose to ignore them.

The fires of frustration and discord are burning in every city, North and South, where legal remedies are not at hand. Redress is sought in the streets, in demonstrations, parades, and protests which create tensions and threaten violence and threaten lives.

We face, therefore, a moral crisis as a country and as a people. It cannot be met by repressive police action. It cannot be left to increased demonstrations in the streets. It cannot be quieted by token moves or talk. It is a time to act in the Congress, in your State and local legislative body and, above all, in all of our daily lives.

It is not enough to pin the blame on others, to say this is a problem of one section of the country or another, or deplore the fact that we face. A great change is at hand, and our task, our obligation, is to make that revolution, that change, peaceful and constructive for all.

Those who do nothing are inviting shame as well as violence. Those who act boldly are recognizing right as well as reality.

Next week I shall ask the Congress of the United States to act, to make a commitment it has not fully made in this century to the proposition that race has no place in American life or law. The Federal judiciary has upheld that proposition in a series of forthright cases. The executive branch has adopted that proposition in the conduct of its affairs, including the employment of Federal personnel, the use of Federal facilities, and the sale of federally financed housing.

But there are other necessary measures which only the Congress can provide, and they must be provided at this session. The old code of equity law under which we live commands for every wrong a remedy, but in too many communities, in too many parts of the country, wrongs are inflicted on Negro citizens and there are no remedies at law. Unless the Congress acts, their only remedy is in the street.

I am, therefore, asking the Congress to enact legislation giving all Americans the right to be served in facilities which are open to the public—hotels, restaurants, theaters, retail stores, and similar establishments.

This seems to me to be an elementary right. Its denial is an arbitrary indignity that no American in 1963 should have to endure, but many do. . . .

My fellow Americans, this is a problem which faces us all—in every city of the North as well as the South. Today there are Negroes unemployed, two or three times as many compared to whites, inadequate in education, moving into the large cities, unable to find work, young people particularly out of work without hope, denied equal rights, denied the opportunity to eat at a restaurant or lunch counter or go to a movie theater, denied the right to a decent education, denied almost today the right to attend a State university even though qualified. It seems to me that these are matters which concern us all, not merely Presidents or Congressmen or Governors, but every citizen of the United States.

This is one country. It has become one country because all of us and all the people who came here had an equal chance to develop their talents.

We cannot say to 10 percent of the population that you can't have that right; that your children can't have the chance to develop whatever talents they have; that the only way that they are going to get their rights is to go into the streets and demonstrate. I think we owe them and we owe ourselves a better country than that.

Therefore, I am asking for your help in making it easier for us to move ahead and to provide the kind of equality of treatment which we would want ourselves; to give a chance for every child to be educated to the limit of his talents. . . .

6

MARTIN LUTHER KING JR.: "IT'S A DIFFICULT THING TO TEACH A PRESIDENT" 17 NOVEMBER 1964

Between two resolute Americans, a black Baptist preacher and a white Roman Catholic President, there smoldered a three-year struggle of the will. The two young leaders agreed on principle, but not upon its urgency (Freedom—Now!) The black man won. Near the end, he shaped events so that the white man had to use every resource, his audacity and skill, to avoid national disaster, and to earn his most likely claim on history.

Martin Luther King, Jr., studied John Fitzgerald Kennedy with the cold insight of an enemy and the warm concern of a friend. "The basic thing about him—he had the ability to respond to creative pressure," says King. "I never wanted—and I told him this—to be in the position that I couldn't criticize him if I thought he was wrong. And he said, 'it often helps me to be pushed.' When he saw the power of the movement, he didn't stand there arguing about it. He had the vision and wisdom to see the problem in all of its dimensions and the courage to do something about it. He grew until the day of his assassination."

"Historians will record that he vacillated like Lincoln," King believes, "but he lifted the cause far above the political level."

Source: T. George Harris, "Eight Views of JFK: The Competent American," *Look,* 17 November 1964, 61–62.

They first met—a Kennedy invitation to breakfast—only a month before the 1960 Democratic convention. King sensed "a definite concern but . . . but not what I would call a 'depthed' understanding." By September, worried about the attitude of Negro voters, Kennedy had King to dinner at his Georgetown home. "I don't know what it is, Senator, but you've got to do something dramatic," said King.

King soon provided by accident the incident for a dramatic move. Back in Atlanta, he was jailed as a probation violator for joining a sit-in. Kennedy, watching for an opportunity, seized it for a substantial act of personal courtesy, the sort that whites seldom extend. He made his famous sympathy call to Mrs. King. "Bobby called the judge," adds King. The gesture inspired record Negro majorities needed to carry close industrial states. "There are those moments when the politically expedient is the morally wise," King observes with a patient smile. "It would have been easy for him to stand by."

A month after inauguration, Kennedy called King to the White House for the first of many visits. The President was going to strengthen the executive order on fair-employment contracts. The move was more important than anybody knew because Vice-President Lyndon Johnson took over the contract enforcement job, spent as much as half his time nudging industrialists and Federal agencies into all-out Negro recruiting. But, to King's dismay, John Kennedy was putting the civil-rights bill on the back burner. "Nobody needs to convince me any longer that we have to solve the problem, not let it drift on gradualism," he said. "But how do you go about it? If we go into a long fight in Congress, it will bottleneck everything else and still get no bill."

King kept the pressure on, urged Kennedy to shape public opinion in TV fireside chats. He even visited the White House on the day of the Bay of Pigs, again the day Christmas lights were turned on. One night before dinner, when President and Mrs. Kennedy showed King the White House renovations, he walked to the room where Lincoln signed the Emancipation Proclamation. "Mr. President, I'd like for you to come back in this room one day and sit down at that desk and sign the Second Emancipation Proclamation." He followed up, at Kennedy's request, with a 120-page document outlining a total attack.

"He was always ready to listen," says King, who once lectured Kennedy on the nonviolence discipline of the early Christians." "They had practiced civil disobedience in a superb manner," explains King. "But it's a difficult thing to teach a President and his brother, who is a lawyer about civil disobedience."

The talks convinced King that the President was slowly coming around. Others doubted it. Kennedy sent the troops to Ole Miss to put down the bloody riot and protect James Meredith, but his behind-the-scenes deals with Mississippi Gov. Ross Barnett made Negroes feel like pawns in a white man's political game. He talked only in specifics, they argued, and did not assert the broad moral issue.

"We were puzzled at the anti-Kennedy sentiment among Southern whites," recalls a candid King deputy. "There was almost that much anti-Kennedy sentiment among Negroes in the movement."

Angry activists suspected Kennedy of exploiting King. In the desperate drive to integrate Albany, Ga., Negroes charged that Kennedy men kept King on the telephone for two solid days, when their leader could have turned failure into victory. Next, in Birmingham, King's men were ready to march twice, and twice Kennedy's men persuaded King to hold off. Robert Kennedy called the campaign ill-timed. It was against the Justice Department's hard pressure that the Negro masses marched, May 3, 1963, on the police dogs and fire hoses.

That settled the White House arguments. Next time King went to talk—hours before the President flew to Europe for his triumphal tour—the two spent an hour and fifteen minutes alone. As they walked in the Rose Garden, their ideas were in step. "Birmingham had caused him to revise his legislative agenda. Civil rights, which had been on the bottom of the list, or not there at all, moved to the top. I liked the way he talked about what *we* are getting. It wasn't something that he was getting for you Negroes. You knew you had an ally."

The ally did far more than King knew. After Birmingham, Kennedy began to call bankers, union chiefs, businessmen, churchmen, lawyers, clubwomen and other leaders to the White House to ask their help in the crisis. A Democratic President was relying on private citizens, many of them Republicans, not only to back a new civil-rights law, but to take action in their own spheres. The Establishment's response was immediate, general, and decisive. "White only" signs fell from most hotel chains, restaurants and theaters in the South. Negro hiring picked up. Bail money flowed to Negro demonstrators. Businessmen sought out the local Negro leaders. Forced by King, Kennedy learned how strong citizens, given leadership, can be.

The sentiments let loose by Birmingham peaked in the August 28 March on Washington. King brought the jubilee throng of 230,000 to tears with his visionary oration: "I have a dream. . . ." That night, he went with other March leaders to the White House. When the President reached out to shake hands, he said, "*I* have a dream."

There were, in fact, two John Kennedys, King believes. "One presided in the first two years under pressure of the uncertainty caused by his razor-thin margin of victory. In 1963, a new Kennedy had emerged. He had found that public opinion was not in a rigid mold. He was, at his death, undergoing a transformation from a hesitant leader with unsure goals to a strong figure with deeply appealing objectives."

7

SURVEY ON THE AMERICAN PRESIDENCY OCTOBER 2000

Rank	President:	Political leadership	Foreign policy	Domestic policy	Character integrity	Impact on history	Total score
1	Lincoln	4.87	4.38	4.75	4.90	5.00	23.90
2	F. Roosevelt	4.96	4.61	4.65	3.94	4.99	23.14
3	Washington	4.57	4.33	4.18	4.99	5.00	23.06
4	T. Roosevelt	4.57	4.28	4.16	4.44	4.32	21.78
5	Truman	3.84	4.38	3.73	4.57	4.28	20.79
6	Wilson	4.01	3.78	4.22	4.24	4.43	20.68
7	Jefferson	4.27	3.52	3.97	3.92	4.55	20.23
8	Jackson	4.51	3.13	3.56	3.81	4.34	19.34
9	Polk	3.88	4.00	3.34	3.82	4.03	19.07
10	Eisenhower	3.63	3.98	3.12	4.48	3.69	18.88
11	Reagan	4.18	3.45	2.69	3.49	3.96	17.78
12	Monroe	3.29	4.03	3.21	3.92	3.25	17.71
13	L. Johnson	4.31	1.99	4.34	2.62	4.00	17.27
14	McKinley	3.36	3.48	2.95	3.81	3.38	16.99
15	Adams	2.51	3.65	2.58	4.71	3.24	16.68
16	Madison	2.99	2.76	3.02	4.44	3.41	16.61
17	Cleveland	3.35	3.00	2.93	3.84	2.87	15.99
18	J. Q. Adams	2.19	3.48	2.74	4.50	2.81	15.73
19	Kennedy	3.47	3.27	3.16	2.71	3.10	15.71
20	Bush	2.69	3.70	2.29	3.71	2.63	15.02
21	Carter	2.21	2.76	2.54	4.37	2.40	14.28
22	Clinton	3.68	2.94	3.16	1.61	2.79	14.17

Rank	President:	Political leadership	Foreign policy	Domestic policy	Character integrity	Impact on history	Total score
23	Nixon	2.96	3.60	2.77	1.17	3.49	13.99
24	Hoover	2.06	2.77	2.10	4.25	2.76	13.95
25	Taft	2.12	2.62	2.70	4.08	2.37	13.89
26	Hayes	2.66	2.30	2.67	3.58	2.31	13.52
27	Van Buren	2.78	2.54	2.52	3.08	2.38	13.31
28	Ford	2.26	2.61	2.28	4.07	1.99	13.20
29	Coolidge	2.28	2.25	2.11	3.82	1.98	12.44
30	Taylor	2.15	2.15	2.20	3.42	1.96	11.87
31	B. Harrison	2.18	2.25	2.21	3.18	1.96	11.77
32	Grant	1.98	2.49	2.00	3.05	2.25	11.77
33	Arthur	2.26	1.98	2.50	2.97	1.90	11.61
34	Tyler	1.83	2.53	2.02	3.07	2.05	11.50
35	Fillmore	1.98	2.05	2.16	2.96	1.72	10.87
36	A. Johnson	1.36	2.16	1.55	2.66	2.40	10.13
37	Pierce	1.47	1.68	1.45	2.79	1.73	9.12
38	Harding	1.58	2.42	1.72	1.61	1.45	8.78
39	Buchanan	1.21	1.61	1.17	2.58	2.11	8.68

Source: *Chicago Sun Times*, 1 October 2000.

SELECTED READINGS

Bernstein, Irving. *Promises Kept: John F. Kennedy's New Frontier.* New York: Oxford University Press, 1991.

Beschloss, Michael R. *The Crisis Years: Kennedy and Khrushchev, 1960–1963.* New York: Edward Burlingame Books, 1991.

Borstelmann, Thomas. "'Hedging Our Bets and Buying Time': John Kennedy and Racial Relations in the American South and Southern Africa." *Diplomatic History* 24 (Summer 2000): 435–63.

Brauer, Carl M. *John F. Kennedy and the Second Reconstruction.* New York: Columbia University Press, 1977.

Brinkley, Douglas, and Richard T. Griffiths, eds. *John F. Kennedy and Europe.* Baton Rouge: Louisiana University Press, 1999.

Chang, Gordon H. *Friends and Enemies: The United States, China, and the Soviet Union, 1948–1972.* Stanford, Stanford University Press, 1990.

Doyle, William. *An American Insurrection: The Battle of Oxford, Mississippi.* New York: Doubleday, 2001.

Freedman, Lawrence. *Kennedy's Wars: Berlin, Cuba, Laos, and Vietnam.* New York: Oxford University Press, 2000.

Fursenko, Alexsandr, and Timothy Naftali. *"One Hell of a Gamble": Khrushchev, Castro, and Kennedy, 1958–1964.* New York: W.W. Norton, 1997.

Giglio, James N. *The Presidency of John F. Kennedy.* Lawrence: University Press of Kansas, 1991.

Graham, Hugh Davis. *The Uncertain Triumph: Federal Education Policy in the Kennedy and Johnson Years.* Chapel Hill: University of North Carolina Press, 1984.

Guthman, Edwin O., and Jeffrey Shulman, eds. *Robert Kennedy in His Own Words: The Unpublished Recollections of the Kennedy Years.* New York: Bantam Books, 1988.

Harrison, Cynthia Ellen. *On Account of Sex: The Politics of Women's Issues, 1945–1968.* Berkeley: University of California Press, 1988.

Heath, Jim F. *John F. Kennedy and the Business Community.* Chicago: University of Chicago Press, 1969.

Herring, George C. *America's Longest War: The United States and Vietnam, 1950–1975.* 4th ed. New York: McGraw Hill, 2002.

Hersh, Seymour M. *The Dark Side of Camelot.* Boston: Little, Brown, 1997.

Hilsman, Roger. *To Move a Nation: The Politics of Foreign Policy in the Administration of John F. Kennedy.* Garden City, N.Y.: Doubleday, 1967.

Hoffman, Elizabeth Cobbs. *All You Need Is Love: The Peace Corps and the Spirit of the 1960s.* Cambridge, Mass.: Harvard University Press, 1998.

Kaiser, David. *American Tragedy: Kennedy, Johnson, and the Origins of the Vietnam War.* Cambridge, Mass.: Belknap Press of Harvard University Press, 2000.

Kaufman, Burton I. "John F. Kennedy as World Leader: A Perspective on the Literature." *Diplomatic History* 17 (Summer 1993): 447–69.

Kochavi, Noam. "Limited Accommodation, Perpetuated Conflict: Kennedy, China, and the Laos Crisis, 1961–1963." *Diplomatic History* 26 (Winter 2002): 95–135.

Kornbluh, Peter, ed. *Bay of Pigs Declassified: The Secret CIA Report on the Invasion of Cuba.* New York: Free Press, 1998.

Kunz, Diane B. *The Diplomacy of the Crucial Decade: American Foreign Relations during the 1960s.* New York: Columbia University Press, 1994.

Leamer, Laurence. *The Kennedy Men, 1901–1963: The Laws of the Father.* New York: William Morrow & Co., 2001.

Levinson, Jerome, and Juan de Onís. *The Alliance That Lost Its Way: A Critical Report on the Alliance for Progress.* Chicago: Quadrangle, 1970.

Logsdon, John M. *The Decision to Go to the Moon: Project Apollo and the National Interest.* Cambridge, Mass.: MIT Press, 1970.

Matusow, Allen J. *The Unraveling of America: A History of Liberalism in the 1960s.* New York: Harper & Row, 1984.

May, Ernest R., and Philip D. Zelikow, eds. *The Kennedy Tapes: Inside the White House during the Cuban Missile Crisis.* Cambridge, Mass.: Belknap Press of Harvard University Press, 1997.

Navasky, Victor S. *Kennedy Justice.* New York: Atheneum, 1971.

Parmet, Herbert S. *JFK: The Presidency of John F. Kennedy.* New York, Dial Press, 1983.

Paterson, Thomas G., ed. *Kennedy's Quest for Victory: American Foreign Policy, 1961–1963.* New York: Oxford University Press, 1989.

Perret, Geoffrey. *Jack: A Life Like No Other.* New York: Random House, 2001.

Rabe, Stephen G. "After the Missiles of October: John F. Kennedy and Cuba, November 1962 to November 1963." *Presidential Studies Quarterly* 30 (December 2000): 714–26.

———. *The Most Dangerous Area in the World: John F. Kennedy Confronts Communist Revolution in Latin America.* Chapel Hill: University of North Carolina Press, 1999.

Reeves, Richard. *President Kennedy: Profile of Power.* New York: Simon & Schuster, 1993.

Rice, Gerard T. *The Bold Experiment: JFK's Peace Corps.* Notre Dame, Indiana: University of Notre Dame Press, 1985.

Rowen, Hobart. *The Free Enterprisers: Kennedy, Johnson, and the Business Establishment.* New York: Putnam, 1964.

Schlesinger, Arthur M., Jr. *Robert Kennedy and His Times.* Boston: Houghton Mifflin, 1978.

———. *A Thousand Days: John F. Kennedy in the White House.* Boston: Houghton Mifflin, 1965.

Shank, Alan. *Presidential Policy Leadership: Kennedy and Social Welfare.* Lanham, Md.: University Press of America, 1980.

Sorensen, Theodore C. *Kennedy.* New York: Harper & Row, 1965.

Sundquist, James L. *Politics and Policy: The Eisenhower, Kennedy, and Johnson Years.* Washington, D.C.: Brookings Institution, 1968.

Wicker, Tom. *JFK and LBJ: The Influence of Personality upon Politics.* New York: Morrow, 1968.

White, Mark J., ed. *Kennedy: The New Frontier Revisited.* New York: New York University Press, 1998.

Wofford, Harris. *Of Kennedy and Kings: Making Sense of the 1960s.* New York: Farrar, Straus, Giroux, 1980.

Zeiler, Thomas W. *American Trade and Power in the 1960s.* New York: Columbia University Press, 1992.

Zelikow, Philip D., Timothy Naftali, and Ernest R. May, eds. *The Presidential Recordings: John F. Kennedy:* Volumes 1–3, *The Great Crises.* New York: W.W. Norton, 2001.

INDEX

ABOUT THE AUTHORS

James N. Giglio is distinguished professor of history at Southwest Missouri State University. He is a scholar of twentieth-century America with particular interest in political history. Besides this study, he has published five books, including *The Presidency of John F. Kennedy* (1991) and *Musial: From Stash to Stan the Man* (2001). He has also published innumerable articles and reviews, many of which have focused on the presidency.

Stephen G. Rabe is professor of history at the University of Texas at Dallas. His field of research interest is U.S. foreign relations, with a special interest in U.S. relations with Latin America. Rabe has written *The Road to OPEC: United States Relations with Venezuela, 1919–1976* (1982); *Eisenhower and Latin America: The Foreign Policy of Anticommunism* (1988); and *The Most Dangerous Area in the World: John F. Kennedy Confronts Communist Revolution in Latin America* (1999). He has also edited, with Thomas G. Paterson, *Imperial Surge: The United States Abroad, The 1890s–Early 1900s* (1992). Rabe has served as the Mary Ball Washington Professor of American History at University College, Dublin, and has lectured on the history of U.S. foreign relations in Ireland, Northern Ireland, Wales, and Argentina. Professor Rabe is currently studying the history of U.S. involvement in British Guiana from 1953 to 1970.

DATE